Cosmopolitan Refugees

FORCED MIGRATION

General Editors: Tom Scott-Smith and Kirsten McConnachie

This series, published in association with the Refugees Studies Centre, University of Oxford, reflects the multidisciplinary nature of the field and includes within its scope international law, anthropology, sociology, politics, international relations, geopolitics, social psychology and economics.

Recent volumes:

Volume 46
Cosmopolitan Refugees: Somali Migrant Women in Nairobi and Johannesburg
Nereida Ripero-Muñiz

Volume 45
Refugees on the Move: Crisis and Response in Turkey and Europe
Edited by Erol Balkan and Zümray Kutlu Tonak

Volume 44
Durable Solutions: Challenges with Implementing Global Norms for Internally Displaced Persons in Georgia
Carolin Funke

Volume 43
Mediated Lives: Waiting and Hope among Iraqi Refugees in Jordan
Mirjam Twigt

Volume 42
Outsiders: Memories of Migration to and from North Korea
Markus Bell

Volume 41

Latin America and Refugee Protection: Regimes, Logics and Challenges
Edited by Liliana Lyra Jubilut, Marcia Vera Espinoza and Gabriela Mezzanotti

Volume 40
Un-Settling Middle Eastern Refugees: Regimes of Exclusion and Inclusion in the Middle East, Europe, and North America
Edited by Marcia C. Inhorn and Lucia Volk

Volume 39
Structures of Protection? Rethinking Refugee Shelter
Edited by Tom Scott-Smith and Mark E. Breeze

Volume 38
Refugee Resettlement: Power, Politics, and Humanitarian Governance
Edited by Adèle Garnier, Liliana Lyra Jubilut and Kristin Bergtora Sandvik

Volume 37
Gender, Violence, Refugees
Edited by Susanne Buckley-Zistel and Ulrike Krause

For a full volume listing, please see the series page on our website:
https//www.berghahnbooks.com/series/forced-migration

Cosmopolitan Refugees

SOMALI MIGRANT WOMEN IN NAIROBI AND JOHANNESBURG

Nereida Ripero-Muñiz

berghahn
NEW YORK • OXFORD
www.berghahnbooks.com

First published in 2023 by
Berghahn Books
www.berghahnbooks.com

© 2023, 2026 Nereida Ripero-Muñiz
First paperback edition published in 2026

All rights reserved. Except for the quotation of short passages
for the purposes of criticism and review, no part of this book
may be reproduced in any form or by any means, electronic or
mechanical, including photocopying, recording, or any information
storage and retrieval system now known or to be invented,
without written permission of the publisher.

Library of Congress Cataloging-in-Publication Data

Names: Ripero-Muñiz, Nereida, author.
Title: Cosmopolitan refugees : Somali migrant women in Nairobi and Johannesburg / Nereida Ripero-Muñiz.
Other titles: Forced migration ; v. 46.
Description: New York : Berghahn Books, 2023. | Series: Forced migration; v. 46 | Includes bibliographical references and index. | Summary: "Exploring the dynamics of identity formation processes in diasporic spaces, this book analyses how gender, cultural and religious practices are renegotiated in a situation of displacement. The author presents the comparative case study of Somali migrant women in Nairobi and Johannesburg: two cosmopolitan urban hubs in the global South. The book is based on and includes ethnographic observations in Nairobi and Johannesburg, first-person accounts of migration journeys across the African continent and women's reflections on what it means to be a Somali woman today"– Provided by publisher.
Identifiers: LCCN 2022036413 (print) | LCCN 2022036414 (ebook) |
ISBN 9781800738188 (hardback) | ISBN 9781800738195 (ebook)
Subjects: LCSH: Women, Somali–Kenya–Nairobi. | Women, Somali–South Africa–Johannesburg. | Somali diaspora. | Identity (Psychology) | Cosmopolitanism–Social aspects.
Classification: LCC HQ1795 .R56 2023 (print) | LCC HQ1795 (ebook) |
DDC 305.48896773–dc23/eng/20220801
LC record available at https://lccn.loc.gov/2022036413
LC ebook record available at https://lccn.loc.gov/2022036414

British Library Cataloguing in Publication Data

A catalogue record for this book is available from the British Library

EU GPSR Authorized Representative

LOGOS EUROPE, 9 rue Nicolas Poussin, 17000, LA ROCHELLE, France
Email: Contact@logoseurope.eu

ISBN 978-1-80073-818-8 hardback
ISBN 978-1-83695-412-5 paperback
ISBN 978-1-83695-774-4 epub
ISBN 978-1-80073-819-5 web pdf

https://doi.org/10.3167/9781800738188

Contents

List of Illustrations	vi
Preface	viii
Acknowledgements	x
Maps	xiv
Introduction. Cosmopolitan Refugees	1
1. The Port and the Island: Somalis in Nairobi and Johannesburg	25
2. The Dynamics of Identity and Placemaking: The Making of 'Little Mogadishus'	51
3. Global and Local Identifications in Dialogue: Expressions of Somaliness in Nairobi and Johannesburg	67
4. Negotiating Religious and Cultural Identifications in Diasporic Spaces	86
5. Somali Women of Nairobi and Johannesburg: Migration, Agency and Aspirations	105
Conclusion. Migrating in and Out of Africa	125
References	131
Index	145

Illustrations

Maps

0.1. Somali migration in and around East and Southern Africa. Map by Quinten Edward Williams. — xiv

0.2. Family-based aspirational migration among Somali migrants. Map by Quinten Edward Williams. — xiv

Figures

1.1. Eastleigh. Photo by Joakim Arnøy. — 28

1.2. Mayfair. Photo by Salym Fayad for the project 'Metropolitan Nomads'. — 29

1.3. Migration route from Somalia to South Africa of one of the participants in the workshop #EverydayMayfair. Published with permission of the participant. — 39

1.4. Woman selling wholesale perfumes imported from Dubai on the upper floor of Amal, Mayfair. Photo by Salym Fayad for the project 'Metropolitan Nomads'. — 45

1.5. Woman selling dresses and *diracs* in her shop in Amal. Photo by Salym Fayad for the project 'Metropolitan Nomads'. — 46

1.6. Travel agency in Amal. Photo by Salym Fayad for the project 'Metropolitan Nomads'. — 47

2.1. A street in Eastleigh. Photo by the author. — 54

2.2. Restaurant and shops in Mayfair, Eighth Avenue. Published with permission of the participants in the workshop #EverydayMayfair. — 57

2.3.	Map of Mayfair drawn by participants in the workshop #EverydayMayfair. Published with permission of the participants.	58
2.4.	Map of Mayfair drawn by participants in the workshop #EverydayMayfair. Published with permission of the participants.	59
2.5.	Prayers in Mayfair during Eid. Photo by Salym Fayad for the project 'Metropolitan Nomads'.	62
3.1.	The 'cultural man' of Mayfair. Photo by Salym Fayad for the project 'Metropolitan Nomads'.	80
4.1.	Somali bride wearing a Western-style dress combined with traditional henna patterns covering her body. Photo by Salym Fayad for the project 'Metropolitan Nomads'.	93
4.2.	Woman dancing during a *toddoba* ceremony in Mayfair. Photo by Salym Fayad for the project 'Metropolitan Nomads'.	94
5.1.	Map by participants in the workshop #EverydayMayfair. Published with permission of the participants.	118
5.2.	Map by participants in the workshop #EverydayMayfair. Published with permission of the participants.	119
5.3.	Mayfair. Photograph taken by a participant in the workshop #EverydayMayfair. Published with permission of the participant.	122

Preface

More than a decade ago, I was visiting Isiolo, the furthermost town in eastern Kenya before the desert begins, which is mostly inhabited by Somalis. They are descendants of Somali soldiers brought there by the British colonizers during the First World War. A Somali-Kenyan friend and colleague, whom I had met at the Kenyan university at which I was working then, had invited me to accompany her there to visit her family during our holidays. We stayed at her sister's house. We were chatting in the living room when one of their many cousins arrived and removed her burka in the room, while telling my friend in Kiswahili: 'Tell your friend that I am not wearing the burka because I am very religious; I am wearing it so people in the village don't recognize me when I go around.' She was justifying her wearing of a garment that she presumed I, a white visitor, would likely associate with a form of ardent religiosity and perhaps even extremism. Her comment changed my perception of what it could mean to wear a burka and the women who decided to do so. I realized that, in many cases, this is a conscious choice that serves other purposes than those perceived by an outsider. In this instance, she sought to hide her movements in a town where everyone knew each other; by wearing a burka, she made her individual identity unclear and was able to navigate very socially gendered and controlled spaces with a certain degree of anonymity. Her choosing to wear a burka was strategic and agentive, a way to retain some freedom to move around in public spaces without being noticed. Her invisibility was chosen, and with it, she avoided potential criticism and gossip concerning her actions, the houses she entered and the people she might be seeing. In this way, she was giving a different meaning to a garment that is normally associated with religious fervour or female submission by the outside world; for her, it was a chosen strategy of invisibility with which to navigate an urban social structure.

This interaction made me aware of the intricacies of being a Somali woman and the layers of meanings associated with it. I realized that their portrayal in the global imagination, fed mostly by mainstream Western media obsessed with 'Islamic terrorism' that insists on seeing Africa as the 'dark continent' and source of multiple maladies, is extremely incomplete, inaccurate and often far from a more complex reality. One can simply run an internet search for the terms 'Somalia' or 'Somalis' and get a handful of news entries about hunger, Al-Shabaab or refugee camps. Under this narrow lens, Somalis are often represented as jihadists par excellence, pirates of the Indian Ocean, helpless refugees, dying malnourished children or constrained women.

During that journey, I realized the need to contribute to other counter-narratives that could challenge the stereotypical representations of Somali women generated mostly from a myopic Western point of view. Far from being constrained victims, these women were highly aware of what they wanted for their lives and those of their families, and of how to achieve it, transnational migration being one of the main ways to fulfil those dreams. By following the lives of Somali women moving across borders on the African continent and beyond, this book is an attempt to mend the 'single story' perspective and present other stories generated in the Global South that are more aligned with current African realities and cosmopolitan ways of being in the world.

Acknowledgements

This book is the result of more than a decade of work with Somali women and men in Nairobi and Johannesburg. Numerous people have contributed to bring together all these years of research. However, this book would never have happened if I hadn't met Fatuma Ahmed Ali – who introduced me to her Somali world in Kenya – in Nairobi when we were both lecturing at United States International University. I thank her for her generous hospitality and friendship, for being a role model and constant inspiration, and for showing me other realities *beyond the veil*, some of which I aim to share in these pages.

Once the formal research for this study began at the University of the Witwatersrand in Johannesburg, my advisors – Ingrid Palmary, former director of the African Centre for Migration and Society (ACMS), and Eric Worby, professor in anthropology – provided invaluable guidance on how best to approach and conduct the research that is the base of this book. I thank them for the support they provided over the years, and for all the long and interesting conversations, their feedback on my writing and their very valuable insights. Professors Lorena Nuñez, Francis B. Nyamnjoh and Catherine Besteman also provided very valuable feedback and encouraged me to take my work further. I thank all of them for their support at the early stages of my research.

I am also enormously grateful to Neil Carrier and Daniel Thompson for their detailed comments and recommendations on the manuscript, which have hugely improved the quality of this work. Thanks also to Lara Jacob for her language editing and proofreading of the final manuscript.

At the University of the Witwatersrand, the Faculty of Humanities Staff Development Grant and the Book Publication Grant were very beneficial for the completion of the manuscript. At the School of Literature, Language and Media, where I am based, I would like to thank the two Heads of School during the period this book was being researched and written – Professor Libby Meintjes and Professor Dan Ojwang – for always being understanding and supportive of my research and granting me the necessary time and funds to complete this book. I would also like to thank my colleagues Isabel Hofmeyr and Nicky Falkof for reading and commenting on the book proposal, and Simon van Schalkwyk for his valuable comments on the early drafts of the manuscript. At the Department of Spanish and Latin American Studies, I thank my colleagues Remei Gonzalez Manzanero and Paula Lerones Robles for their help and support through their teaching in the last years of completing this book. At the African Centre for Migration and Society (ACMS), I benefitted from the conversations had over the years with different researchers working and visiting the centre. I would like to thank Zaheera Jinnah for initially introducing me to Mayfair, and especially Jo Veary, current director of the ACMS, for her constant support, encouragement and friendship along the years in Johannesburg. I also benefitted enormously from the wonderful seminars and workshops in the anthropology department. The reading group on narrative enquiry initiated by Jill Bradbury – which over the years became NEST: Narrative Enquiry for Social Transformation – was also a very enriching place to learn about and discuss the power of narratives.

In Mayfair, I am enormously grateful to all the women and men who gave their time to participate in this research, for opening the doors to their homes and lives. Especial thanks go to Saytoon and Muna, whose help was invaluable in navigating Mayfair. Thanks also to Hanad, Ibrahim, Mohamed, *Kings* and all their friends for their collaboration, support, openness and trust. Thanks to Salym Fayad, for the collaborative project 'Metropolitan Nomads: A Journey through Joburg's Little Mogadishu', which added new layers of meaning to this research, and for the beautiful photographs from it, some of which are included in this book. This project was also possible thanks to MOVE: Methods. Visual. Explore at ACMS; I thank them for their support, which made possible several exhibitions and the free e-book that resulted from them. I would also like to thank the participants in the participatory research arts methods workshop #EverydayMayfair, for their time, creativity and engagement; some of the maps they created and photos they took have also been included in this book. The workshop was conducted in collaboration with Elsa Oliveira, and sponsored by the Security at the Margins (SeaM) project at the University of Edinburgh and the Migration and Health Project Southern Africa (MaHp) at Wits University. Thanks also to Quinten Edward Williams for the careful creation of the maps concerning Somali migration that open the book, which were designed based on women's stories of migration and some of the maps produced at this participatory research arts methods workshop.

In Nairobi, I would like to thank all the women who generously gave their time for the interviews, especially Sukria, Hamdi and Faiza. Thanks to Dr. Warsame and his team at Tawakal Clinic in Eastleigh for being so welcoming and for letting me be present in their weekly women's meetings. Thanks to Amina 'Taylor', Amina and Hafsa for helping me to navigate Eastleigh.

To Fatuma and her family for their hospitality and practical advice. Thanks also to Joakim Arnøy for his photo of Eastleigh.

In Minneapolis, I thank my colleagues and friends Dr. Jamal Adam and Dr. Ahmed Ibrahim for introducing me to their city and the Somali community living there. Thanks to Jamal also for his assistance with some Somali-language terminology that gave me some deeper insights, and especially for his hospitality and support during my visit. Thanks to the women who gave their time to talk to me in Cedar Riverside and to other members of the Somali community who spent time in interviews and conversations. This field trip was also possible thanks to a research grant from the Andrew Mellon Foundation: Research and Publication Support for Young and Emerging Scholars.

At Berghahn Books, thanks are due to Tom Bonnington and Anthony Mason for their patience and support over the years that this book was in the making. Thanks also to Harry Eagles for his careful edits and to Keara Hagerty for her guidance during production.

Earlier versions of Chapters 4 and 5 were published in a journal article in the *African Studies Review*, as part of the forum 'Migration in Sub-Saharan Africa: The Somali Refugee and Migrant Experience'. The maps on Somali migration that open the book also appeared first in this publication. I thank the special issue editors – Ahmed Ibrahim, Aditi Malik and Cori Wielenga – for their insights and feedback on my work.

Parts of the introduction's theoretical framework and Chapter 3 appeared as a book chapter, 'The Port and the Island: Cosmopolitan and Vernacular Identity Constructions among Somali Women in Nairobi and Johannesburg', in *Mobile Urbanity: Somali Presence in Urban East Africa*, edited by Neil Carrier and Tabea Scharrer for Berghahn Books.

Finally, on a more personal level, I would like to thank Sonsoles Vázquez at the Spanish Agency for International Cooperation and Development (AECID), and their *lectorados* programme for changing my destiny by sending me to Kenya and later to South Africa. I am also enormously thankful to my friends and family, who have accompanied me along this long journey, providing the emotional support needed to complete this work: to Javier, for all the invaluable shared moments and conversations along the years in Africa and beyond; to Ignacio and Monica, Mari and Oscar, Lucy and Mike and Sarah and her wonderful family for making the years of writing in Johannesburg more pleasurable and joyful. To Cecilia, Miren, Carlota and all other long-time friends for their constant encouragement and moral support. Thanks to my sisters, Dyana and Alejandra, for always, always being there, since the beginning, for always keeping close even if we stay far apart, and for all the love. Thanks also to Claudia, Valentina, Elena, Luis, Jan and Lola for the moments of play and joy. And last but not least, thanks go to my parents: to my mother, for being the woman she was and for all the love, and to my father, for his constant support, not only throughout this process but throughout my entire life, for his encouragement and understanding, for his endless patience, for his always wise advice and for his unconditional love. This book is dedicated to them.

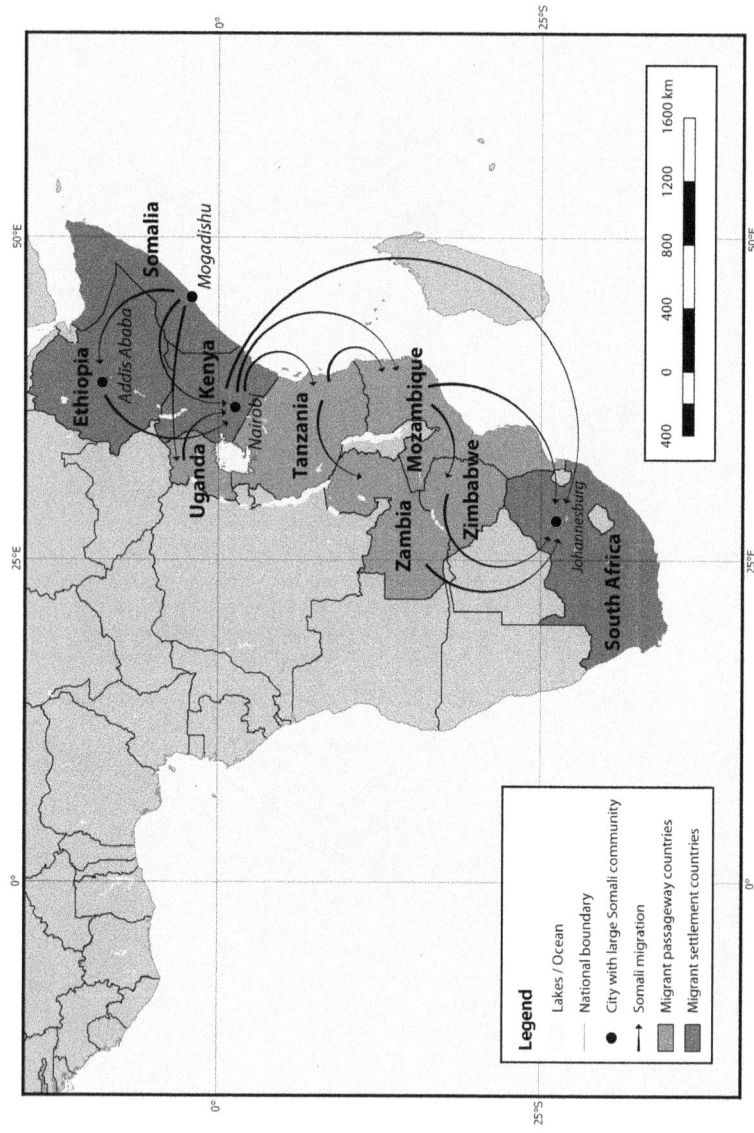

Map 0.1. Somali migration in and around East and Southern Africa. Map by Quinten Edward Williams.

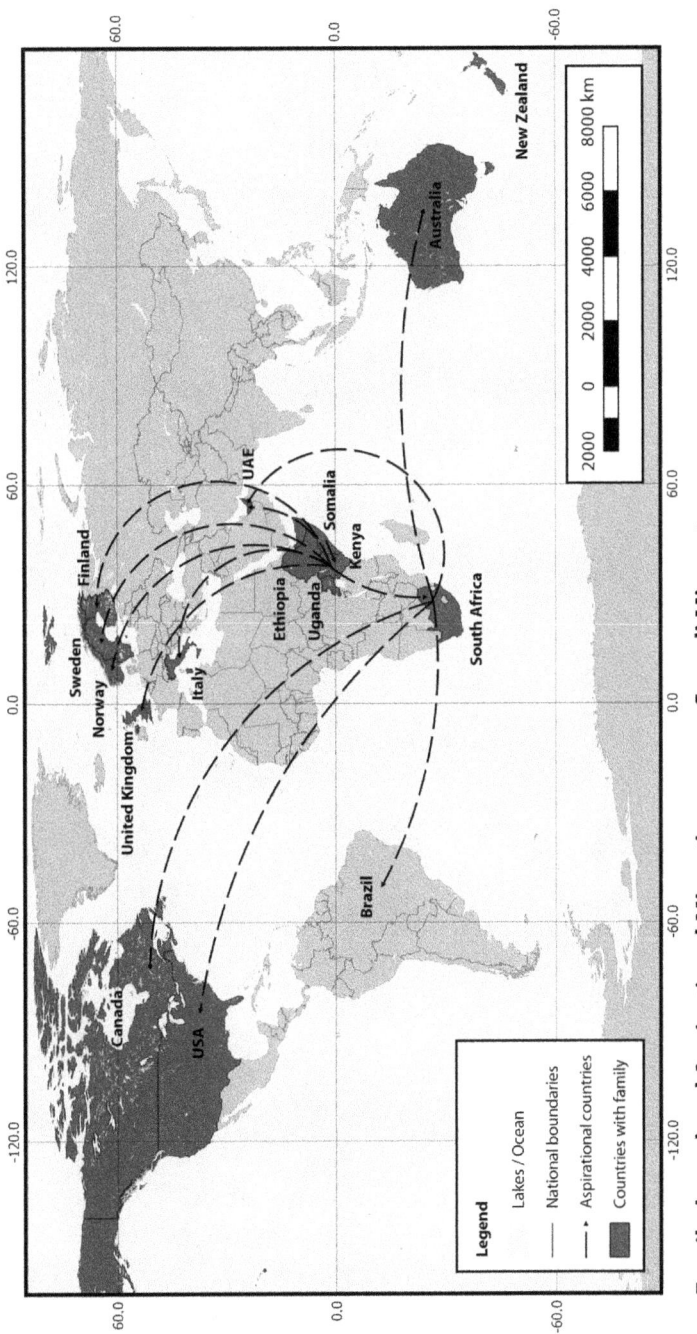

Map 0.2. Family-based aspirational migration among Somali migrants. Map by Quinten Edward Williams.

Introduction
Cosmopolitan Refugees

I am a civil war child. I survived murderers. I survived hunger, I survived diseases, I survived refugee camps. I survived many borders. I am strong. I stand strong.

On a hot December day, some years after my visit to Isiolo, I was in Eastleigh, the predominantly Somali neighbourhood of Nairobi. Amal, a young Somali woman I had previously met in a women's meeting at Tawakal Clinic, took me to a beauty salon to have our hands done with henna. Her cousin, who had returned from Saudi Arabia a couple of years back, owned and ran Sacdiya Beauty Salon, situated along Jam Street in the heart of Eastleigh. On our way there, we stopped at Dallas International College of Modern Teaching. 'Your way to success', declared the sign on the building. Amal had been learning English and Community Health there and needed to collect her degree certificate. At the beauty salon, just below Dallas College, preparations for a wedding were under way in the back room; the bride and bridesmaids were readying themselves for the evening celebration. The beauticians were busy doing the bride's hair and decorating her whole body with henna.

In the front of the salon, Amal and I sat down with four other women who were also having their hands done with henna – a new pattern trend from Sudan of big flowers on your forearms. Nasra and Fatuma were visiting from Sweden, where they have been living for the past ten years. A mother of two sets of twins, Nasra likes coming to Nairobi during the Swedish winter with her children. Fatuma, a medical student in Stockholm, in Nairobi on holiday, was keen to show us some pictures of her wearing a white coat next to a model skeleton. Daris was preparing to travel to Sudan to see her husband who was working there. She explained that she liked to have henna done at least once a month to please her husband. 'You have to keep active', Amal clarified; 'if you are not active, your husband will get bored and look for another woman.' She went on to explain how you need to have the house clean, cook a good meal, do your henna and your hair, put lotion in your body, wear a nice *dirac* and burn some *unzi*.[1] 'Then your husband will come home and be very happy, never wanting to leave.' All of us laughed. Amal was getting married very soon and seemed to know very well how to keep 'active' in order to keep a husband. She was travelling to Ethiopia the following week, where she was meeting her husband-to-be, a distant cousin who was coming from the UK to marry her in Addis Ababa. The plan was for her to join him in the UK after the marriage. Six months after our visit to the beauty salon, she was already there.

All the women at Sacdiya Beauty Salon were, or had at some point been, forced migrants from a country generally portrayed as the epitome of a failed state. The political chaos that came after Siad Barre was overthrown, alongside the frequent droughts, consequent famines and the rise of Al-Shabaab, forced thousands of Somalis to leave their country, turning Somalia into a 'refugee producing nation' (Hopkins 2010: 523). Today, Somali migrants can be found not only in the refugee camps of northern Kenya, but in many of the metropoles around the world, such as London, Minneapolis or Toronto, and also in the African urban hubs of Cairo, Nairobi and Johannesburg.[2]

This is not a static diaspora because Somalis constantly traverse boundaries. The women at Sacdiya Beauty Salon were all coming from or going to another country, and their lives take place across national boundaries – as can be observed in Map 0.2 at the beginning of this book, which shows the countries with established Somali communities, as well as aspirational countries of resettlement.[3] This transnational cosmopolitanism is not unique to the clientele of Sacdiya Beauty Salon; it can be found in every corner of Eastleigh, where everyday practices are performed in a translocal context of displacement.

Transnational Nomads

Even if transnationalism is a relatively new concept in the social sciences, connected to discourses on postmodernity and globalization, it has been present in the lives of Somalis for centuries preceding the creation of African nation states by the colonial powers.[4] The traditional pastoralist and nomadic life that many Somalis had led them to move along the Horn and through East Africa, reaching as far south as Tanzania (Carrier 2016; Weitzberg 2017).[5] There was also a history of international migration among Somalis outside Africa before the armed conflict started in the 1990s, as Somalis migrated as sailors or soldiers during and after colonial times and ended up settling in the UK, and travelled to Saudi Arabia during the 1950s and 1960s to work as oil workers (Kleist 2004); as Abdi (2015) and Carrier and Scharrer (2019) also point out, the geographical position of the Horn, close to the Gulf countries, has permitted a fluid mobility for religious, business or work reasons over the years.

Nomadism is considered by many Somalis to be a natural disposition and 'way of being', and 'the nomadic imaginary still remains a key aspect of identification for many, also for those now living very different lives in towns and cities' (Carrier and Scharrer 2019: 9). In fact, Somalia is one of the few countries in the world where a nomadic way of life is praised and admired instead of demeaned (Harper 2012). Jamal, a young Somali man who used to live in Mayfair, Johannesburg, and ran a lodge before being resettled in Canada, where his wife-to-be had been waiting for him, explained during an interview that it was common practice for people living in urban centres to send their children for some months to relatives living 'in the bush' so that they could learn the arts and perils of the nomadic lifestyle. Even if this way of life has been threatened in recent decades, mostly due to the security situation in the country, it has not completely disappeared. On the contrary, it could be seen to have increased, as Somalis have gone from being local nomads to transnational ones (Horst 2006a). It was striking to see how many Somalis were eager to move somewhere else in order to improve their lives and those of their families. People living in Somalia maintain strong links with their relatives in the diaspora, who also play a key role in the migration process of their siblings, spouses, parents, cousins or nephews living in the country. Most of the women I spoke to in Johannesburg had previously lived in at least two countries. Those living in Nairobi had either returned from abroad or were on their way to somewhere else. Even for those who have not left Somalia, contact with relatives overseas through new technologies provides access to new cultural practices and ways of being. Somalis are eager users of the internet, with Somalia having been one of the first African countries 'to develop a mobile phone system' (Harper 2012: 10), and the Somali diaspora today is hyperconnected through social media (Ponzanesi 2021), creating a new space not only to keep in touch but to recreate a shared collective identity, as this book will further explore. As an example, when I asked Amal for her email address, so that we could keep in touch, her response was: 'Which one should I give you? I have thirteen.' Thus, the nomadic imaginary is still very present in the Somali collective identity, and the wish to move is even reflected in the Somali language through different terms or expressions: *reer-guuraa*, meaning 'nomad', also reflects a constant desire to move from one place to another, and, as Jamal explained, this concept also refers to the 'nomad we all have inside', emphasizing again the importance of movement in the Somali collective imagination. Then there is the saying *Nin aan dhul marini dhaayo maleh*, meaning 'He who has no travel has no understanding', which is a way of praising the knowledge that comes with seeing other places and therefore reflects a certain degree of cosmopolitanism. Even more interesting is the concept behind the word *buufis*, that refers to the unfulfilled desire to migrate and the anxiety generated by the impossibility of moving, which can result in depression or even temporary madness. Old Somalis identify *buufis* with *saar*, the spirit of travel that possesses the person affected and only leaves after this desire to travel is fulfilled (Horst 2006b). As Horst argues, *buufis* are sometimes the result of the strong transnational connections of the Somali diaspora, through which those staying in Somalia or in refugee camps get constant updates from relatives residing in Western countries with better living standards, creating a constant desire for improvement by migrating. Moreover, as Horst notes, it is important to understand this desire to move within a historical culture of migration, as Somalis 'are part of wider cultural discourses and practices that place migration at the centre of Somali culture' (ibid.: 155). This 'culture of migration' together with the harsh conditions they find in their home country are what makes most Somalis eager to relocate to a place that can offer better opportunities to improve their lives and those of their families. Somalis can be found today all around the world, and in these foreign contexts, they constantly renegotiate what it means to be Somali and Muslim, and the implications that these identities carry into contemporary life in a globalized world.

A *Nomadology* from the Global South

Even if Somalis are spread all around the world, and despite the fact that Somalia is normally referred to as the classic example of a collapsed nation state, the people in the Somali diaspora share a very strong sense of ethnic, national, religious and cultural identifications. These collective identifications connect Somalis across borders, generating a strong sense of belonging to a collective that is not contained within the boundaries of nation states, as authors such as Appadurai (1996), Malkki (1992, 1995) and Keesing (1974, 1990) already pointed out decades ago; more recently, Weitzberg (2017) has examined this in relation to Somalis in Kenya. For the Somali diaspora, feelings of belonging to a collective expand across borders. Apart from the historical nomadic past of many Somalis, the current transnational situation in which many of them live generates translocal networks that connect them to home and to other locations where Somali communities are settled, at the same time as new identifications are simultaneously established in the new places inhabited, as the denominations Somali-Kenyan, Somali-American or Somali-Canadian reflect. Many of the women interviewed for this work, especially those returning from the Western diaspora, identified themselves as 'hyphenated', showing dual feelings of belonging to different cultural realities (a phenomenon also noted in other contexts, as Kebede (2017) explores among second-generation Ethiopians in the US). Thus, by analysing the translocal identity-formation process and dynamics of the Somali diaspora, one of the main objectives of this book is to explore how identities in a postmodern world have become increasingly deterritorialized and reterritorialized with feelings of belonging to a collective that expand across national boundaries, and in this way to contribute to 'a new "sociology of displacement" a new "nomadology"' (Malkki 1992: 38).

At the same time, this book seeks to present alternative narratives and discourses that move beyond the stereotypical representation of Somalis in the global imagination that mainstream media and international discourses have repeated for decades (Hawkins 2002; Klep and Winslow 1999; Mermin 1997; Besteman 1996a), in which Somalis tend to be portrayed as 'gun-toting gangsters' (Farah 2000: 192), or as the helpless Black from a war-torn country, the refugee, the Indian Ocean pirate, the radical Muslim or the Al-Shabaab terrorist. These are reductionist representations that are still very present: a recent search on online news sites about Somalis produced headlines such as: 'Somali Refugees Flock to Camps Amid Devastating Drought'; 'At Least 13 Killed by Suicide Bomber in Central Somalia'; 'Daughters of Somalia, a Continuous Pledge to End Female Genital Mutilation'.[6] These headlines convey images based on stereotypes that seem to fit perfectly with the negative discourses used to represent Africa (Mbembe 2001), in which 'its people appear as victims many times over' (Ferguson 2006: 8). Victimizing stereotypes are still present in the global imagination because there is no 'personal, concrete familiarity of the other' (Hurst 1995: 6). They are a reductionist and simplistic way to look at the other, making certain characteristics fixed and unchangeable, whereas the different identifications that define a person or a group of people continually change and adapt to certain contexts (Brubaker and Cooper 2000; Eidson et al. 2017), something that becomes especially apparent in a context of displacement and diaspora.

The stereotypical narrative of victimization around Somalis is exacerbated even further in representations of Somali women. Even though some attempts have been made to present alternative narratives – such as the books *Aman: The Story of a Somali Girl* (Barnes and Boddy 1994), *Somalia – the Untold Story: The War through the Eyes of Somali Women* (Gardner and El Bushra 2004) and more recently *Women of the Somali Diaspora: Refugees, Resilience and Building after Conflict* (Lewis 2021) – Somali women are still largely perceived in the global imagination as helpless victims of a patriarchal society that relegates them to second place, making them passive subjects of their circumstances, or as alienated women without rights or voice who need to be saved from a culture and religion that suffocates and oppresses them (Abu-Lughod 2013). This widespread and dominant representation resonates with the powerful stereotype of 'Third World Women' as Black, Muslim and uneducated (Mohanty 1988) and does not take into account the more complex scenario in which Somali women participate: they migrate by themselves, start businesses on their own, organize themselves into support groups, take control of many of their cultural practices, express their agency and handle the displacement that such movement has generated in Somali society (Ripero-Muñiz 2019; Abdi 2015; Jinnah 2010; Al-Sharmani 2010; Hopkins 2010; Langellier 2010; Gardner and El Bushra 2004; Farah 2000; Bryden and Steiner 1998).[7] Showcasing and emphasizing the agency and decision-making power of Somali migrant women in Nairobi and Johannesburg is another aim of this book. The book presents alternative narratives and discourses that explore the dynamics of identity formation that Somali women undergo in relation to cultural, religious and gender practices in these two African contexts.

In these two African cities, Somalis challenge the widespread stereotype of the refugee in Africa, enclosed in a camp, a victim figure unable to provide for their family and completely dependent on humanitarian aid. Furthermore, these two African urban hubs are connected by the migration route of many Somalis, and in both places, Somalis have transformed neighbourhoods: Eastleigh in Nairobi and Mayfair in Johannesburg, both of which have come to be known popularly as 'little Mogadishus'. Both cities have become transitional places for Somalis to stop on their way to somewhere else, but at the same time more than temporary homes away from home, and nodal hubs for the Somali diaspora in the Global South and beyond. This comparative study of the two cities reveals a variety of transnational connections among the Somali diaspora. While allowing for and noting the similarities and differences of experiences in the two contexts, that constitutes the main contribution of this work, it is the first comparative study of how the Somali diaspora operates in two African cities that are themselves interconnected.

In order to fulfil these aims, I analyse how people on the move constitute themselves as a collective in a foreign land, proving the assertion that refugees are not people 'without culture' just because they have been uprooted from their place of birth (Malkki 1992); in the case of Somalis, a culture of migration, together with the translocal reproduction of cultural and religious practices, creates a sense of belonging to a collective that is independent of the territorial boundaries of the nation state. By focusing on Somali migrant women living in or transiting through two interconnected urban hubs of the African continent, the book addresses questions about collective and individual identities. It explores how women, as carriers of national, cultural and religious identifications, renegotiate them in a context of displacement. In some cases, this becomes a way to exercise their agency while they try to fulfil the expectations placed upon them by the local and translocal community. Using a cosmopolitan standpoint and focusing on two African urban hubs of the Somali diaspora, I argue that Somali migrant women, far from being uprooted beings without a 'culture' to belong to, strategically renegotiate their cultural and religious identifications, generating new forms of agency and mobility in translocal urban contexts that are both interconnected, at the same time than exclusionary and full of opportunities. In broader terms, the book contributes to current debates about the dynamics of how collective identities operate in the context of displacement, in an interconnected, postmodern world in which migration and displacement have become more common than ever, identities are not as certain as they used to be, and a translocal sense of being connected surpasses fixed national borders.

Cosmopolitan Refugees

Tawakal Clinic, where I had previously met Amal, was established in Eastleigh by two doctors, initially as a gynaecological and physicians' clinic. However, they noticed that the patients coming over and over again, complaining of physical pains such as headaches, insomnia or high blood pressure, were really suffering from symptoms of post-traumatic stress disorder. They decided to start offering psychological counselling, together with weekly group meetings in which women could speak freely and share their experiences and anxieties. As the years went by, the meetings, run by young women, developed to cover a wider range of topics, such as healthy eating, forgiveness, dealing with everyday cohabitation problems, family members and daily exercise. Two groups of women meet on Saturday mornings and afternoons to talk about these topics with facilitators, whom the participants regard as 'teachers'. The topics at one such meeting were physical and mental well-being, nutrition and how to deal with older relatives. At the end of the meeting, I stayed to talk to Hibo, one of the teacher-facilitators; at the time, she was a 22-year-old student of Islamic studies at UMMA University in Thika, a small town north-east of Nairobi. She explained that she loved preparing for the meetings and talked with joy about how beneficial it is for women to have a safe space to talk freely about their worries and experiences. Our conversation took place around January 2014, when the Kenyan police started raiding Eastleigh in search of 'undocumented migrants' and Al-Shabaab members, just months before the launch of the Operation Usalama Watch scheme by the Kenyan government.[8] Hibo was outraged by the raids and her joy turned into anger as she told me about these events, especially when she referred to the stereotypical image that people project onto Somalis, as ignorant refugees with terrorist aspirations. 'People think we are stupid that we don't even know who Rihanna is!' she said, raising her voice and gesticulating, her arms emerging from under the *jilbaab* covering her head and half of her body; her henna-decorated hands, smartphone in one of them, moved in expression of her outrage.[9] This view of Hibo's is not unique to her, but shared by many young Somali women, who move between the expression of global trends, which they consume and generate, and the weight of stigmatization for being refugees, Somalis and Muslims. The consumption of global popular culture and the sense of belonging to the modern world are not just the result of transnationalism or globalization, but also denote the great cosmopolitan experience lived by women in the Somali diaspora.

Beyond translocal experiences and aspirations, Hibo, Amal and the other young women at Sacdiya Beauty Salon also adopted a cosmopolitan standpoint in relation to the world, in which 'cosmopolitanism [was] not only embodied, but also felt, imagined, consumed and fantasized' (Skrbis et al. 2004: 121). In the case of young Somali women in Nairobi and Johannesburg, this cosmopolitanism was felt, embraced and consumed in the form of cultural expressions and lifestyles, at the same time as being imagined and fantasized in the hope of further migration.

Cosmopolitanism, as a theory of enquiry in the social sciences, has had a revival in the last couple of decades (Appadurai 2013; Werbner 2008; Appiah 1997, 2006; Beck 2006; Beck and Sznaider 2006; Furia 2005; Gilroy 2005; Darieva et al. 2012; Breckenridge et al. 2002; Pollock 2000; Pollock et al. 2000; Waldron 2000). The vast use of the term has caused its meaning to multiply, and cosmopolitanism can be understood as a sociocultural condition, a philosophy, a political project, an attitude or a social practice (Vertovec and Cohen 2002). In this book, I take into account cosmopolitanism both as an attitude and as a social practice. Cosmopolitanism appears as an attitude or standpoint that many young Somalis adopt in relation to their world, at the same time as it is produced, consumed and performed in everyday social and cultural practices. In the contexts of Nairobi and Johannesburg, the cosmopolitanism that Somali women expressed operated both as the result of the migration experience and as a motivation to migrate further.

Even if some authors have associated the cosmopolitan condition with migrants or refugees (Landau and Freemantle 2010; Kothari 2008; Werbner 1999; Malkki 1995), cosmopolitanism is not normally attributed as a characteristic of refugees or forced migrants; the term tends to be associated with a cultivated elite from Western countries (Appadurai 2013; Skrbis and Woodward 2007; Waldron 2000; Hannerz 1996), an elite embodied in the traveller or the expatriate who pursues 'the freedom of travel, and the luxury of expanding the boundaries of one's own self by expanding its experiences' (Appadurai 2013: 197). However, this approach to cosmopolitanism is narrow and incomplete, as it leaves out other forms of cosmopolitanism taking place in the world today. Challenging the contemporary and Eurocentric connotations of the term, Gilroy (2005: 289) proposes South Africa, especially Johannesburg, as the cradle of 'a new cosmopolitanism centred in the global South', an idea developed further by Achille Mbembe in his concept of Afropolitanism (2007; see also Nuttall and Mbembe 2008). This is a cosmopolitanism born and practised in Africa with a long history, in which Johannesburg is presented as the main cosmopolitan hub of the continent. However, African cosmopolitanism is not a new, postmodern phenomenon: Laviolette (2008) explores the centuries-old cosmopolitan nature of the Indian Ocean's Swahili coast, while Diouf and Rendall (2000) analyse the historical cosmopolitanism among the Senegalese Murid diaspora.

Regarding refugee studies, Landau and Freemantle (2010) propose a 'tactical cosmopolitanism', adopted by many migrants to South Africa as a strategy to negotiate inclusion in a foreign society. Kothari (2008) also observes this strategic cosmopolitanism taking place among peddlers from South Asia and West Africa living in Barcelona, who

> are members of transnational networks who accumulate and share knowledge about how to cross spatial and cultural borders. They create, exist in, and invoke global networks as they travel across the world, producing cross-cultural interactions and sensitivities. (ibid.: 501)

However, even if some of the characteristics of a strategic cosmopolitanism were present among Somalis in Nairobi and Johannesburg, the cosmopolitanism they expressed was not only tactical or strategic, but the result of a transnational experience in which they reinvented themselves in the diaspora.[10] These findings resonate with Liisa Malkki's study *Purity and Exile* (1995), in which she explored the cosmopolitan constructions of identity that Hutu refugees experienced in Kigoma. She observed that 'in the process of managing these "rootless" identities in a township life, they were creating [...] a lively cosmopolitanism' (ibid.: 36). Among Somali women in Nairobi and Johannesburg, the embraced cosmopolitanism is brought about by the migration experience of exposure to new urban contexts and the further cosmopolitan aspirations of relocating somewhere else. It is a cosmopolitanism that emanates from below, that 'builds on the practices of the local [...] but which is imbued with a politics of hope [...] It builds towards global affinities' (Appadurai 2013: 198). This is a grounded cosmopolitanism in which the local interweaves with the 'politics of hope', the desire of having a better life than the current one, which speaks directly to the strong connection between migration and hope (Pine 2014). For the women interviewed in both cities, the main motive behind their decisions to migrate was the aspiration to improve their lives, a constant desire for a better future, hoping to improve their lives and those of their families through transnational migration. All of them expressed a strong desire for membership in the 'new world order' (Ferguson 2006), in which they could work, study and move freely around the world. This cosmopolitanism from below, emanating from the 'politics of hope' intrinsic to the migration process (Appadurai 2013; Pine 2014), becomes a powerful engine for moving across borders. In the case of the Somali diaspora, this embraced cosmopolitanism does not erase certain characteristics of Somaliness, but is compatible with them. As Anthony Appiah (1997) points out, the cosmopolitan ideal actually resides in taking your roots with you wherever you go. The cosmopolitan experience brought about by transnational migration does not make Somalis leave their ethnic, cultural and local identifications behind; instead, they are re-enacted in new cosmopolitan urban contexts that at the same time are imbued with further desires for migration. The dialogue between local and cosmopolitan expressions becomes especially apparent in the Facebook and Instagram accounts of young Somali women, where motivational quotes of encouragement towards a better life cohabit with nostalgic representations of a lost Somalia and Islamic messages. The epigraphs that open each chapter of this book are taken from these sources, as they showcase how this popular cultural practice reflects the subjectivities and identifications of young Somalis on the move. Thus, aspirations for membership of and inclusion in the 'new world order' do not mean abandoning local practices and ways of being; these are still very present and relevant in Somalis' everyday lives. Rihanna may be one of Hibo's favourite singers: that is perfectly compatible with wearing her *jilbaab*, having her hands decorated with henna for special occasions and studying the Qur'an.

Translocal Identities

The rooted cosmopolitanism or cosmopolitanism from below that Somali women embrace in Nairobi and Johannesburg takes place in a context in which the Somali diaspora has transformed two urban spaces, Eastleigh and Mayfair, into 'little Mogadishus'. This may seem contradictory, in the sense that the cosmopolitanism described takes place in spaces that are physical and symbolic reproductions of a lost homeland, and around which Somalis cluster together. However, this situation can be better understood through translocality, a concept also introduced by Appadurai (1995) and further developed by Brickell and Datta (2011). Translocality emphasizes the agency of migrants in the transnational experience, which can be considered a 'grounded transnationalism' in that all transnational ties and links take place and are embodied in a particular locale. In the streets of Eastleigh and Mayfair today, one can find plenty of internet cafes that, apart from providing internet services, also sell Somali music on CDs and DVDs burned to the customer's specifications in a few minutes. This 'traditional' Somali music is mostly produced in the Western diaspora, especially in London, and then exported all around the world. The music video clips showcase mostly images of Somalia, and are a good example of how a translocal situation can bring together such different and distant places as London, Mogadishu and Johannesburg, 'enabl[ing] the symbolic and affective bridging between locations as well as a heightened sense of home' (Rios and Watkins 2015: 212). Places are also embedded with social practices deeply linked to our sense of identity (Giddens 1990) and 'constructed thought the patterned repetition of behaviours in one location' (Oakes and Price 2008: 254). Thus, the repeated performativity of social, cultural and religious practices in diasporic spaces reproduces certain lifestyles with recognizable identifications. And it is this repetition of behaviours that leads Brickell and Datta (2011) to apply Bourdieu's concept of *habitus* to the reproduction of spaces that migrant communities carry out in their new locations.

In this sense, translocality is a useful concept with which to explore the different dimensions of identity formation in relation to places that are interconnected through both 'symbolic representations' and 'material and physical dimensions', as it can 'describe socio-spatial dynamics and processes of simultaneity and identity formation that transcend boundaries' (Greiner and Sakdapolrak 2013: 373). Such is the case of the Somalis living in Eastleigh and Mayfair: the two neighbourhoods are interconnected for Somalis, and are also linked to Somalia and any other places in the world where Somalis can be found. A translocal situation links together migrants' imagined places, which materialize in spatial recreations embedded with cultural meanings. These connections among the Somali diaspora have become even more fluid now that new technologies and social media allow faster and easier communication across borders (Ponzanesi 2021), and what Sadouni (2019) defines as pan-Somalianism, which is a sense of being Somali extended all around the world.[11]

Narratives of the Self

The qualitative research for this book started with a focus on women's life stories and the analysis of their narratives related during in-depth interviews about their experiences of migration and relocation to a new diasporic space. Self-narratives provided an excellent tool to simultaneously access lived experiences and the subjectivity of the people that lived through them. They also became a way to move beyond generalizations about cultures by focusing on individual stories (Abu-Lughod 1993). The different first-person narratives produced by women constitute the basis of this work. Maria Tamboukou (2008) applies the Foucauldian senses of power and discourse to how narratives are produced. She states that power 'intervenes in creating conditions of possibility for specific narratives to emerge as dominant and for others to be marginalized' (ibid.: 104), which is the case for women's narratives, that have historically been relegated to second place, silenced or suppressed. She argues that 'the self is a discursive formation, emerging from the margins of the hegemonic discourses … Auto/biographical narratives thus constitute a discursive regime creating the conditions of possibility for counter-discourses to arise' (ibid.: 106). Creating a space for Somali women to narrate their stories allowed for the emergence of reflections about what they considered to be their identity features or identifications and what these meant to them; at the same time, it opened up a space for individual subjectivities to emerge, which permitted access to their own discourses on culture, religion and gender. First-person narratives also challenge the 'taken-for-granted', dominant discourses about Somali women, offering a counter-narrative that is fundamental to a better understanding of how Somaliness is constructed across borders. They also allowed women to reflect on the influence of migration on their lives and to consider how it had been a factor of change, and enabled the exploration of how Somali women's stories 'connect with other stories, discourses and practices' (ibid.: 111). Moreover, in a situation of displacement, the migrant leaves behind a familiar reality to inhabit a new one; this uprooting can create, in Edward Said's words, a 'discontinuous state of being' (1984: 50). Narrative can help to put this 'discontinuity' together, acting as a link between past, present and future and creating a new sense of self that inhabits the three temporal spaces, giving a sense of continuity and meaning in a fragmented life.

When listening to others' stories, one has to move between the hermeneutics of faith and the hermeneutics of suspicion (Ricoeur 1970). Faith refers to believing what we are being told, and suspicion points to what is elicited in a narrative, what is not said. The hermeneutics of suspicion pay attention to layers of meaning in the shadows that are not obvious or apparent. Throughout this research, I moved between the two. I did, however, generally give preference to the hermeneutics of faith; as Josselson (2004) asserts, the hermeneutics of faith aim to restore meaning:

> This approach is of paramount value when our aim is giving 'voice' to marginalized or oppressed groups and thus representing their experiences. Meanings may be assigned through consensus between the researcher and the researched and understood to be co-constructed through conversation between them […] The hermeneutic stance from this position is one of trying to re-collect and reorder meanings. (ibid.: 6)

This approach to 'restoring meaning' was taken into account concerning the life stories and in-depth interviews, as well as during the informal conversations I had with Somali women in Nairobi and Johannesburg, creating a space in which they could freely express their views and opinions. The narratives they produced in both cities provided a rich resource with which to explore identity dynamics in situation of migration.

The concept of 'identity' has recently been criticized in some anthropological circles due to its multiplicity of meanings and the potential ambiguities it presents; instead, terms such as 'self-understanding' or 'identifications' are proposed (Brubaker and Cooper 2000). In this research, the use of the term 'identifications' was helpful as an approach to the study of identities from a dialogical perspective, as it places emphasis on the intention of the actor and the agency of subjects who identify themselves with certain discourses, narratives and practices. As Eidson et al. (2017) suggest, this terminology bridges between the 'inside' world of the individual self and the 'outside' one of material, social, religious and cultural practices. At the same time, identities, in the sense of 'self-understanding' (Brubaker and Cooper 2000), are deeply linked to narratives (Somers 1994; Ochs and Capps 1996), as the 'self' is performed and takes shape in the autobiographical narratives produced during social interaction. As Ochs and Capps (1996: 19) put it: 'narrative and self are inseparable in that narrative is simultaneously born out of experience and gives shape to experience [...] Narratives bring multiple, partial selves to life'. Toni Morrison (1994: 22) goes further when she affirms that 'narrative is radical, creating us at the very moment it is being created'. Our sense of self emerges from the stories we produce to present ourselves to the world and from the stories that circulate about us, which may sometimes differ from the ones we tell about ourselves (Brubaker and Cooper 2000). This operates both for individual and collective identities; these are understood here as 'an activated category of perceived, felt, to feigned likeness, distinction and solidarity among human actors' (Eidson et al. 2017: 341). Such is the case for Somalis, who, as stated, are normally portrayed as 'the refugee', 'the pirate' or 'the terrorist' par excellence, a narrative that does not match the narratives they produce about themselves, as explored in these pages. These perspectives on identity, as 'self-understanding' or 'identifications', are applied throughout this book, as they provide helpful models in explaining how the positionality of Somali women operates in regard to their own self-identifications and narratives. However, having clarified the approach to 'identity', this book employs the term with all its ambiguity, as it seems unavoidable for the analysis of some of the questions that the book seeks to answer, which are directly linked to cultural, national and religious identity (or identifications).

Finally, this book approaches the study of identities from a dialogical perspective (Bakhtin 1981), whereby within a dialogical framework, our sense of self always emerges from a dialogue, in whatever form it may take: with ourselves, with others, with the world or with the spatial and temporal contexts we inhabit. Identifications are thus constantly constructed in dialogue with the different factors or intersections surrounding the life of a person and the context in which they take place. I treat the various identifications that the Somali women expressed as performative (Butler 1990, 2010) and interactional, always constructed in relation to others and to the particular translocal spatial context in which the women find themselves.

An Ethnographic and Dialogical Approach to Somali Studies

As mentioned, initially the methodology for this book was intended to be exclusively narrative-based, based on life stories of and in-depth interviews with Somali women in Nairobi and Johannesburg. However, as the fieldwork advanced, some women were not sure what kind of self-narrative they were expected to produce; many of them were also anxious about the fact that the interviews were recorded. At the same time, more meaningful data was emerging in the casual conversations I had with them before or after the interviews. Some of the anecdotal stories they told seemed more relevant than those they related during interviews. They were also more relaxed and open during these casual interactions, which made me adopt a more ethnographic approach, as this allowed access to the 'small stories' happening at a local level, in addition to the 'big stories' circulating on a more global scale and interconnected through transnational channels. The multiple conversations held with young women informally or in focus groups also provided access to the narratives being constructed in the virtual spaces of Instagram and Facebook. These constituted direct reflections of the participants' subjectivities, values and desires and provided a useful entry point to understanding how Somaliness is constructed through a collective narrative taking place in the virtual space. In this sense, moving between the local and the global, the virtual and the physical became an exceptional tool for the study of change (Bruner 1986).

There is an unavoidable subjectivity presented by any ethnography, leading it often to be criticized as an inaccurate knowledge-production form, a subjective representation of someone else's world (Abu-Lughod 1993; Clifford and Marcus 1986; Leach 1984; Ruby 1982) or an interpretation of reality (Geertz 1973, 1988; Behar 1993; Clifford and Marcus 1986). This subjective factor in ethnographic writing makes it very similar to literature (Collins and Gallinat 2010; Fassin 2014). Approaching ethnography as a story constructed by the ethnographer, based on what they observed and reflected upon, makes ethnography a kind of narrative, a particular representation in which the views of the ethnographer are always going to determine what is told and how it is told. Ruth Behar (1993) not only sees the whole ethnographic research project as an interpretation between cultures, but also highlights how through this process, the researcher is firstly a listener who later becomes a storyteller. Nevertheless, ethnographies are always co-created between the ethnographer and their informants, and the ethnographer could be seen not as a 'creative scholar [...] but more as a material body through whom a narrative structure unfolds' (Bruner 1986: 150). In this sense ethnographies are representations of reality, not accurate descriptions of it, as reality is always bigger and far more complex than the stories told about it. However, it cannot be forgotten that narratives are not only structures of meaning, but also structures of power (Tamboukou 2008; Bruner 1986), something that speaks directly to the politics of representation and the story being told, and explains the common representations presented under a colonial gaze, in which subjects are objectified. Anthropology has been heavily criticized for this, and more recently, in the postcolonial world we live in today, accused of losing its object of study, *the native* or *the savage* (Comaroff 2010; Forte 2014). However, ethnographies keep proliferating in the postmodern world, offering valid representations with which to understand fragments or aspects of reality. I argue that the dialogical process between ethnographer and informants is fundamental for providing a fair representation of the realities studied and for the co-creation of knowledge (Jakobson 1960; Ricoeur 1986; Bakhtin 1981; Josselson 2004). Within a dialogical framework, meaning is what emerges in the encounter we have with the other, which is always mediated through dialogues in whatever form they may take – this is what Bakhtin calls 'an intersection of two consciousnesses' (1984: 289). It is from this intersection of consciousness that ethnographic writing should emerge.

In the field of Somali studies, although Richard Burton (1856) provided some of the first accounts of Somalis to the Western colonial world of his time,[12] I.M. Lewis is considered by many the founding father of Somali ethnography. However, his views and approach to the study of Somalis, focusing mostly on kinship relations (Lewis 1961), have often been criticized, as many see a strong colonial gaze in his representations of Somalis. Probably his best-known detractor is Catherine Besteman. In her 1996a essay, she critiques Lewis's characterization of the Somali conflict as being based exclusively on divisions among the clans, in line with Western political and media discourses. Besteman (1996a: 123) points out that 'shifting cultural constructions of difference such as race, language and status, [...] occupation and class' also played a key role in the breakout of the violent conflict of 1991, followed by the collapse of the Somali state, which cannot only be understood based on clanship conflicts. Moreover, Besteman (1996a, 1998) strongly criticizes the static representation of the conflict in Somalia as based purely on seminary lineages and unchangeable traditions. This is a still-relevant debate today in contemporary Somali studies, with the emergence of *Cadaan* studies, in which young Somali scholars are contesting and rebelling against the constant study and representation of the Somali world by

Western scholars. These scholars are questioning the production of knowledge and the gaze through which it is carried out (Aidid 2015a, 2015b, 2015c). *Cadaan* studies – *cadaan* means 'white' in the Somali language – emerged in 2015 as a contestation of the reductionist approach to Somali studies. This contestation was initiated by Safia Aidid, at the time a PhD candidate in history at Harvard University, as a reaction to the launching of a new journal on Somaliland whose editorial board did not include any Somali scholars (Aidid 2015a; Hassan 2015). The debate, which started on Facebook and Twitter, was ignited by the response of Markus Hoehne, one of the editors of the journal, who attributed the non-inclusion of any Somali scholars on the editorial board to a lack of young Somali scholars. This generated a collective response in an open letter titled 'Can the Somali Speak?', signed by Aidid and two hundred young Somali intellectuals from all over the world, questioning Hoehne's assertions and, moreover, the production of knowledge within Somali studies. This is an ongoing debate linked to other forms of decolonizing knowledge production currently taking place at universities in the Global South.

There are, however, other ethnographic works that, in line with what Besteman pointed out decades ago, provide a different approach to Somali studies. Best known is probably the work of Lidwien Kapteijns (1999), who provides an interesting account of Northern Somali women's voices through oral poetry and songs. Her work is among the few ethnographies that focus on women's voices, exploring how oral poetry can become a way to 'diagnose' the state of gender roles and relations among Somali women and men from the precolonial era to the 1980s. More recent ethnographies, like Cindy Horst's (2006a) study of Somalis in Dadab, Neil Carrier's (2016) ethnography of Eastleigh or Cawo Abdi's (2015) comparative study on the Somali diaspora, also move away from a static representation of Somali society, offering a more fluid and organic picture of Somalis. It is along these lines that this book aims to contribute, by bringing into focus Somali women on the move in the two African urban centres of Nairobi and Johannesburg.

In order to achieve this, it was important to create a space in which Somali women could express themselves freely with regard to their own identifications and what it meant for them to be Somali in the world today. In this sense, the dialogical process was of great importance in representing 'the other' based on their own opinions and their views on their own lived experience. In the book, I have tried to reveal other meanings, usually hidden under the heavy weight of the stereotypes attached to Somali migrant women, and to represent them in an open and honest way, based on the stories I heard from them during interviews and fieldwork I carried out in Eastleigh and Mayfair. I have tried to do so in the most dialogical way possible, taking into account their views and ideas, and allowing their own voices, often silenced or unheard in the public domain, to guide this research, in order to showcase their agency and decision-making power and to present a counter-narrative to the mainstream representations normally constructed around them. I do not intend to present an over-optimistic account of Somali women's lives or to deny the hardships they face; however, to overcome the narratives of victimhood with which they tend to be portrayed, it is important to create a space in which their voices can be heard. The information I chose to include in these pages has been carefully selected so as not to compromise any of my informants' reputations or their well-being. Names have been changed, as well as some distinctive personal details, in order to ensure the anonymity of the women who participated in this research. All the women who decided to participate did so in an open and enthusiastic way; even if their circumstances at the time may have been far from ideal, they were happy to talk and to be listened to about their views and opinions on what it means to be a Somali migrant woman in today's world.

In the Field

The data for this book was collected during three years of ethnographic research in Johannesburg and Nairobi, between 2012 and 2015. During this time, I interviewed forty Somali women and ten men in the suburbs of Mayfair and Eastleigh. The interview sessions involved exploring life stories, followed by in-depth interviews with each participant, as well as some group discussions. Participants were all over 18 years of age and their names have been changed to protect their anonymity. The body of narrative data collected was treated using thematic analysis. I grouped the narratives collected in Nairobi and Johannesburg in thematic clusters, compared what was said in the two contexts and contrasted it with my notes and observations from the field in order to find similarities and differences between the two interlinked cities. I present case studies of particular women to illustrate the theoretical analysis, but I have also retained quotations directly from interviews to show what the women said, and in this way to showcase their voices.

In 2015 I also conducted the project 'Metropolitan Nomads: A Journey through Joburg's Little Mogadishu', a collaboration with a photojournalist that used ethnography and photography to visually document the everyday life of Mayfair in order to portray a different approach to the representation that Somalis normally receive in South Africa. Some of the ethnographic data gathered for this project has also been used for this book, which is also illustrated with selected photos from the project.[13] A workshop on participatory arts methods, #EverydayMayfair, was also conducted in Mayfair in 2017, in which five participants produced different sets of maps showcasing their migration routes, aspirations and lives in Mayfair, together with photographs that they took of their everyday lives in the neighbourhood. Some of the maps that they produced and the photos they took are also included in this book.[14] Finally, some fieldwork also took place in Minneapolis in 2017, where I travelled to follow in the footsteps of some of the women I had met in Mayfair, who had relocated to the USA.[15]

The interviews, focus groups, workshops and informal conversations with women took place either in English, which the majority of participants were fluent in, or in Somali when they were not able to speak English fluently. A Somali research assistant was always present during the interviews and further conversations with women, and she played the role of interpreter when needed. The interpreter and their role in the 'making-meaning' process of a social research interview should also be taken into account, not as someone who distorts the original meaning of the speaker, but someone who adds meaning to the interview-construction process by acting as an intercultural mediator (Palmary 2011; Venuti 2000; Alexieva 1997). Social interactions become situations for the creation of meaning (Bakhtin 1981; Elliott 2005), and when an interpreter is needed, they also become part of the meaning-construction process. This can create questions regarding transparency and accuracy; however, interpreting is not just about translating languages, but also about 'translating' cultures (Alexieva 1997; Venuti 2000); in this sense the interpreter becomes a mediator between different cultures, adding any supplementary information that may be needed and becoming key to the co-production of knowledge (Cronin 2002). I am extremely thankful to the several research assistants that I had in Nairobi and Johannesburg – whose names have been anonymized as per their request – for acting as 'mediators of meaning' for this study, and some of them became friends in the process.

The views of women about their homeland expressed in these pages have not been contrasted with fieldwork in Somalia or Somaliland, and they reflect women's personal opinions on their country and how their lives there were before migrating. Some of these women considered life in Somalia to be ruled by stringent traditional and religious codes of conduct, and for them, migrating and being exposed to new contexts have created opportunities to question some of their attitudes and beliefs.

While conducting fieldwork, I was also aware of the role played by my own identity, as a non-Somali, white, foreign researcher. This sometimes gave rise to misunderstandings and suspicion, as both Mayfair and Eastleigh are not especially frequented by white researchers. Many of the women assumed I was working for the UN or some other NGO. In Nairobi, it was common that women brought me their documentation to check if I could help. In Mayfair I was initially met with a lot of suspicion; people in the neighbourhood initially thought that I was a missionary who wanted to transform their faith, or that I was working undercover for the FBI looking for members of Al-Shabaab in the area (Ripero-Muñiz 2017). A woman even gave me a nickname – Surprise – because for her, my presence in the neighbourhood was always unexpected. However, after a while, people got used to my presence and trust could be built with research participants. Nevertheless, during the interviews and participant observation, the fact that all the claims and observations that women made were addressed to me also had implications for the way in which they wanted to be seen and portrayed. This has been taken into account when analysing the data, and I have moved between faith and suspicion (Ricoeur 1970; Josselson 2004), not only in relation to participants' stories, but also to the field and the role my own identity played in conducting research with a group of people from a very different background to my own, and to how I was perceived as someone to trust or to suspect. This was a suspicion that further escalated during a fieldtrip to Minneapolis some years later, when I tried to follow up with some women I had met years before in Mayfair, who had then relocated to the USA, the details of which I relate in Chapter 4.

Finally, it should be noted that the last period of the fieldwork for this research was affected by a tragic event: on 21 September 2013, the world witnessed with horror an appalling terrorist attack in Kenya. In the attack, several armed men entered Westgate Shopping Mall in the upper-income neighbourhood of Westland, killing sixty-seven people and wounding 175. The ensuing siege lasted four days, with confusing information coming from the government and the media about the fate of possible hostages. The role of the Kenyan police and army was later deeply criticized, as it emerged that they were actually the ones who had looted the shops, restaurants and casino. Part of the mall was later demolished by the army, who alleged that this was the only way to end the stalemate with the attackers, but some media denounced this as a way to cover up the looting.

After this event, the Kenyan government decided to pass a law against the freedom of the press. Accounts by witnesses described this operation as having been directed by a woman with a British accent, prompting claims that one of the heads of the operation was Samantha Lewthwaite, popularly known as the 'White Widow'. Lewthwaite is a British woman who converted to Islam and later joined the jihad, and was married to one of the 7/7 London bombers. Information emerged that she had entered Kenya with a South African passport and had actually resided in Mayfair for some months.

One week after the Westgate attack, an imam was murdered in Mombasa and riots followed. Police raids increased in Eastleigh as they sought to identify members of Al-Shabaab, who were believed to have infiltrated the country to plan the attack. Al-Shabaab claimed responsibility for the attack. This jihadist group had been operating in Somalia and throughout

East Africa from 2006, with the intensity of their operations increasing since the Kenyan army entered Somalia in 2011. Smaller blasts later took place in busy areas of Mombasa and Nairobi, as well as the kidnapping and killing of British tourists in the northern Kenyan town of Lamu and the kidnaping of two humanitarian workers for Médecins Sans Frontières (MSF) in the Dadaab refugee camp.

The Westgate attack had enormous repercussions for Somalis all over the world, but especially for those in Nairobi, who, months later, from around January 2014, experienced constant harassment by the Kenyan police that culminated in the passing of a government bill against undocumented Somali refugees and the arresting of thousands of Somalis at the Kasarani stadium in April 2014 during Operation Usalama Watch.

I went to Nairobi in January 2014, four months after the attack, and found that the city had profoundly changed: security checks were in place for entering almost any public building and even to board some buses, and people looked at each other with suspicion as they did their weekly shopping at Nakumatt and other major shops in Nairobi. Locals and foreign expatriates feared going anywhere in the city and Nairobi's vibrant nightlife had become almost non-existent. In Eastleigh the atmosphere was more intense, as regular police raids descended on the neighbourhood. Eastleigh was unofficially declared a 'no-go' area for any foreigner, and walking along its dusty streets became a stressful mission. I remember one occasion when, as I walked along First Avenue, a mattress displayed in front of a shop fell down, making a noise similar to a small explosion; everyone screamed and started to run, only to laugh minutes later when they realized what had actually happened, but the tension was palpable.

Even in Johannesburg, the consequences of the event could be felt, especially in the month following the September blast, as reports that Lewthwaite had lived in Mayfair some months before the attack emerged. Mayfair became quieter, with people staying indoors and commercial activity decreasing. Residents were worried about a possible backlash from the Black South African population, from whom they already felt threatened in the wake of xenophobic attacks that had targeted foreign nationals from other African countries (Worby et al. 2008; Landau 2012; Steinberg 2014).

This event impacted Somalis all over the world, and to some extent across the Muslim world in particular. Since 9/11, every time there is a major 'Islamic' terrorist attack, Muslims, and in this case Somalis in particular, are perceived as a major threat to international security – as several respondents asserted, especially Somali-Americans and Somali-Canadians residing in Nairobi. This had and has repercussions on the way in which collective identity is built and strength is drawn as a form of resilience against dominant international media discourses – a theme I explore in the chapters that follow.

Outline of the Book

The first chapter, 'The Port and the Island: Somalis in Nairobi and Johannesburg', describes in detail the two contexts studied in relation to Somalis. Both cities are transitional places for them, but the creation of 'little Mogadishus' also generates the sense of a temporary home and feelings of belonging and non-belonging. I propose the metaphors of Nairobi as a port and Johannesburg as an island based on the meaning that these two cities have for Somalis, on how they experience and live them based on expectations built before arrival. By offering first-hand accounts of migration between the two cities, the chapter focuses on how historical and social factors shape the relationship that Somalis have with these two cities and the links that exist for the Somali diaspora between them and the rest of the world.

The second chapter, 'The Dynamics of Identity and Placemaking: The Making of "Little Mogadishus"', expands on Chapter 1, analysing in more depth the transformation of Eastleigh in Nairobi and Mayfair in Johannesburg in the last few decades since the arrival of Somali refugees. It explores the translocal connections taking place in both neighbourhoods and the ways that the implementation of cultural and religious practices has contributed to the transformation of the areas at the same time as creating translocal identification ties among Somalis and Muslims around the world.

Chapter 3, 'Global and Local Identifications in Dialogue: Expressions of Somaliness in Nairobi and Johannesburg', focuses on how a Somali collective identity – *Soomaalinimo* or Somaliness – is constructed in a diasporic context. It explores the different cultural and national identifications that Somali women use to define themselves and compares how this process takes place in the two contexts studied, distinguishing between different approaches to identifications in the two cities. However, Somaliness cannot be fully understood without taking into account the role of Islam in the construction of a strong collective identity; thus, in Chapter 4, 'Negotiating Religious and Cultural Identifications in Diasporic Spaces', I focus on how Islam became a unifying factor and a core identifier among Somalis. I explore how women negotiate their Somali and Muslim identifications and reflect on the intersections between cultural and religious practices. Moreover, the fact that more women access the Qur'an gives them the power and agency to contest some cultural practices that they wish to discontinue, such as female circumcision.[16] I explore how, in this regard, the difference between Islam and Somaliness becomes strategically used to contest and even discontinue some cultural practices.

Chapter 5, 'Somali Women of Nairobi and Johannesburg: Migration, Agency and Aspirations', focuses on how migration has transformed gender practices and roles among Somalis, increasing women's agency and decision-making power. Building on the previous chapter, it explores the politics of marriage and how women navigate them in order to exercise their agency. It also follows the journey of some women who further relocated to the USA to explore whether their dreams were finally fulfilled in this desired destination.

Finally, in the conclusion, 'Migrating in and Out of Africa', I reflect on all the factors that constitute Somalis as a collective in diasporic spaces and link them to broader current discourses about identities, migration and their consequences in our postmodern world.

Notes

1. A *dirac* is a 'a long, loose-fitting dress … made of printed cotton voile (a semi-transparent fabric) which is worn with a fancy slip called *gorgorad* which hangs several inches below the dirac' (Akou 2011: 82). *Unzi* is a 'cooked' incense made by women, different from frankincense (a natural resin). It is made by mixing sugar with different perfumes or essences.
2. For Somali refugees in Dadaab, see Cindy Horst's (2006a, 2006b) seminal works, as well as Crisp (2000). Harris (2004), Cole and Robinson (2003), Holman and Holman (2003) Lewis (2021) examine the situation of Somalis in the UK, while Hopkins (2010) compares the situation of Somali women in London and Toronto. For Somalis in African urban hubs, see: Carrier (2016) and Carrier and Lochery (2013) for Somalis in Eastleigh, Nairobi, Carrier and Scharrer (2019) for Somalis in East Africa and beyond and Weitzberg (2017) for the situation of Somali in Kenya; Al-Sharmani (2010) for Somalis in Cairo; and Jinnah (2010), Sadouni (2009, 2019) and Thompson (2016) for Somalis in Johannesburg. Abdi (2015) offers a comparative ethnographic study of Somalis in South Africa, the USA and the UAE and Ripero-Muñiz (2019, 2020) compares the situation of Somalis in Nairobi and Johannesburg
3. These maps were created based on the migration routes described by participants in this research, as well as on the maps produced during the participatory arts methods workshop #EverydayMayfair, carried out in Mayfair in 2017.
4. For a general approach to transnationalism, see the works of Vertovec (2009), Brettell (2006) and Portes et al. (1999). Other works that specifically deal with cultural transnationalism are Morris and Wright (2009) and Mahabir (2004). For the effects of transnationalism on identity, see Erol (2012), Bradatan et al. (2010), Butcher (2009) and Vertovec (2001).
5. Historically, only Somalis settled in the fertile lands of the south of the country, between the Juba and Tana rivers, had a sedentary agricultural lifestyle (Besteman 1996b, 1998; Lewis 1998).
6. See Valmary (2022); 'At Least 13 Killed by Suicide Bomber in Central Somalia', *Al Jazeera*, 19 February 2022, https://www.aljazeera.com/news/2022/2/19/at-least-13-killed-by-suicide-bomber-in-central-somalia (accessed 28 June 2022); 'Daughters of Somalia, a Continuous Pledge to End Female Genital Mutilation', *UN News*, 4 February 2022, https://news.un.org/en/story/2022/02/1111242 (accessed 28 June 2022).

7. Recent publications on gender and migration also challenge these stereotypical notions of migrant women as invisible victims without any voice or power, and have emphasized the agency and decision-making power of many female migrants and the consequences that displacement can generate in regard to gender roles, relations and practices. See Palmary et al. (2010); Wright (2008); Jolly and Reeves (2005); Boyd and Grieco (2003); Pessar and Mahler (2003); Curran and Saguy (2001); Yeoh et al. (2000); Willis and Yeoh (2000).
8. Operation Usalama Watch – *usalama* meaning 'peace' in Kiswahili – was an operation launched by the Kenyan government following the Westgate terrorist attack and subsequent armed incidents in Eastleigh and Mombasa, with the idea of 'cleaning up' terrorist suspects. Initially, it targeted Eastleigh and was later extended to the neighbourhood of South C in Nairobi and the city of Mombasa. Raids and arrests of undocumented Somalis led to the arrest of thousands at the Kasarani stadium, some of whom were deported back to Somalia (see Carrier 2016 for further details about the policing of Eastleigh; and Wandera and Wario 2019 on the media coverage of this event and its consequences. Human Rights Watch 2014 a/b and Amnesty International 2014 give a detailed account of these events, and denounce them as violations of human rights).
9. A *jilbaab* is 'an outfit consisting [of] three pieces made from opaque fabric … a triangular-shaped headwrap (*masaar*), a matching skirt or dress (*gunno*), and a much larger cone shaped head covering that fits tightly around the face and drapes down under the shoulders and chest' (Akou 2011: 77).
10. This, however, does not mean that expressions of cosmopolitanism are absent in Somalia. For instance, Mogadishu was a commercial node for centuries (Farah 2002), making the city one of the most cosmopolitan hubs of the Indian Ocean. During the 1960s and 1970s, the city also saw the renaissance of a cosmopolitan art scene, and more recently, diaspora returnees, such as the public figure Ugaaso Abukar Boocow (known as Ugaasada), have documented though social media their cosmopolitan lifestyles in the city.
11. See also Maps 0.1 and 0.2 at the beginning of the book, and Figures 5.1 and 5.2 in Chapter 5, for a visual representation of the global connections of the Somali diaspora.
12. It is interesting to note that Burton ridicules the Somalis of that time for believing that malaria was caused by the bite of a mosquito (Aidid 2015c).
13. 'Metropolitan Nomads: A Journey through Joburg's Little Mogadishu' was a collaborative project carried out by researcher Nereida Ripero-Muñiz and documentary photographer Salym Fayad, supported by the African Centre for Migration & Society (ACMS) and MOVE: Methods. Visual. Explore at the University of the Witwatersrand. Using photography and an ethnographic approach, the project explored the daily lives of Somalis in Mayfair, Johannesburg. The outcomes were several photographic exhibitions and a free e-book (Ripero-Muñiz 2017).
14. The workshop was conducted with Elsa Oliveira. Funding for #EverydayMayfair was received from Security at the Margins (SeaM) and the Migration and Health Project Southern Africa (MaHp). For more details about this project, see: https://www.mahpsa.org/everyday-mayfair/ (accessed 08 August 2022)

15. This field trip was made possible thanks to a research grant from the Andrew Mellon Foundation: Research and Publication Support for Young and Emerging Scholars.
16. I have chosen deliberately to use the term 'female circumcision' throughout this book, as this was how Somali women referred to it. This practice is normally referred to as 'female genital mutilation' (FGM) or 'female genital cutting' (FGC). I consciously avoided this terminology as many women found the nomenclature of mutilation harmful, imposing and even derogatory. I also refer to it as 'infibulation', the medical term that refers to the most drastic forms of female circumcision, as will be explained in Chapter 4.

1

The Port and the Island
Somalis in Nairobi and Johannesburg

Every morning you have two choices: continue to sleep with your dreams or wake up and chase them. The choice is yours.

I met 23-year-old Waris, from Puntland, in Johannesburg when she was living in a room in Mayfair with three other Somali women in 2014. She had come to Johannesburg two years before, yearning for 'a better life', after having previously resided in Nairobi for three years, where she studied community development at one of the many Eastleigh colleges. Her family had sent her to Kenya with an aunt to further her education and pursue better opportunities, but after finishing her studies and still being unable to find a job there, she came to Johannesburg, again with economic support from her family. Once there, things did not go as she and her family had expected. She was unable to study any further and after a failed business in Jeppe Street, she could not find another job, so she remained economically dependent on her relatives.[1] One day, she disappeared. Her phone was found switched off and she was not replying to messages. I later learned from some of her friends that her relatives could not keep supporting her and she went back to Nairobi. Some months later, when I was in Nairobi, I tried to contact her via Skype so we could meet, but to my surprise she was now in Indonesia. During our conversation, she related how, in a period of six months, she went from Johannesburg back to Nairobi, then to Somalia, and after finding herself in some 'trouble' there, back to Kenya, where she took a boat to Australia. She was unable to reach her desired destination, ending up instead on an Indonesian island, where she was initially helped by locals and then resettled in a UNHCR camp. I would hear from her from time to time while she was living in the camp, but our contact became less and less frequent until I completely lost touch with her. Five years later, in Minneapolis, I was at the Twenty-Four Mall, one of the several Somali malls in the city, when she suddenly appeared in one of the shops. We warmly greeted each other and she told me how after several years in the refugee camp in Indonesia, she was finally resettled to the USA. She initially arrived in Las Vegas, but she did not like it there and moved shortly afterwards to Arkansas, where she worked in a meat factory. At the time we met, she had just arrived in Minneapolis and was living with another Somali woman in Cedar-Riverside – the predominantly Somali neighbourhood in the Twin Cities – while she looked for a job in one of the warehouses. After finally arriving in the USA, Waris wanted to be close to other Somalis and in Minneapolis specifically, and she finally felt a sense of home, surrounded by the community.

Where is Mogadishu?

Waris's case described above is not unique; similar transnational movements are also made by many other Somali women and men who look to settle in Somali 'enclaves' around the world as well. Such as in Waris's case, transnational migration sometimes includes a return home first, in order to get some economic support with which to endure the journey, leaving the country again soon after. The transnational networks that Somalis have created around the world are shaped by multilayered connections in which people, goods, money, ideas and practices move. In this sense the Somali diaspora appears to incarnate 'the five dimensions of global cultural flows' (Appadurai 1996: 33): ethnoscapes, mediascapes, technoscapes, financescapes and ideoscapes.[2] Exemplifying these dimensions, one can find women like Heda, a mother of five young children and a successful businesswoman who used to run Nuura Lodge in Mayfair and previously resided in London, Egypt and Nairobi; cultural products, like music video clips featuring Somali 'traditional' music – in which women appear with 'open' hair and white robes in a Horn of Africa setting – produced in London and consumed in Toronto and Nairobi; the thirteen email accounts of Amal, which she uses to communicate with family and friends all around the world; money transfer systems such as *hawala*, which allows money to quickly and reliably travel from the USA to the streets of Eastleigh so that a relative can start a business; and political ideas about the fate of the country and the role of the terrorist group Al-Shabaab, which are discussed as vigorously by Somalis in Mogadishu as in Minneapolis. The transnational situation in which many Somalis live has also transformed families such that their members can be spread around several continents (Al-Sharmani 2007), and investment from the diaspora plays a crucial role in the reconstruction of Somalia itself (Farah

2009; Lindley 2010; Carrier 2016). Forced migration has transformed many aspects of the lives of those who had to flee Somalia in the aftermath of the conflict, affecting individuals and also 'economic, social and political processes of various locations' (Kusow and Bjork 2007: 4).

Nairobi and Johannesburg are two of the main urban hubs in sub-Saharan Africa, and attract migrants and refugees from other African countries. They are also deeply connected in the migration routes of many Somalis, as many members of the Somali community in Johannesburg have previously lived or transited through Nairobi, a situation that generates strong social networks connecting the two African cities. This is a migration route that, in some cases, is also taken the other way round, from Johannesburg to Nairobi. Such was the case of Waris, related in this chapter's introduction, and other Somali refugees in South Africa, who, once they have obtained their pertinent legal documents for travelling outside the country, also go back to Nairobi to visit family, seek economic support or invest in goods that they bring back to resell in Johannesburg. This route was also taken in larger numbers in the aftermath of a wave of xenophobic attacks in South Africa in early 2015, which led many Somalis to go back to Nairobi after temporarily transiting through Mayfair in Johannesburg.

Both cities have also become transitional places for Somalis, as many of them journey through or temporarily inhabit these two cities and use them as platforms to get to Western countries – and in the case of Nairobi, to temporarily go back to Somalia, as many diaspora returnees do. However, a more stable Somali population also exists in both places.[3] In Nairobi, even if ethnic Somalis reside in different areas of the city – such as South C, Kilimani or Komorock – the vast majority are concentrated in Eastleigh, or 'Isili', as it is popularly known. The Somali community in Nairobi, formed by refugees, Somali-Kenyans and diaspora returnees, is bigger and more established than the one in Johannesburg, and offers a larger network of support for Somalis transiting through or living in the city. In Johannesburg, the Somali population is smaller in number and mostly resides in the area of Mayfair. Many respondents expressed feelings of isolation and lack of support from their extended families. Even if the city is also perceived by many Somalis as a transitional place on the way to more desired destinations in the West, it is also seen as a land of opportunities; its thriving economy, quite unique in the African context, makes it a treasure island for many African migrants. This is also the case for Somalis, who endure a tough journey through the African continent full of great expectations that start to disappear as soon as they reach the city. This chapter will approach the description of the two cities and their further analysis based on the meaning that they have for Somalis, the way that they are interconnected for Somalis living on the continent and abroad, and the way that the latter imagine and experience these two places, the expectations they bring and the realities

Figure 1.1. Eastleigh. Photo by Joakim Arnøy.

they find. In the next sections, I will describe the context that Somalis encounter in South Africa and Kenya, and then focus specifically on Nairobi and Johannesburg, and the journeys that they endure between the two cities.

Between Hostility and Cosmopolitanism: The Situation of Somalis in Kenya and South Africa

Kenya and South Africa are two of the countries in Africa that attract the most Somali migrants (see Maps 0.1 and 0.2), with Ethiopia also being home to large numbers of Somalis. Kenya has a long history as a Somali refugee-receiving nation, due to its geographical proximity to Somalia, its historical ties and its own large indigenous Somali-Kenyan population. By 31 July 2022, UNHCR gave a figure of 287 913 registered Somali refugees, making up more than 50 per cent of the total refugees that Kenya received up to that date (UNHCR 2022). This figure is an estimate, as it is mostly based on refugees living in the northern camps, where UNHCR carries out its population counts. The figure does not take into account urban refugees in Nairobi and other Kenyan cities (Campbell 2006). Additionally, the 2019 Kenyan census

Figure 1.2. Mayfair. Photo by Salym Fayad for the project 'Metropolitan Nomads'.

provides a figure of 2,780,502 Somali Kenyans living in the country (Kenya National Bureau of Statistics 2019: 423)

There is no exact data on the number of Somalis in South Africa. Krause-Vilmar and Chaffin's (2011) report estimated between twenty-seven thousand and forty thousand Somali forced migrants or asylum seekers in 2011 – mostly young and in urban areas – and UNHCR estimated a figure of 27,396 by the end of 2021 (UNHCR 2021). In the last few decades, large numbers of Somali migrants started arriving in South Africa after the outbreak of civil war and the droughts that devastated the country in the early 1990s. Two other waves of Somali migration to South Africa took place subsequently: in 2006, after the Ethiopian invasion of Somalia to oust the Islamic Courts Union; and in 2010–11 as a result of the droughts and famines (Jinnah 2010). However, Somali presence in South Africa can be traced back to the early 1900s, when they were brought to the region by the British during the Anglo-Boer War, as Sadouni (2019) examines in her historiographic account of Somalis in Southern Africa.

Even if the contexts and experiences that Somalis find in both countries are different, Kenya and South Africa also share some characteristics for Somalis: both countries can become transitional places in the migration journey outside the continent (see Maps 0.1 and 0.2), and in both, Somalis also encounter some form of hostility, either from members of the local population or government organizations (Abdi 2015; Jinnah 2010; Murunga 2009; Sadouni 2009). In Kenya, hostility against ethnic Somalis – either Somalian refugees or Kenyan Somalis – is not a new phenomenon, as they have been stigmatized both by the government and the police for a long time. This hostility has been present since colonial times due to conflicts in both countries caused by the territorial division and introduction of borders during and after rule by Western countries. The pastoralist way of life of many Somalis did not recognize borders, and Somali nomads moved freely around the different regions of the Horn and East Africa (Weitzberg 2017). The introduction of borders during colonization divided Somalis into different territories administered by different colonial powers.[4] The disputes between Somalia and Kenya originated in the North-Eastern Province (NEP), a semi-arid area inhabited by Somali nomads that the British colonial authorities annexed to Kenya at the beginning of the twentieth century (Otunnu 1992). During the independence process in Kenya in 1963, both the Somali inhabitants of this region and the Somali government in Mogadishu asked for this territory to be returned to Somalia, following the idea of reunification of all territories inhabited by ethnic Somali people under the unique territory of Greater Somalia, a request that was rejected both by the British and the later government of Jomo Kenyatta (Al-Safi 1995; Otunnu 1992). This generated an independent and dissident vision of the Somalis living in this region in the Kenyan imagination. Somalis in Kenya are normally stigmatized both by the government and the country's citizens. As the writer Nuruddin Farah (2000: vii) notes: 'In Kenya a Somali is either a *shifta*-bandit or a refugee.' This stereotypical vision of the Somali as a criminal has become part of the 'state imagination' that filters down to the lower layers of the Kenyan citizenry (Murunga 2009). Current events, such as the military intervention of the Kenyan army in Somalia since October 2011 and the consequent terrorist attacks in Nairobi and Mombasa in the last decade, have exacerbated the hostile relations between the two countries, and Somalis living in Kenya, especially in Nairobi, are constantly harassed by police, who demand bribes that Somalis must pay to avoid arrest on a regular basis. The massive arrests carried out by the Kenyan police in April 2014, in the aftermath of the Westgate terrorist attack, during Operation Usalama Watch serve as another example of such hostility and stigmatization.

Unlike Kenya, South Africa does not share a conflict-ridden history with Somalia. Nevertheless, Somalis encounter hostility in South Africa from 'government officials, public servants, hospitals and government departments and from ordinary citizens' (Jinnah 2010: 93). South Africa, being the most prosperous country in sub-Saharan Africa, attracts great numbers of migrants from the rest of the continent. But it is also a country of great social and economic inequalities. As happens in many other places, the immigrant population is willing to undertake low-paid jobs or to start businesses through which they offer products at low prices; Somalis are no exception. Due to the above-mentioned inequalities, this is not well received by some of the local population, and hostility against migrants has tragically materialized in recurrent xenophobic attacks (Landau 2012). Probably the most significant attacks took place in May 2008, leaving sixty-four dead and thousands displaced (Hassim et al. 2008), and more recently in January 2015. This xenophobic violence is more significant in townships, where many Somalis live, running spaza shops (as explored further in the next chapter).[5] As Worby et al. (2008: 16) note, the ideal of South Africa as the 'rainbow nation' is pure idealism, and the social fabric of the country could be better described as an onion in which 'degrees of national belonging [are] layered around an authentic core [...] the fragile outer skin is made up of black immigrants: Somalis, Congolese, and Zimbabweans.' Therefore, it could be said that while the hostility Somalis face in Kenya has a conflicted historical background, in South Africa it takes the form of xenophobic attacks that are mostly the result of the post-apartheid state's failure to create an egalitarian society, with respect to both the guarantee of rights and access to resources (Hassim et al. 2008; Pillay 2008; Mngxitama 2008).

Nevertheless, as well as hostility, xenophobia and marginalization, Somalis in Kenya and South Africa also find the cosmopolitan hubs of Nairobi and Johannesburg, where an African modernity flourishes and where they are able to recreate cosmopolitan practices and tactics (Landau and Freemantle 2010; Thompson 2016; Ripero-Muñiz 2019). The strong transnational links between the two cities also generate new forms of fluid dynamics expanding across borders in the form of transnational trade (Carrier and Lochery 2013; Thompson 2016) and in the fluidity of cosmopolitan practices and beliefs.

Nairobi: The Port of Somalia

Nowadays, Nairobi is one of the most rapidly changing urban metropolises in sub-Saharan Africa, with a construction boom in the past decade transforming the city centre and its surrounding suburbs, mostly due to Chinese investment: flashy glass office buildings have mushroomed in the Central Business District (CBD), Westlands and Kilimani; new flats and houses are being built almost everywhere to accommodate a rapidly growing middle class; and main roads are being expanded in order to ease the nightmare of the city's traffic, which in fact has not been solved. The old Thika Road, nowadays renamed the Thika Superhighway, with its six lanes, flyovers, tunnels and ring roads connecting it with other parts of the city, is probably one of the most representative of the roadworks that have transformed the face of the city. Along its sides, blocks of flats and chalet compounds have also proliferated, together with shopping malls such as Garden City, a massive 32-acre compound that includes 'the biggest mall in East Africa', five hundred houses and leisure facilities. All this urban development contrasts enormously with the unpaved muddy roads of the townships surrounding the development boom areas. Just a few kilometres away from the Thika Superhighway lies Mathare, a slum in which around half a million people live in metal shacks without electricity or running water. In the streets of Nairobi's city centre these stark contrasts come together in the inhabitants of the city. In the early afternoon, businessmen and women wearing their best suits come for meetings at Java House in Koniange Street, avoiding the street kids who are inhaling glue they find on their way. On busy Moi Avenue, populated by disabled beggars and street vendors selling fruit, a Masai wearing a *shuka* blanket and colourful bead necklace looks for a building he cannot find and asks busy passers-by for directions. As the sun sets, queues of *matatus*[6] wait to be filled with people to drive to all corners of Nairobi, while sex workers start to arrive in their designated spots along Koniange Street, passing some scared tourists in khaki outfits going for sundowners at the Norfolk Hotel. The central mosque sounds the call for evening prayers. Among this mix of people populating Nairobi's streets, ethnic Somali men and women are fully part of the everyday life of the city as they come to town to shop, work, meet friends in cafes or pray at the central mosque, as many other people living in Nairobi would do.

Along Mboya Street, hundreds of *matatus* accumulate, as they wait to leave for the northern neighbourhoods of Nairobi. The chaos is continuous. The street is always busy with people selling and buying things. But the road is even busier, full of white or colourful *matatus*, some moving, others waiting to be filled up with people. The majority are just stuck in traffic. Loud music is played from most of them as people melt and sweat inside. At one side of the road, opposite the fire station, the 6/9 minibuses that are going to Eastleigh make a perfect moving line, waiting their turn for departure. The bus has a double number – 6/9 – because it can take two different routes to Eastleigh, either through Pangani or via Kariokor Market and River Road. Some Somali men and women wearing black burkas are about to board the first one, which is already getting full. The buses are a bit bigger than the average *matatu*. Some are pink, blue or yellow, but the great majority are painted black, as if they were wearing a burka too.

The entrance to Eastleigh begins here. I get into one of these buses. I am going to visit Amal in Eastleigh; she has invited me for lunch at her sister's flat. We go via Pangani. Stalls and shops at the sides of the unpaved roads display their goods out front: sofas, beds or gravestones. After spending a long while sitting in very slow-moving traffic on Juja Road, the driver decides to take a detour on an unpaved side road, covered in bumps, in the back streets of Eastleigh, where Kenyan street kids collect and pile up plastic bottles, rubbish spread around them, rotting under the hot sun. The bus route ends at Eastleigh's First Avenue, a muddy road full of massive potholes filled with brown, stagnant water.[7] Amal is waiting for me there. After years of negligence, Nairobi Council is finally building properly paved roads. According to some passers-by, the company undertaking this task is Israeli: 'That's why they are taking so long and everything is so messy', they say. Tractors alternate with *matatus* and *boda-bodas*[8] along the avenues that have become a construction site, covered with improvised street vendors. I accompany Amal to pick up a suitcase she has bought, as she is travelling to Addis Ababa the next week, where she will meet her future husband from the UK, a country she will move to once the family is reunified after the wedding. After getting her suitcase in Jam Street, we get a taxi to her house in Pumwani, which she says is not far, but the road is dusty and dirty. The taxi stops outside her compound of several blocks of flats. She is staying in a top flat in the corner, with her sister's family. She has been staying with them for a couple of years. We enter the flat from the kitchen, where Muna, Amal's niece, just a few years younger than her, greets us. Today, she did not go to school because she was not feeling well, so she is staying at home and taking care of her younger brothers. There is also a house help, a Kenyan woman. The kitchen has a small balcony with astonishing views of Nairobi city centre, on which they do the laundry and some of the cooking in a charcoal stove. They are cooking a 'Somali pizza', Amal explains, a wheat base with goat meat and tomato on top. She removes her hijab and takes her new suitcase to the big living room, an ample space with a large plasma TV on one of the walls. She brings a pile of clothes and packs them, together with a couple of body lotions and books from the courses in English and community development that she took at Dallas School.

Her packing is now done. I wonder what kind of dreams and fears she also put in there. When the pizza is ready, we eat it sitting on the living room floor, accompanied by salad and soda. The kids join us. After we finish, we chat for a bit. Muna, who was born in Kenya, tells me she wants to study medicine at Nairobi University, but even though she got very good marks in her A levels, they are giving her problems registering. She thinks she is being discriminated against as a Somali-Kenyan.

When we are ready to leave, Amal puts on her hijab. This time we walk back to Eastleigh First Avenue and we pass the garbage dump and the kids. Amal tells me they are orphans. We get to Jam Street through the back roads. It is a very hot afternoon. People come and go, especially women, all wearing hijabs. Others cook and sell snacks on stoves in the streets. 'It feels like home!' Amal exclaims as she takes me to the bus stop. Eastleigh has become a home away from home for the majority of its inhabitants; even if it is only a transitional one, they feel integrated in the everyday life of the neighbourhood, where a 'Somali' way of life takes place everywhere and where the movement of people and goods is constant.

Three distinct groups form the Somali population in Nairobi today: Somali-Kenyans (Kenyan nationals of Somali ethnicity), diaspora returnees coming back from Western countries and refugees fleeing Somalia. Somali-Kenyans, with Kenyan nationality, lived in Nairobi and other regions of Kenya – mostly on the coast and in the north-eastern region – for generations before colonial borders were imposed (Weitzberg 2017). Kiswahili is their mother tongue together with English. Some of them also speak Somali, but very few in the younger generations do. Depending on their class and economic status, they live in different areas of Nairobi, such as Westlands, Kilimani, Pangani, South C, Komrok or Eastleigh. As I will further explore in subsequent chapters, they identify themselves as Kenyan nationals with a 'Somali' ethnic background, as they perform and reproduce many of the cultural practices that they consider truly 'Somali', such as ways of cooking or dressing or the rituals at special events like wedding celebrations. However, they are normally looked down on by Somalis from Somalia on the grounds that they cannot speak Somali properly and don't know 'Somali culture' well enough. They are referred to as *Sijui*, which literally means 'I don't know' in Kiswahili. As Weitzberg (ibid.) explores, Kenyan citizens also consider them 'foreigners' in their own country despite their having been residents in East African territories since before colonial borders were created, making them 'the archetypal "other"' (Carrier 20166 :35). Often, they also suffer discrimination from Kenyan nationals and institutions (as was the case for Muna, mentioned above), due to their perceived 'foreignness'. And sometimes they even experience harassment from police, who treat them as undocumented refugees, something that became routine during Operation Usalama Watch.

During the last few years, there has been an increased number of Somali returnees from the Western diaspora. They hold American, Canadian or British passports and mostly settle in the upper-class suburb of Kilimani. They have chosen to settle in Nairobi, a place where they can live in peace, enjoy its cosmopolitan facilities and at the same time be close to Somalia, to which many of the women I spoke to routinely travel back and forth. The motives for their return are various: from wanting to 'give back' to their motherland communities to the desire of their children to grow up in an African setting, far from the West, so that they do not become too 'Westernized'.

Somali refugees have been fleeing to Nairobi and settling in Eastleigh since the beginning of the war in Somalia in 1991, even though the first Somalis – including Somali-Kenyans – started living in this area from the 1970s (Steinberg 2014; Carrier 2016), as further explained in the next chapter. The number of refugees has increased in the last ten years as a result of the security situation in Somalia, the severe droughts, the consequent famines and the rise of Al-Shabaab in the country. The majority of refugees cross the permeable border to Kenya and go directly to Nairobi. Others register and stay for a while at the refugee camps in northern Kenya, but as they do not want to live there, they settle in Eastleigh and go back to the camps when UNHCR conducts its recounts in order to keep their refugee status and 'papers', which they can show the police in case of harassment or arrest. They have become the main target of the Kenyan police, who constantly run raids in Eastleigh, harassing Somalis and asking them for bribes to avoid being arrested due to their undocumented situation. This harassment is a constant fact affecting Somalis living in Nairobi, whether they are refugees or not. These raids were taken to another level altogether when the massive raids and arrests took place in Eastleigh in April 2014 during Operation Usalama Watch. Refugees from Somalia come not only from Mogadishu or the south of the country, where the presence of Al-Shabaab is stronger and conflict is part of everyday life, but also from the more peaceful, semi-independent and relatively stable regions of Somaliland and Puntland. When I asked some of the women from these more stable areas for their reasons for leaving, their responses were always similar: *There is nothing there, I want to have a better life, I want to help my family* ... Poverty and lack of opportunities become the motor of migration here rather than war and conflict. Somali refugees have made Eastleigh a transitional place par excellence; some are happy to stay there, but they are a minority, as most arrive in Nairobi with the desire to go somewhere else, staying for a period of transit that can last from just a couple of weeks to several years. However, some are never able to leave as planned, due to their lack of money or travel documents; for them, Nairobi becomes not a port but an enclosure or trap that they are unable to leave – as is the case of Samira, related below. Nevertheless, for the majority of Somali refugees and diaspora returnees, Nairobi constitutes a transitional place through which to get into or out of Somalia. Its geographical position and the historical, cultural and social links between the city and Somalia have made it an entry and exit point for the country, not only for people but also for goods, money, ideas and various cultural and social practices, making Nairobi, and specially Eastleigh, one of the busiest ports of Somalia. Moreover, Eastleigh is also connected to other areas of Kenya that are Somali-dominated, such as Isiolo, Garissa, Mandera or Moyale. In this sense, 'the port' of Nairobi is also connected to other Somali-inhabited towns in the country.

Even if the majority of Eastleigh inhabitants are in transit – a floating population – there are certain structures in place that remain, allowing the transit to continue. Probably the most important is a thriving transnational economy based on strong kinship links. Newcomers to Eastleigh normally rely on the help of their relatives. This help can take many forms, from offering a space to sleep in Eastleigh during the time of the newcomer's transit, to sending remittances from the Western diaspora for the person to live on. If the family is wealthy, some distant uncle or cousin living in Canada can decide to invest in a business in Eastleigh that his relative will run. Relatives often (but by no means always) decide what will be the next destination of the person in transit and economically support the move, something they call being sponsored. Sometimes this decision can take a long time, or things can go wrong and a relative who was supposed to sponsor you can no longer do so. This is one of the reasons that transit through Nairobi can sometimes take years. This was the case for Samira, a young woman who left Bossaso in Puntland, following in the footsteps of her sisters, one in Johannesburg, another in Addis Ababa. A distant cousin offered to sponsor her to go to London, but after she arrived in Eastleigh her cousin changed his mind. According to the stories related by other informants and corroborated by my Somali research assistant, this is a situation that happens often. Samira has now been in Eastleigh for several months, living with some relatives that support her, together with her sisters who send her 'little' money when they can. After the London plan did not work out, Samira thought of going to Libya via Sudan so that she could reach Europe from there, but her sisters persuaded her not to, as this route is very dangerous and she could be robbed, raped or even die at sea. For now, then, she is staying in Eastleigh, and even if she is stressed and suffering from *buufis* due to lack of money and the impossibility of helping her family back home, she is also happy because now she has hope, founded on the desire of belonging to a 'better reality'. In this sense, the port can also become an island, with some of its inhabitants unable to move until the right opportunity arises.

Contrary to the widespread belief supported by politicians and the international security agenda of fighting terrorism, Eastleigh is not an Al-Shabaab recruiting site. In fact, most Somalis living there left Somalia because of the terrorist group, and as most informants repeated, they have no intention of engaging in that kind of political activity in their new destination and disregard the radical extremism that has caused so much harm in Somalia. Botha (2014) corroborates this fact, affirming that most Al-Shabaab recruits in Kenya tend to be from other Kenyan ethnic groups, or even non-Kenyan nationals. Normally, they are poorly educated youths who have been recently converted to Islam and in some cases manipulated by religious leaders, who find in the organization a sense of collective belonging lacking in their everyday lives, in which they feel frustrated and forgotten by the government. Some NGO programmes are trying to address this matter, especially in the slums of Majengo and Mathare, and are trying to empower young men in order to keep them away from joining the terrorist group. One of these programmes is focused on several areas: working with government, leadership and development, rehabilitation support, cultural and recreational activities, and livelihood support. They have also facilitated workshops with the Kenyan police to build trust in governmental organizations; funded meetings supporting groups at Tawakal Clinic; created a basketball team and a drama workshop; and invested in Eastleighwood, where young Somalis are producing films (Carrier 2016). Nevertheless, the stigma of Al-Shabaab operating in Eastleigh has a profound effect on the everyday lives of Somalis inhabiting the neighbourhood and the rest of the city, especially after the Westgate terrorist attack, with police periodically conducting raids in the area. One of the most widespread complaints of Somalis residing in Eastleigh is the harassment that they suffer from the Kenyan police, who constantly raid the neighbourhood under the excuse of finding and detaining undocumented refugees and possible terrorists. Somalis claim that they are seen as 'walking ATMs' by the highly corrupt Kenyan police, who constantly demand bribes that Somalis must pay to avoid arrest.[9] One young man declared that he never leaves home without a KES 1,000 note in case of possible arrest. These arrests have been happening constantly on and off, but have increased since the Westgate terrorist attack in September 2013. From January 2014 police started detaining women and children for the first time, which led to many women deciding not to leave their houses in the evenings for fear of being arrested. These arrests also create bizarre situations, like the case of a Somali-Kenyan woman who left her house one evening in a hurry to buy some food without taking her ID and ended up being arrested because of the claim that she was an undocumented refugee (Al Jazeera 2013). The constant harassment by police culminated in April 2014 with the arrests of thousands of Somalis under Operation Usalama Watch, which was intended to fight 'Islamic Terrorism'. A bill was passed by the Interior Ministry that allowed police to detain any undocumented migrants, with the government even encouraging Kenyan citizens to denounce any undocumented persons they may know. Hundreds of men, women and children were taken to the Kasarani stadium, where they remained for several days with scarce food, water and toilet facilities.[10] The media and humanitarian organizations were banned from accessing the premises. This event made many Somalis leave Kenya, either returning to Somalia or going somewhere else. However, those who could not leave had to live with the stigma of being considered undocumented migrants or terrorists. This is probably worst for Somali-Kenyans, who are Kenyan citizens in their own right, but are considered 'dangerous' foreigners. A Somali-Kenyan I interviewed in Nairobi complained of how this has made her everyday life and interactions with people extremely difficult, as the police are always suspicious of her, as Weitzberg (2017) also describes.

In addition to these police raids, some respondents reported that another danger of Eastleigh's streets was gangs of young Somalis who committed petty crime, like stealing smartphones or money. According to them, these gangs were mostly formed of young Somalis from the Western diaspora, who had been deported and had no strong family links in Nairobi. They explained that these gangs operated in different areas of Eastleigh, and fights between the different gangs over operating territories were common. The biggest and most popular gang at the time of my research was the Superpowers.[11]

To recapitulate, Nairobi, and especially Eastleigh, where the majority of the Somali population in the city is concentrated, functions as a central port for the Somali diaspora; the latter uses the city's proximity to Somalia either to leave the country, as refugees do, or to get into it, as diaspora returnees are increasingly doing. Nairobi also functions as a cargo port, as it is probably the main node of commerce for the Somali diaspora, providing goods not only for Kenya but for East and Southern Africa too, and also for other places around the globe where Somalis can be found.

Journeys to the South

For Somalis, the journey to Johannesburg, as to many others places, begins in Nairobi. Somalis from different regions of East Africa come to Eastleigh, which has become a kind of central station where one can find transport to get to anywhere else on the African continent. Somalis arrive in South Africa by crossing the border from either Mozambique or Zimbabwe by road – either in cars, minibuses or simply by walking. This is the last part of a journey that started weeks, months or even years before in faraway East Africa. Refugees normally head from Somalia to northern Kenya, crossing the northern border on foot. From there they continue to Nairobi, although some may stay in the refugee camps for a while and others may pass through Ethiopia or Uganda first, depending on the region of Somalia they are leaving from and whether they have family there. Once in Nairobi, the journey to South Africa is organized through *mukhalasiin*, or smugglers, who charge a considerable amount of money to smuggle people over the different borders they have to cross. They are also of Somali origin and operate in every country that Somalis cross on their route to South Africa. The journey can be organized in two ways. The migrants sometimes pay the full amount at the beginning of the journey, normally in Nairobi. This full amount includes transport, accommodation on the journey, bribes to pay border officials and the smuggler's commission. Others pay off the amount bit by bit as they reach the different countries that the journey includes.[12]

There are three possible routes to South Africa. The most common way that Somalis undertake this journey is by road. They normally go from Kenya to Tanzania. Once there, there are two possible routes: crossing directly to northern Mozambique and Maputo, where the last steps of the journey are then organized, or detouring from Tanzania to Zambia, Malawi and finally Zimbabwe. However, a small minority are also able to fly from Nairobi or

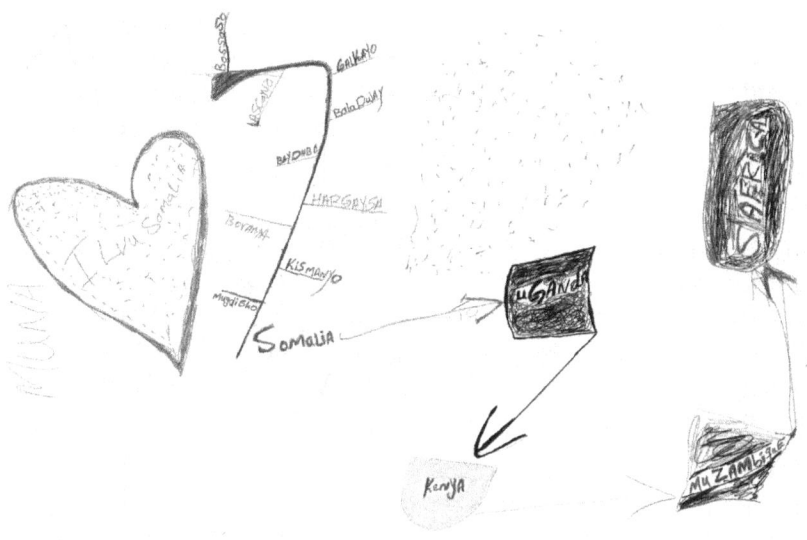

Figure 1.3. Migration route from Somalia to South Africa of one of the participants in the workshop #EverydayMayfair. Published with permission of the participant.

Addis Ababa to Maputo, and from there cross the border to South Africa by road. Figure 1.3 illustrates the migration journey of one the participants in the workshop #EverydayMayfair, who went from Somalia to Uganda and Kenya, then flew to Mozambique before crossing into South Africa. In other cases, people travel by boat from Somalia or Kenya to northern Mozambique. The journey can take from a couple of weeks to several years, depending on whether migrants have the money to pay for the full journey upfront or stop at different places along the way. Small Somali enclaves are found along the route, such as those in Dar es Salaam or Nampula, so if the migrant knows someone from their family or clan staying there, they are able to stay there for some months before continuing their journey. People who have paid just for part of the journey may need to stay, relying on other Somalis' help and hospitality until they raise the necessary funds to continue the journey, either by working for somebody or waiting for the sponsorship of a relative, who would send money through *hawala* rather than the more common money-transfer facilities MoneyGram or Western Union.

This is a journey full of perils. Migrants, normally travelling individually, regroup in small bands of ten to fifteen people. The border authorities and the police are some of the main concerns along the journey, but the smugglers can also become a problem, especially for women. Even if they are normally reliable, in the sense that they deliver the service they have been paid for, there is no guarantee that they will do so. Many of them were described as criminals who drop undocumented migrants in the middle of nowhere. Women travelling alone can become the target of rape and are subjected to constant sexual harassment by smugglers, who demand sexual favours from them in return for taking them across borders. Such was the case of Zahara, one of the women I interviewed in Mayfair. She was in her late thirties and had not had children, something she resented. At the time we met she was running a humble convenience shop in Mayfair West. Her husband, working in another shop in Limpopo, visited her from time to time when he came to Mayfair to buy wholesale items to resell in Limpopo. She had left Somalia in December 2008 and did not arrive in South Africa until March 2010. Her journey to South Africa was full of risks. She left Kismayo for Kenya by boat, but they could not drop anchor on the Kenyan shores as the authorities were patrolling. They continued to Tanzania in a small, overcrowded boat, 'piled like sheep'. When they were approaching the Tanzanian coast, the boat's engine collapsed. They spent six days stranded at sea, with very little water and no food. When they finally approached the coast of Sima in northern Mozambique, police spotted the boat, so the smuggler ordered everyone to get into the water and then sailed away; half the people in the boat, unable to swim, died. Zahara was luckily helped to reach the beach along with some other people. Once they were ashore, the police came and took their money and the few belongings they had carried with them. Without anything, they were taken to Maratane refugee camp in Nampula province. Zahara related that there was no food or water there for them, and they had to ask some Congolese refugees to build their huts for them. After three weeks there, a Somali man from the same clan came and invited her to go with him to Sima. He said he would help her. In Sima, he told everyone that she was his fiancée. Some people warned her about him: that he was a bad man, a smuggler who drank a lot and often raped women. She got confused and scared. Another woman helped her to get the 'refugee papers' from the police station. The smuggler found out and got very angry; he was obsessed with her. After getting the refugee papers, she started working at the house of some Somali men, but had to leave shortly afterwards because the smuggler was causing trouble for them. When she took a plane to Maputo, he was seated two rows behind her. In Maputo she arranged with other smugglers for her trip to South Africa, but when she was at the border, the smuggler who was following her appeared. He was a powerful man in Mozambique, with a lot of money made from smuggling people. He knew the police at the border, who would accept his words – he was painting a bad picture of her – and his money to not let her into South Africa. She became very sick and was taken to the hospital. One of the men that she was working for in Sima came to help her; he took her out of hospital and ran with her until she was on the South African side of the border. She arrived in Johannesburg, where she got her refugee papers. This long, dangerous and anxious journey did not stop her from making it again in the opposite direction after staying in Johannesburg for some months. While working for an Ethiopian man in Jeppe Street, she found out that her mother, who she thought was dead, was still alive and living in Ethiopia. She managed to get a refugee passport and went up again by road to Addis Ababa, crossing Mozambique, Malawi, Tanzania and Kenya in order to see her mother again. She did not have any problems this time because now she had her 'travel papers'. Zahara's migration story showcases the dangers many migrants undergo while crossing half the continent, especially those with meagre economic means; at the same time, all the hardship experienced does not stop them from travelling again when the need arises.

Once Somalis arrive in Johannesburg, normally at Park Station – the main train and bus station in central Johannesburg – a family member picks them up or they call one of the Somali taxi drivers operating in Mayfair. They would have got this number already, at their previous stop. A driver picks them up, and on the way to Mayfair figures out what region or clan their passenger belongs to and drops them at the house of someone related to them. If no kinsmen are found in the city, the migrant attempts to find possible friends or acquaintances. Sareedo, a young refugee in Johannesburg who wanted to become a sports journalist and was a big fan of football, had arrived in the city some years previously from Nairobi, where she lived for some time with an aunt until she could not support her any more. She flew from Nairobi to Mozambique and then travelled to South Africa by land. She recounted her arrival in Johannesburg as follows:

> Before I left Mozambique, I asked a Somali guy there, 'Do you know anybody who drives a car or maybe a taxi driver in the Somali community?' and he gave me this guy's number. So, when I got here, I phoned him, I said, 'Hello, my name is … I am from there … I am at Park Station, can you come, please?' He came to pick me up, firstly because I was paying him and secondly because I was speaking in Somali and he was speaking in Somali. He brought me to Mayfair and while we were on the road, he was asking me where I was from, and I tell him, 'My mother is that family, my father is that family but I was born and grew up in that town'. And he said, 'Yeah, I know some people from that town'. And he mentioned one of the families that I knew and he took me to them. I didn't know that guy but I knew the family and we were talking and I told the guy that his brother and I used to go together to the same school. So, I was staying in the house for two nights and then I decided to go to Durban because there was this lady … her and my mother were friends, and she said, 'When you're in South Africa, why don't you come and visit us?' And I went there and I stayed there for three months. And when I had stayed

three months I couldn't stay longer, I couldn't stay jobless. I hate to be jobless, and then I said, 'Thank you very much for your hospitality, I appreciate I could stay with you but I want to move either to Cape Town or Joburg where I can work'.

Sareedo's journey from Mozambique to Johannesburg showcases the various human connections that enabled her to arrive safely in Mayfair. This human network provides great support for early arrivals, who rely on the help of relatives or friends to start their lives in South Africa. Sareedo also noted that after staying with friends in Johannesburg and Durban for a while, she felt the need to look for a job and be independent, as being a burden to others is something that Somalis always try to avoid. They seek economic independence to support themselves and their close relatives back home. The way in which Sareedo started her life in South Africa is quite common among young women and men, who initially seek the support of others. However, for Somalis it is hard to be unemployed, especially after they have migrated, due to the importance they give to their own economic independence, and especially so that they can support those back home and give back to those who helped them on their migration journey. Once in Johannesburg, Somalis get their asylum seeker or refugee permits and then either settle in Mayfair or continue to somewhere else in the country, like Durban, Cape Town or any township where they can start a business or work for another Somali who already has one. Women normally prefer the first option due to the safety that Mayfair offers, unless they have family living in another South African town. Life in townships, or as they call them, 'locations', is dangerous due to the constant xenophobic attacks and harassment by the local South African Black population, so only men tend to go to these places (Thompson 2016).

Johannesburg:
The Treasure Island of the African Continent

Somalis endure these tough journeys to South Africa, during which they face enormous, even life-threatening risks, because of the big dreams, desires and expectations that they have built about this part of the continent, where they believe they can have a better life. Stories circulate, travelling miles, reaching those in East Africa: stories about the wonderful things and good life to be found in the south of the continent: access to good education and the possibility of finding a good, remunerated job, starting a successful business, making a lot of money, and so on.

However, as days pass and they start to settle in South Africa, they realize, as Waris did, that education is expensive and, in most cases, inaccessible to them; that the jobs they may get working for other Somalis, Ethiopians or Indians give them barely enough money to eat and pay their rent in a shared bedroom; and that starting a business in a township can be life-threatening. Somalis in South Africa become 'third-class citizens', foreigners constantly discriminated against by the local population and the South African authorities, the 'skin of the onion' that can be easily peeled off and discharged (Worby et al. 2008). Johannesburg, a city normally portrayed as the most modern, multicultural and cosmopolitan hub south of the Sahara, and even considered the cradle of 'Afropolitanism' (Nuttall and Mbembe 2008), is actually a city that constantly excludes. The metropolis developed with clear demarcated ethnic enclaves, making it very obvious who belonged where. The spatial rules imposed by the apartheid regime meant that Blacks belonged to 'locations' or Bantustans and whites to the urban centres. Even if these spatial rules no longer exist, their consequences are still felt in the urban landscape and the life of the city. These boundaries are still present in the collective imagination of the city, fed by narratives of fear that have become as difficult to surpass as the numerous electric fences anchored to the ground. Dogs bark behind house fences when Black gardeners or house help walk along the streets of the wealthy northern suburbs, and many white people will never go to the CBD, or if they do, it is on an organized tour. It is still very clear who belongs where. This exclusion becomes even more apparent for migrants, as Grant and Thompson (2015: 181) note: 'Paradoxically, Johannesburg is a quintessentially migrant city and also ranks among the least immigrant-friendly cities in the world.' From this divided spatial perspective, Somalis, considered Black foreigners by the South African authorities, should have settled in townships or the urban migrant areas of Yeoville or Hillbrow. However, as Abdi (2015) notes and as the next two chapters will further explore, Somalis do not identify themselves as Black, and do not fully fit the racial divisions of the post-apartheid nation state (Tewolde 2020), instead choosing Mayfair to settle due to the Islamic connection with the area, which is populated by Indian Muslims.

Mayfair, much smaller than Eastleigh, consists of a small central area along Albertina Sisulu Road and Eighth Avenue, surrounded by a more residential area, with Fordsburg to the east and Brixton to the north-east. At the heart of the neighbourhood is Amal, a Somali shopping mall – a branch of a similar, bigger one in Eastleigh with the same name and owner, who has recently opened another one in Mogadishu. It is situated between Albertina Sisulu Road and Eighth Avenue. Inside, the two-storey mall centres around an open-air food court, always busy with Somali men eating or drinking tea as they chat. Around it, on the ground floor, which always smells of incense, one can find travel agencies, money transfer outlets and small shops run by women, selling clothes, perfumes and a mix of Indian Ocean products. In Halima's shop, for instance, you can find spices such as cardamom and cinnamon, colourful clothes like dresses, *diracs* and scarfs, plastic sandals, *unzi* and incense, whitening creams, sesame oil, perfumes, tea and coffee, and small bottles of *Zam-zam*, the holy water from Mecca. One day Halima showed me a kind of electronic pen that you scan over the verses of the Qur'an and it reads them out for you. She imports all her products from Nairobi or Dubai. Other shops, like Basra's, concentrate only on clothes for women. Her shop is small but full of things: there are scarfs all around, on the wall, on hangers and on shelves. She also sells jeans, T-shirts, skirts, dresses, handbags and suitcases. Inside the small glass counter at the front of the shop are make-up, skin lightening creams, incense, henna and teeth-brushing sticks. In a corner at the top of the shop, hidden from the view of passers-by, is women's underwear on white mannequins. The shop has a back room that initially served multiple purposes: storeroom, prayer room, lunch room. Later it was transformed into a tailor's workshop. Basra gets all her goods wholesale from China Mall or Dragon City, just a few kilometres away, and then resells them, increasing the prices slightly so she can make a profit.

On the upper floor of Amal, bigger shops sell wholesale products, normally imported from Nairobi or the Arab countries. Somalis staying in townships come periodically to get their goods here. As in many cases, the journey to Mayfair is long, those who have no family to stay with in Johannesburg during their business trips stay overnight in lodges that have proliferated around Amal. The streets around the mall burst with life. Eighth Avenue, popularly known as Jahanama or Hell Street because it is always dirty and busy with traffic, has transformed very quickly during the last ten years. When I started going to Mayfair in January 2012, just a couple of lodges, cybercafes and restaurants could be found. These businesses, run by Somalis or Ethiopian Muslims, have doubled in number in the last couple of years, making Eighth Avenue a very lively street. Somalis and Ethiopians enjoy good relations in the city, with many Ethiopians who run businesses in Jeppe Street tending to hire Somalis as shopkeepers. At night it becomes particularly striking that the 'Ethiopian side' of Eighth Avenue becomes extremely quiet, with most businesses closed after dark, while the 'Somali side' bursts with life and activity. There seems to be an unspoken hierarchy among migrants living in Mayfair, with Somalis sometimes working for Ethiopians, as mentioned, but hiring Malawians or Zimbabweans to work in the houses as help or in restaurants as kitchen porters. The shops along Eighth Avenue sell food wholesale, like rice, sugar and tea. There are several restaurants, and a couple of convenience stores and small clothes shops, although many of these are multipurpose spaces, where it is common to find, for example, a cybercafe that is also a hairdressing salon. Several of these businesses also hide a *mafrish*, or khat café, behind them. Passing through a back door, you enter an underworld filled with the smoke of shishas being puffed by Somali and Ethiopian men as they chat or watch

Figure 1.4. Woman selling wholesale perfumes imported from Dubai on the upper floor of Amal, Mayfair. Photo by Salym Fayad for the project 'Metropolitan Nomads'.

a football match on a big plasma TV while chewing khat – a plant with amphetaminic properties traditionally consumed in the Horn of Africa.[13] As one walks further away from Amal along Eighth Avenue, the streets become quieter and the residential area begins. Some businesses can still be found, like Nuura Lodge on Albertina Sisulu Road, which was one of the most luxurious hotels in Mayfair. Before changing ownership, it used to have a nice restaurant on its ground floor where men ate and had tea as they talked, and as they watched the news on a Somali TV channel. The Embassy of Somalia in South Africa began there, in one of its rooms, before being fully established in Pretoria in 2013. The lodge was owned and run by Heda, who arrived in Johannesburg a few years ago with her husband from London, where they owned three prosperous businesses (a restaurant and two internet cafes). But she didn't like it there. She had four young children and didn't want them to grow up in the West. So she went from London to Egypt where her mother and sisters were. She was not working there, 'just relaxing for two years'. Then her husband came to South Africa and she followed with the kids. They used to have a supermarket near Church Street, also called Nuura, but one night it was looted and they closed it afterwards.

Even if Mayfair has transformed in the last decade into another 'little Mogadishu', the hostile and xenophobic situation that Somalis face in South

Figure 1.5. Woman selling dresses and *diracs* in her shop in Amal. Photo by Salym Fayad for the project 'Metropolitan Nomads'.

Africa, the spatial boundaries that still exist in the post-apartheid city and the lack of direct family support create strong feelings of insecurity, alienation and isolation among the Somali community living there. This generates a strong collective feeling of *buufis*, the Somali concept that expresses the anxiety generated by the desire and the impossibility of moving somewhere else. In this sense, Mayfair becomes a small island that is difficult to leave. Most Somalis residing in the neighbourhood, especially women, rarely leave it – unless they work in the CBD – and have seldom been to other parts of the city, as is explored further in next chapter, even if they often visit other relatives in Durban or Cape Town. From this perspective, Mayfair is very different from Eastleigh, in which there is a constant movement of Somalis coming from or going to somewhere else. Eastleigh is also more integrated into Nairobi's life, with many Kenyans choosing to shop there due to the prices, which are cheaper than anywhere else in the city. However, Mayfair is rarely visited by other South Africans, except for the few Indians still residing in the area. In this sense, Somalis living in the neighbourhood feel quite isolated, with few links, if any, to the rest of the city. This isolation contrasts enormously with the various commercial and social connections they maintain with other Somalis spread across South Africa, and with the tight transnational social networks maintained with

Figure 1.6. Travel agency in Amal. Photo by Salym Fayad for the project 'Metropolitan Nomads'.

Somalia and other Somali diasporic spaces on the continent and around the world. Grant and Thompson (2015: 197) corroborate that '[Mayfair] appears as an enclave less connected to an urban or national grid, but operates more widely in transnational networks that link dispersed spaces to immigrant enclaves, creating specific local milieus'.

Nevertheless, this isolation also offers a kind of protection. Some Somali businessmen in Mayfair are aware that they could be making much more money opening shops in townships, but they choose to stay as they feel more secure inside this island or protective nest. Even if petty crime occurs in Mayfair and Somalis are sometimes verbally abused by Black South Africans, especially in public taxis, there has never been any major xenophobic attack against Somalis in this neighbourhood. Moreover, as will be further explored in the next chapter, during the xenophobic attacks in 2008 and 2015, the numbers of Somalis in Mayfair multiplied, with shopkeepers from the townships coming to the area in large numbers looking for protection. In January 2015 the lodges were full to capacity, hosting people for free, with some even sleeping in the corridors. Weeks later, Mayfair began to empty, with many Somalis leaving South Africa in February and March, either returning to Somalia or travelling to Kenya or Brazil (in order to reach the US, a new extended migration route popular among Somalis). Even if the majority of Somalis leaving South Africa were those staying in townships, where most of the xenophobic violence took place, this had an effect on Mayfair, as many of the spaza shop owners buy their goods from the area. With no customers to provide for, many businesses had to close due to lack of income and their owners had to go somewhere else to start afresh. Strikingly, during this time, I noticed that the number of Ethiopian businesses increased in the area; probably, those Ethiopians who ran businesses in townships had decided that Mayfair was also safer for them. However, this was contested by a Somali informant who, when asked about this, declared: 'When Somalis leave, everyone else leaves, as we are the ones who resist longer when things go wrong' – a sentence that reflects the Somali sense of resilience and pride at being the toughest even in the most hostile circumstances. In any case, in a period of a few months, the island became first a protective nest and soon after a temporary port – a busy transitional place from which to leave South Africa; this shows the ephemeral nature of the place, open to constant transformation depending on the always-changing circumstances of the people inhabiting its streets.

The Port and the Island

The fluidity of the Somali diasporic networks in Nairobi and Johannesburg makes these two cities interconnected at different transnational levels: through the commercial route of goods that leave the Kenyan capital in the direction to South Africa, and through the bidirectional migration routes of Somali migrants. The two cities are cosmopolitan hubs in the Global South, which have become important nodes for the Somali diaspora around the world. At the same time, the two cities act as transitional places for Somalis on their way to the Global North, the ultimate desired destination for many of them (Abdi 2015). Nevertheless, a sense of temporary home also emerges along these transits. The geographical and historical links between Somalia and Kenya present certain characteristics, such as a bigger Somali population, including refugees, Somali-Kenyans and diaspora returnees, that provides a larger network of support. This situation does not exist in the South African context, where a smaller population of Somali refugees is found and feelings of insecurity and isolation seem to be the general norm.

Based on the meaning that these two cities have for Somalis – on how they imagine, experience and interact with them – I propose the metaphors of Nairobi as a port and Mayfair as an island, as I believe that these are especially illuminating in describing the different relationships that Somalis have with each place. Due to a more extended network of support in Nairobi, Somalis develop greater feelings of belonging in this city. Eastleigh has become a home away from home to the people temporarily inhabiting its streets. The fluidity of Eastleigh, in which Somalis from different backgrounds cohabit, together with notable transnational commercial activity, make Eastleigh a cosmopolitan hub for the Somali diaspora. However, in Johannesburg, Somalis do not develop the same feelings of belonging as in Nairobi, as they lack the direct networks of support that operate in the latter city; in many cases this creates strong feelings of isolation. Johannesburg, a city normally portrayed as an example of Afropolitanism or African cosmopolitanism, does not operate in that way for Somalis, who in fact demonstrated stronger cosmopolitan interactions in Nairobi. This has some implications for collective identification processes and the way that cultural and religious practices are reproduced, performed and transformed in the two cities, as further chapters will analyse. At the same time, members of the Somali diaspora all around the world have contributed to the formation of an imaginary diasporic community, shaped by diverse transnational links and connections. Moreover, in the two cities, Somalis have transformed the urban landscapes of Eastleigh and Mayfair, creating what are popularly known as 'little Mogadishus', a phenomenon that will be further explored in detail in the next chapter in relation to placemaking and translocal identity-formation processes.

Notes

1. Jeppe Street in Johannesburg CBD is populated by Ethiopian businesses and popularly known as 'Little Addis'. Some Somalis work for Ethiopian businesses. For more about the economic dynamics of the area, see the works of Tanya Zack (2015; Zack and Estifanos 2016; Zack and Govender 2019).
2. These characteristics refer to different globalization flows: technoscapes to the movement of people as refugees, migrants or tourists, and mediascapes to the circulation of information across the globe. Technoscapes emphasize the use of new technologies in transmission of cultures across borders that takes place in the technological space. Financescapes refer to the rapid movement of money and currencies in the global world, and ideoscapes to the movement of ideas and narratives that expand and circulate across the globe.
3. There is no exact data on how many Somalis live in each city.
4. During colonial times, Somalia was divided into British Somaliland, in the north of the country (and the north-east region of today's Kenya); French Somaliland (today Djibouti); Italian Somalia in the south; and what is today Region 5 or the Somali Regional State of Ethiopia (also called Ogaden) (Murunga 2009: 200).
5. Spaza shops are small convenience shops in townships. Today, many of these businesses are run by Somalian or Ethiopian nationals. They constitute the most important aspect of the Somali economy in South Africa, as they tend to be successful businesses. However, there are high risks involved in working in or owning one of these businesses, as they are the main target during the waves of xenophobia in the country. This fact makes them dangerous destinations for

women, and only Somali men tend to work in them (with some exceptions, for instance the women documented in Abdi 2015).
6. Kenyan minibuses.
7. This road has now been repaired.
8. Motorbike taxis.
9. For a historical reflection on the treatment received by Somali refugees in Kenya, see Otunnu (1992) and Carrier (2016). Weitzberg (2017) also documents these abuses with regard to Somali Kenyans. Human Rights Watch (2009, 2010, 2012 and 2013) has also reported this constant harassment and violation of human rights.
10. For an account of how these events unfolded, see: UNHCR (2014), Kushkush (2014), Human Rights Watch (2014a, 2014b), Migiro (2014), Muhumed (2014) and Miller (2014).
11. This information is based on some respondents' assertions, and could not be contrasted with the literature or in-depth research to confirm how these gangs operate and to what extent they disturb the lives of residents of Eastleigh.
12. Towards the end of my fieldwork in 2014, the price to travel from Nairobi to Johannesburg was around $800. The money for the journey is raised among the family.
13. See chapter five for more details about khat consumption and the effects of this habit on households.

2

The Dynamics of Identity and Placemaking

The Making of 'Little Mogadishus'

> Some nomads are at home everywhere.
> Others are at home nowhere.
>
> –Robyn Davison

Shamso is a 45-year-old, well-educated Somali-Kenyan who, after obtaining her PhD overseas, came back to Nairobi to work for the UN. At the time of our interview, she was residing in a spacious flat in Kilimani with her young children and sister, as her husband was working overseas and visiting once a year. Although she was happy living in Kilimani, she grew up in Eastleigh, which she often visited for shopping or to see relatives, and during our interview, she gave a first-hand account of how the area used to be during her childhood. She was the eldest daughter of a wealthy Somali businessman, who owned a fleet of lorries and distributed goods across East Africa. She described the neighbourhood where she grew up as being very different to how it is today, emphasizing how much it had changed in recent decades. It used to be a very clean neighbourhood, she related – 'super-clean' – a residential area full of trees, inhabited by Europeans and Indians as well as ethnic Somalis. She recounted how different religious groups cohabited peacefully. Everyone knew each other, and she used to play in the streets as a child, as there was no danger at all. She went to a Christian school run by nuns for her primary education, and she proudly explained that they were a mixed community that celebrated various religious festivities together: 'When [it was] Christmas, our neighbours cooked and invited us. When it was Eid, we did the same thing.' She also recalled that at that time, there were no shops or restaurants in the area, 'only two places to buy chips'.

They had to go to Ngara, a neighbourhood bordering Eastleigh, to buy their clothes. However, everything started to change in the 1990s when Somali refugees began arriving in Nairobi after the outbreak of the civil war in Somalia. 'Somalis everywhere in the world look for other Somalis', she stated, explaining why most Somalis arriving in Nairobi settled in Eastleigh and thrived by opening shops, restaurants and lodges to meet the demands of the new refugee population.

As Shamso relates, in the last few decades, Eastleigh has become a Somali enclave par excellence, similar to Mayfair, and both neighbourhoods are popularly known as 'little Mogadishus'. Even if other African ethnicities and nationalities cohabit in both neighbourhoods, they are a minority compared to the Somali population.[1] The strong presence of ethnic Somalis in both areas has created a particular landscape that recreates and encapsulates a very significant 'Somali' way of life. Even if Eastleigh is more integrated into Nairobi life – with many Kenyans often shopping in the area – than Mayfair is in Johannesburg (where South Africans rarely visit the neighbourhood and Somalis rarely leave it), both areas have become a kind of 'foreign' land for other inhabitants of their respective cities. A South African colleague once told me that she used to go often to eat in Mayfair, but once the presence of Somalis increased, she stopped going there because she could not find 'South African' food and the place was full of Somalis, which made her feel *as if she were in a foreign country*. And at the opening of the exhibition *Metropolitan Nomads: A Journey Through Joburg's Little Mogadishu*, which took place at the Anthropology Museum of the University of the Witwatersrand, some people who attended thought that the photos exhibited were from India and not the neighbourhood just a few blocks away. These anecdotes highlight the extent to which Mayfair has become a Somali enclave in the city, in which the presence of 'the other' becomes something strange, reinforcing again the sense of Mayfair as an island. This recreation of a home away from home in Eastleigh and Mayfair also generates a lack of self-awareness in the new context. It mitigates the feeling of being 'the other' in a foreign environment, because Somalis are surrounded by people who look like them and who carry out very similar routines and lifestyles to those they left behind. It also creates a situation in which 'the other' becomes any non-Somali who trespasses the borders of the 'little Mogadishus'. At the same time, the neighbourhoods become an initial welcoming point when Somalis arrive in the new country, a place where Somali migrants know they will find assistance and support for their first few months after arrival – a kind of 'decompression chamber, allowing each individual to readjust to the new condition and facilitating insertion in the host country' (Sinatti 2008: 74).

Shamso's account of how Eastleigh has transformed over the years also illustrates how the transformation of space affects the everyday practices of a particular area or neighbourhood, and how places are socially and culturally constructed (Gupta and Ferguson 1997; Massey 1994, 2005). In both areas, Somaliness and Islam have become the materialization of a way of being that is able to transform spaces into very distinctive places. The businesses, objects of consumption and recreational places (such as restaurants or tea houses) recreate on a small scale the social, economic and cultural everyday life of a peaceful Mogadishu that no longer exists. Moreover, these symbolic recreations of the lost city – spaces in which everyday practices take place – also maintain some of the commercial and cosmopolitan spirit that the Somali capital once had, as one of the main hubs on the Indian Ocean. Eastleigh and Mayfair have likewise become commercial and economic global hubs for the Somali diaspora around the world in place of the homeland. This chapter expands on the previous one, exploring the relationship between collective identities and placemaking in diasporic spaces, giving more historical background on Eastleigh and Mayfair and addressing the questions of how place matters in relation to identity and how cultural, religious and gender practices shape urban landscapes in translocal diasporic contexts.

Eastleigh

Neil Carrier, in his book *Little Mogadishu* (2016), gives a detailed account of the history of Eastleigh and the Somali presence in it that echoes Shamso's recollection of the neighbourhood of her childhood. At the beginning of the twentieth century, during the first years of colonialism, Somalis were brought by Europeans to the city and settled firstly in Ngara. However, due to their growing numbers and the cattle that they owned, the colonial authorities decided to move them to other parts of the city, especially to the south. The Somalis refused to relocate there, arguing that it was far from town, where most of them worked. Eastleigh did not exist at that time, and it was formed from the two estates of Nairobi East and Egerton, which were initially intended for European settlers. However, the white population never settled there due to the lack of transportation between the neighbourhood and the city. Indian businessmen showed an interest in this residential area and started to buy plots of land there. Somalis followed due to the connection that they had to Indian merchants. These were ethnic Somalis born in Kenya, and it was not until the 1990s that refugees from Somalia started to arrive due to the outbreak of the armed conflict. As Shamso noted, Somalis always look for other Somalis when arriving in a new place – or if there is not a significant Somali population, they look for Muslim enclaves, as is explained later in this chapter. The arrival of large numbers of Somali refugees in the 1990s changed the landscape of the neighbourhood completely, transforming 'a quiet residential suburb to a major East African

Figure 2.1. A street in Eastleigh. Photo by the author.

commercial hub' (Carrier and Lochery 2013: 334). Refugees began informal businesses, such as selling gold in the lodges they were staying in, to survive and to continue their journeys to somewhere else. This informal business started to transform and grow, and twenty years later, Eastleigh has become an economic hub where banks are open for twelve hours a day, seven days a week (Kantai 2011), making the neighbourhood a global business centre (Carrier 2016; Herz 2007; Campbell 2006).

The businessmen and women of Eastleigh import mostly electronics and textiles from Asia and the Middle East, and sell them at very competitive prices, not only in Nairobi but all over the East African region and the world, due again to the strong transnational links among the diaspora. It is also important to note the role that remittances from family members living abroad play in building this thriving economy (Lindley 2010), and how many members of the diaspora continue to invest in it (Carrier 2016). Eastleigh businesses are distributed thematically: there is, for example, the TV mall and the *bui-bui*[2] mall, specializing in electronics and women's clothes respectively. Beauty products are sold, neatly piled on top of one another according to size and colour, along Second Avenue, and there is also a gold market.

The businesspeople of Eastleigh are not only men. Many women also run or own businesses; indeed, it was a Somali businesswoman who saw the potential of Garissa Lodge and transformed it into a shopping centre (Herz 2007).[3] During the 1990s the phenomenon of 'Dubai Mammas' appeared: women who travelled to the Middle East to buy textiles and electronic products to resell later in Eastleigh (Kantai 2011). This trend is still quite common, especially with gold, as many women travel to the United Arab Emirates to invest in and bring back the finest jewellery made of this precious yellow metal, which is a sought-after commodity in any Somali woman's dowry. It is women who mostly run the gold market in Eastleigh: several stalls selling rings, necklaces, bangles and earrings of yellow gold that they carefully weigh on their scales according to the price of gold of the day.

Today, walking through the lively streets of Eastleigh, the whole world seems to be represented in the shops and stalls populating the busy street and avenues: the latest version of an iPhone, imported directly from China, soft textiles from Indonesia, Palestinian scarfs, fabrics from different origins to make any kind of dress, incense and gold from Dubai, coconuts, oranges and pineapples from Kenya, and spices from every corner of the Indian Ocean. Then there is the Good Star School and the Disney Bar and Restaurant, a rusty stall that is so far away from any Disney movie that the name seems ironic. The streets are very dirty and messy, the unpaved roads contrast with some of the more modern buildings, with their glossy and shiny glass-and-metal look, and as Carrier (2016: 243) describes it, Eastleigh has become:

> a peculiar place, full of apparent contradictions: a place deeply associated with refugees and social marginality, yet also a thriving and dynamic hub of trade, a place long associated with a decayed public infrastructure, yet a place of great private wealth.

This peculiarity of Eastleigh, full of contradictions, is also the context in which individual lives unfold, with Somali refugees and migrants coming to the neighbourhood in search of better opportunities, or the 'Eastleigh dream' (Carrier 2016). Refugees have brought with them a different lifestyle that has completely transformed the area, with repercussions for Somali-Kenyans previously residing in the city. Shamso finished the description of the neighbourhood that opens this chapter with the following statement: 'before the war we were only Kenyans, but then with the war, refugees started to arrive, and we became all the same thing. Now they see us as [if] we are all from Somalia. Somalis from Somalia can always return home ... The only home I know is Kenya.' Thus, the enormous transformation that the neighbourhood underwent from the 1990s led to Somali-Kenyans becoming equated with Somali refugees. They went from being one more ethnic group of Kenyan nationals to carrying the stigmatized label of 'refugees', which had consequences for their daily lives, as they became discriminated against and treated as foreigners in their own country, even if they were Kenyan citizens in their own right (see Weitzberg 2017 for a detailed historical account of Somalis in Kenya).

To summarize, it was the massive arrival of Somali refugees in the 1990s that completely transformed both the physical landscape and the nature of Eastleigh, creating a global business hub for the Somali diaspora; as this was the result of forced migration, the transformation of Eastleigh was a response to the demands of the new migrant population.

Mayfair

As stated in the previous chapter, Somali presence in South Africa also dates back to the early twentieth century, when Somalis arrived with British soldiers for the Anglo-Boer War. These small numbers of Somalis ended up mixing with the Malay and coloured populations of the city (Sadouni 2019). Somalis started arriving in South Africa in large numbers as refugees after the civil war started and droughts devastated Somalia during the early 1990s, with three other migration waves following: in the mid-1990s; in the early 2000s due to conflict with Ethiopia; and in 2010–11 following severe droughts in the country (Jinnah 2010). In Johannesburg, Somalis chose to settle in Mayfair, which was formerly a poor Afrikaner settlement during apartheid (Sadouni 2019), bordering the Muslim Indian neighbourhood of Fordsburg. With time Mayfair also became a predominately Muslim Indian neighbourhood. Somalis chose this area to settle due to the economic and religious ties they shared with the Indian population (Jinnah 2010; Sadouni 2009, 2019; Abdi 2015).

The transformation of Mayfair in the last few years has also been striking. It has gone from being a predominantly 'Indian' suburb with a Somali shopping mall (Amal) to being a Somali neighbourhood, mimicking the 'little Mogadishu' of Eastleigh, which is much bigger and longer established. Sadouni (2019) explains how the economic and business activity of Somalis has transformed the neighbourhood together with Islamic practices taking place there. Distinctive Somali businesses, such as restaurants, coffee shops, hostels and shops, have mushroomed in the last few years, as well as mosques and *madrassas*; this is a materialization of two of the main identifications of Somalis in the urban landscape, as successful entrepreneurs and devoted Muslims. It was this economic and religious connection that led Somalis to settle in Mayfair instead of Yeoville or Hillbrow, where other African migrants to Johannesburg normally settle.

Mirroring Eastleigh and other Somali enclaves around the world (such as Cedar-Riverside in Minneapolis), various objects of consumption from

Figure 2.2. Restaurant and shops in Mayfair, Eighth Avenue. Published with permission of the participants in the workshop #EverydayMayfair.

Somalia, the UAE and East Africa can be found in any corner of Mayfair. When I started conducting interviews in Mayfair, one of the questions I asked women concerned what 'things' they found different in the new place. I used the word 'things' to allow the question to be as open as possible. I thought that the answers would be about different behaviours, lifestyles, opportunities and so on. However, most respondents understood 'things' literally, as material things, and answered thus: 'Nothing is different; you can find everything you need here: Somali clothes, Somali food, Somali perfumes.' Products consumed by Somalis arrive weekly in Amal and nearby shops from the Middle East and Nairobi, allowing the residents to continue a very similar form of material consumption to that which they are used to, something that also highlights the interconnection existing between the two neighbourhoods. Moreover, inside Amal, one could be in Nairobi or Minneapolis, as the distinctive objects of consumption offered are the same in all Somalis enclaves around the world. However, in the case of Mayfair and Eastleigh, the reproduction of space occurs not only through material objects and physical places, but also through the rhythms of street life. On an early Friday afternoon, one can see the streets of both neighbourhoods start to empty for the midday prayers. Shops and restaurants close and the streets become deserted, only to burst back to life a couple of hours later. Somalis love to stay in the street talking to neighbours, friends and passers-by until late at night, a custom also common in many Arab and Mediterranean countries, probably due to the extreme heat experienced

Figure 2.3. Map of Mayfair drawn by participants in the workshop #EverydayMayfair. Published with permission of the participants.

during the day, which keeps people indoors and makes the cooler evenings the time when everyone goes out to socialize. This is a practice also reproduced in Mayfair and Eastleigh, where the nightlife goes on until the early hours of the morning. This also makes Mayfair one of the few neighbourhoods in Johannesburg where life continues in the streets after dark and one can safely walk around.

Somalis residing in Mayfair maintain strong links with Somalia, Nairobi and other locations around the world where Somalis settle, and also with townships in the area, where many Somalis work in small spaza or convenience shops. However, in contrast to these strong transnational connections, many Somalis inhabiting Mayfair do not leave the neighbourhood and its surroundings, venturing no further than the CBD, and just to work in shops on Jeppe Street, which is populated mostly by Ethiopian businesses for which Somali women sometimes work. Apart from a few women who own cars and drive to the malls in Rosebank or Eastgate in the northern suburbs of the city, most women hardly leave the neighbourhood and surrounding areas. This emerged during the #EverydayMayfair workshop when in one of the activities, we asked participants to draw a map of the places they visited or inhabited during their daily lives; in those maps (Figures 2.3 and 2.4) we observed that most of their activities took place around Mayfair

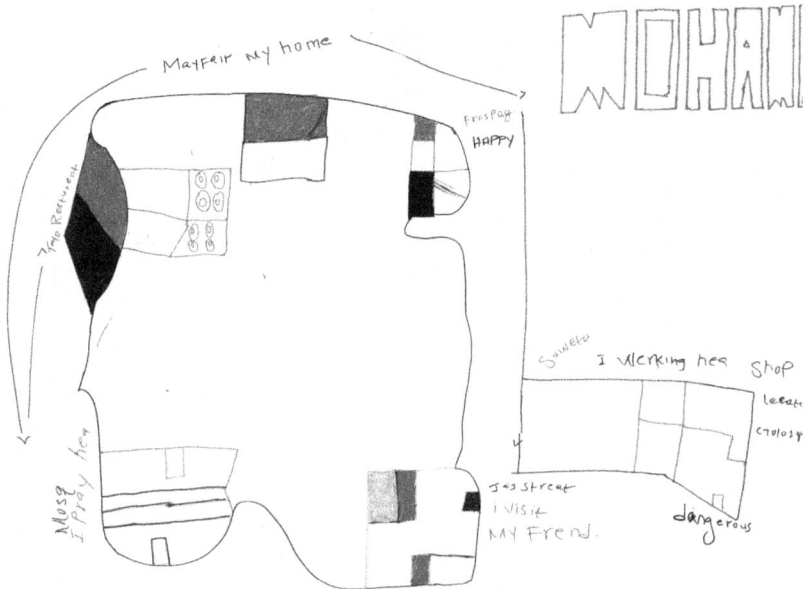

Figure 2.4. Map of Mayfair drawn by participants in the workshop #Everyday-Mayfair. Published with permission of the participants.

and the neighbouring area of Fordsburg. In these sets of maps, the mosque always appeared as a prominent, 'happy' place, as did Amal and its shops, and Fordsburg appeared as a recreational place. In one of the maps (Figure 2.4), one can observe how outside the confines of the neighbourhood and closer to the CBD, the word 'dangerous' is written. In this sense, the neighbourhood is perceived as a safe place or a protective nest for Somalis, a place where they know they can be safe or find protection if needed. This became especially apparent during the various waves of xenophobic attacks in townships targeting Somali migrants.

Many Somalis in South Africa work in or own spaza shops in the townships. These tend to be very successful businesses and constitute the most important aspect of the Somali economy in South Africa (Gastrow and Amit 2013; Gastrow 2018). They have strong transnational links, as many Somalis living abroad in the Global North invest in these businesses (Thompson 2016). Even if business in the townships provides a successful income, however, Somalis face recurrent hostility that from time to time materializes in fatal xenophobic attacks; this makes the 'locations' a dangerous destination, and only men tend to work there, while women stay in the safer urban areas, as also corroborated by Thompson (2016).[4]

Such xenophobic attacks targeting Somali migrants living and working in spaza shops in townships have happened in the last couple of decades; Black South Africans have started attacking these shops, looting them and physically attacking or killing any Somalis they find. Jonny Steinberg (2014) gives a detailed account of the events of 2008. Asad, the main character in Steinberg's book *The Man of Good Hope*, narrates the hardship, fear and horror of those days. One of the most striking episodes in Asad's narration is when Somalis are assaulted by their South African customers and neighbours, who, after the violence they have provoked, simply apologize to them and continue to buy from them as if nothing has happened. Another significant wave of attacks occurred in 2015 when I was still doing fieldwork in Mayfair. These attacks were partly instigated by King Goodwill Zwelithini, a traditional Zulu leader who declared in vernacular language that all foreigners must pack and leave the country. Following this declaration, migrants of different nationalities were attacked across the whole country over several weeks, and many of them, such as Zimbabweans and Malawians, went back to their countries of origin. Somalis around the country were also attacked, and most of them sought refuge in Mayfair after fleeing the rural areas and townships where they ran successful spaza shops. During this time, the numbers of Somalis in Mayfair multiplied for a couple of weeks, with people sleeping on the floors of overcrowded lodges and restaurants serving food for free to those who had lost everything. After the wave of attacks passed, some Somalis returned to their businesses in the townships. Many others decided to leave the country in search of a better and less threatened life elsewhere. Thus, although Mayfair is often considered a transitional place on the migration route for many Somalis, and few feelings of belonging are developed in the area, in the particular context of xenophobic attacks the neighbourhood became a symbolic home, with Somalis who had been isolated in the townships coming there en masse, looking for support and a safe environment. Such was the case of Ahmed, a Somali man in his twenties who had arrived in South Africa in 2010. He firstly settled in Limpopo, where he co-owned a small convenience shop, and then moved to Gauteng. He was running a shop in Soweto when the xenophobic attacks took place and his business was targeted. He said that only a couple of shops were owned by South Africans in the area of Soweto where he was staying; the rest were run by Somalis or Ethiopians, and those were the ones that were targeted. He related how Black South Africans looted everything they could and then ran after him, wanting to kill him. He reported the incident to the police, who told him that they could help save his life, but not his business. He came to Mayfair after the attack as he had nowhere else to go and he knew someone who ran a lodge and let him stay until he recovered; he did not have the money to start the business all over again, and his family could not support him either. He said that he had suffered around thirty similar attacks in the past five years. When I asked why he thought South

Africans targeted Somali and Ethiopian business, he replied: 'Not sure what is the problem, they don't respect us, they have more opportunities than us for business but they don't use them.' He yearned to go to another country where he could find more peace; indeed, many Somalis left South Africa after this wave of xenophobic attacks, either going back to Somalia or travelling to new destinations such as Brazil. Ahmed said that until he can leave, he is fine in Mayfair because he feels safe, 'because here I know they would help me, here is safe, there is peace and we are too many, so in case something happens we can defend ourselves'. He also pointed out that in this sense, Mayfair is preferred to Belville – where many Somalis settle in the Cape Town area – because of the numbers; there are more Somalis in Mayfair, so they can defend themselves better, and there is rarely a xenophobic incident in the area. He concluded that he wanted to stay in Mayfair because there he has 'peace', but that 'I cannot choose, I will go, wherever I find a job'.

Ahmed's hardships are shared by many of the Somali men who work in townships, and his words express very well the meaning of home that Mayfair represents for many Somalis: it is a refuge where they know they will be welcomed and taken care of. Moreover, in this sense, Mayfair becomes not only a temporary island of protection, but also a port from which to leave to other, safer destinations, indicating how the meaning of space is fluid according to the ever-changing circumstances faced by migrants and refugees.

Although the metaphors of the port and the island have been used to define both Nairobi and Johannesburg in relation to Somalis, Eastleigh can also become an isolated place for those who arrive there with plans to leave, as sometimes they spend years trapped in this place where they did not choose to stay (as was the case of Samira, described in the previous chapter). At the same time, Mayfair can also operate as a port in some ways for Somalis in the South African context: it is the entry point for many migrants arriving in the country, who stay with relatives until they find work, either in the neighbourhood or somewhere else in the country. It can also act as a 'cargo port' for those Somalis working in townships running spaza shops, who periodically come to the neighbourhood to buy new wholesale goods to resell later in their shops, as Grant and Thompson (2015) document. And after a wave of xenophobic attacks, the area is again used as a port of exit from the county.

Gendered Spaces and Belonging to the Umma

Just before the evening prayers, the streets around Amal start to empty, the shops along Eighth Avenue close and men walk in small groups to the mosque. Women also close their shops to pray inside. Behind the counter, they lay out prayer mats and kneel. I can see the mosque's entrance from

Figure 2.5. Prayers in Mayfair during Eid. Photo by Salym Fayad for the project 'Metropolitan Nomads'.

where I am, where men also kneel down to pray. The neighbourhood suddenly becomes quiet. The prayer does not take long; men emerge from the mosque and women reopen their shops. Life comes back to the streets of Mayfair. Along Eighth Avenue, small groups of men chat outside the lodges, and restaurants become busy serving dinner, their diners all men.

Although Eastleigh and Mayfair have been transformed by the significant presence of Somalis and the implementation of their cultural and material practices, Islam has also played an important role in the transformation of these neighbourhoods. As Chapter 4 will explore, Islam constitutes a strong identifier among Somalis, and is sometimes inseparable with their sense of Somaliness. Islam is considered an integral way of life. The implementation of Islamic practices in the everyday life of the neighbourhoods has also contributed to their transformation into 'little Mogadishus'. For instance, the urban rhythms and landscapes of both neighbourhoods are completely regulated by Islamic practices; their streets empty following the call to prayers and burst back to life after they are finished, the restaurants and butchers offer only halal meat, and small bottles of *Zam-zam*, the holy water from Mecca, are found in almost every shop.

At the same time, Islam also has an effect in regulating the use of public and private spaces according to gender, as gender relations among Somalis in both cities are very much determined by Islamic precepts: men and women who are not from the same family are not allowed to interact, sexual relations before marriage are completely forbidden and the uses of spaces are highly regulated, with women inhabiting mostly the private sphere and men the public sphere. Even if women who work inhabit public spaces, they do so for a reason: business. Women in both cities work in public spaces, running shops or restaurants, or working as cashiers or employees for other Somalis or Ethiopians, and some places belong entirely to the women's domain, such as beauty salons or the gold market in Eastleigh. However, recreational spaces, such as restaurants or coffee shops, are mostly visited by men, and one will never see a woman sitting in the terraces of such establishments in Mayfair and Eastleigh; when women do go to these places, they have a dedicated space inside, normally separated by a wall or a folding screen from the rest of the establishment. The navigation of spaces for young unmarried women is highly controlled, especially in the smaller community of Mayfair, where rumours play an important part in controlling women's movements (Shaffer 2014; Dreby 2009; Isotalo 2007) – hence the justification for wearing a burqa as a way to hide the movements of the woman discussed in the preface to this book. Rumours become a tool of social control, not only within the local community but also within the Somali diaspora as a whole, as they travel transnationally, especially those regarding the behaviour of women and their senses of virtue and decency. These rumours have to do with the relation between gender and place and who is allowed to be where. Women are very aware that any wrongdoing on their side is likely to reach faraway relatives back home or in other places around the world. Such was the case of Ambro, a young Somali-Kenyan woman I knew in Mayfair, who was married to a successful Somali businessman with whom she had a few children, and was staying at home with them as a housewife. She firmly refused to go with me to Amal on several occasions, stating that her husband did not let her go out. But she had no problem with coming with me to other places around Mayfair. Then, one day, she explained that there was an old woman working in a shop in the mall who often criticized her, as she had attended a boarding school in Kenya during her youth, which caused this woman to have great doubts about her virginity. She spread these rumours around, which ended up controlling Ambro's activities in the neighbourhood. What is interesting here is that rumours tend to exist at a very local level; however, in the global interconnectedness of the Somali diaspora, rumours also migrate transnationally, carrying with them the power to control people's actions, as they can damage or boost their reputations. Women try to keep their reputations undamaged so that an image of being a 'good Muslim' is maintained in the local and translocal community, as they are aware that if they break any of the unwritten rules of spatial governance, they run the risk of ruining their reputations, not only in the community where they live but in the various translocal 'imagined communities' that they inhabit and belong to, such as the umma, the greater community of Muslims spread around the world.

It was important for the women I met to earn a respectable place among the umma; belonging to the umma adds another layer of belonging to a bigger collective identity that provides an extended network of support and solidarity all around the world, and, as stated throughout this chapter and in the previous one, also plays a role when migrating to a new place. Sareedo, the young refugee whose entry into South Africa was related in Chapter 1, had previously resided in Nairobi and later ended up being relocated to Ohio by the UNHCR. She explained how being Muslim always came before being Somali, 'because if I go for example to Spain and I don't find Somali people then I can look for Muslims. First you look for your family, then for Somalis, then for Muslims, so first always a Muslim.' Falis, a middle-aged woman and head of an extended family, who resides in Nairobi but travels overseas often to buy goods to resell, offered a similar opinion:

> I have seen many Arab countries [and] there is not difference between us, only the language ... I went to Egypt, Syria, Qatar, Kuwait, Emirates, Pakistan, India ... The language is different but wherever you go, there is the religion, and because it is your habit, it's not difficult.

Sareedo and Falis's words reflect how Islam acts as a bigger category, erasing local and national identifications and connecting Somalis to an extended group that share the same religion regardless of where they come from in the world. This also explains why Somalis initially chose to settle in Mayfair, close to Fordsburg, a Muslim Indian neighbourhood, instead of other areas of the city like Yeoville or Hillbrow, which are normally preferred by other African migrants arriving in Johannesburg. In this sense, Islam becomes a common thread that enables Somalis to belong to a bigger structure that surpasses national or cultural boundaries. The everyday practice of Islam enables this belonging to a bigger structure, to a network of people who, independent of their place of origin, share a particular world view and belief that transcends national boundaries.

Today Muslims can be found all around the world, something that has cosmopolitan implications for Somalis, as it enables them to relate and engage with something bigger than themselves. This also generates a feeling of belonging to a greater community that is translocally connected. Therefore, the implementation and repetition of Islamic practices in their everyday lives connects Somalis from Eastleigh or Mayfair to the greater global community of the umma. This generates a sense of cosmopolitan collective identification that transcends Somaliness.

Translocality explains dynamics of identity formation across boundaries (Greiner and Sakdapolrak 2013). These dynamics or processes are normally multilayered, and the same Somaliness plays an important role in the construction of a strong collective identity, erasing identifications with the clan, as explored in the next chapter. Islam and the implication of belonging to the umma dilutes feelings of national and ethnic identification in favour of a cosmopolitan sense of belonging to the world. The umma, in this context, can be seen as another supra-structure of modernity, an alternative to Western globalization and at the same time compatible with it.

The Dynamics of Identity and Placemaking

As explored in this chapter, the making of Eastleigh and Mayfair into 'little Mogadishus' was not intended by any urban planning authority. The neighbourhoods began to transform as Somali migrants started to arrive and settle in them, bringing along their material and symbolic practices. Somalis living in both neighbourhoods reproduce habits of the lost homeland through different sets of cultural and religious practices. These reproductions are created by the combination of strong cultural, ethnic and religious identifications with a homeland and connections with other Somali diasporic spaces around the globe. This generates a translocal situation that recreates the lost homeland in a new place, at the same time as connecting these two neighbourhoods to each other and other places around the world where Somali communities can be found. These translocal ties also carry with them an implicit cosmopolitanism, in the sense that people in different locations share expressions of material culture that are products of a global modernity embedded in local objects of consumption. At the same time, these translocal ties generate and maintain cosmopolitan aspirations in the form of hopes of improvement of people's lives through further migration.

For Somalis, Eastleigh and Mayfair are both transitional places and temporary homes connected with distant places. This establishes a temporal continuity and a dialogical relationship between migrants, the places they now inhabit and those they have left behind (Datta 2011). The sense of belonging to a translocal 'imagined community' (Anderson 1983) becomes an important identity anchor and a 'meaning-making practice' (Wise 2011: 97), as the next chapter will further explore. Eastleigh and Mayfair have thus become known as 'little Mogadishus' not only because of the large numbers of Somalis inhabiting them, but because of the transformation of their urban space by distinctive 'Somali' businesses, shops, restaurants and coffee shops and by the reproduction of social, cultural and religious practices generated in them. This proves that migrants and refugees are active agents who reproduce lifestyles and practices from their homelands in new diasporic spaces.

The two neighbourhoods are also in constant change due to their transitional nature, something that is more apparent in Mayfair. When xenophobic attacks occur across the country, affecting Somalis living and working in townships, the latter come back to the neighbourhood looking for protection among their compatriots, and the neighbourhood operates as a protective nest. Although women tend to stay in Mayfair, as it is safer to work there than to run a business in a township, in both neighbourhoods, the use of space is also gendered and women's movements are highly controlled by socio-spatial rules. Rumours play a key role in controlling women's actions, as their whereabouts are known not only in their local communities, but also in transnational ones – a fact that was more noticeable in Mayfair, reinforcing the sense of it as an island. In addition, Muslim identity plays an important role in connecting Somalis to the umma, something that can be understood as another form of cosmopolitanism, connecting Somalis to Muslims around the world, and to a bigger network of support when they migrate.

In recent decades, both Eastleigh and Mayfair have become diasporic spaces that manifest 'the intersectionality of diaspora, border and dis/location as a point of confluence of economic, political, cultural and psychic processes' (Brah 1996: 181), making them nodal centres of diasporic life, in place of the lost 'homeland'. The fact that these nodes are in two African hubs also offers a counter-modernity to Western-centric thinking about sites of the production of cultural dynamics. The ways that women navigate these spaces and define themselves in these two diasporic contexts, and in relation to a transnational community, will be explored in the next chapter.

Notes

1. Oromo, for example, inhabit both Eastleigh and Mayfair (see Carrier and Kochore 2019 on Oromos in Eastleigh). In the case of Eastleigh, traders from other East African countries, such as Uganda, also work in the area. In Mayfair, it is common to find Zimbabwean or Malawian domestic workers in the houses of wealthier Somali families.
2. The Kiswahili word for *abaya*: 'a simple, loose over-garment, essentially a robe-like dress, worn by some women in parts of the Muslim world' (Yarwood 1978: 9).
3. Situated on the corner of Jam Street and First Avenue, Garissa Lodge is an iconic place in Eastleigh. It was one of the first lodges to which a newly arrived Somali in Eastleigh would go to stay in the early 1990s. There, people, especially women, started to sell their gold in their rooms as a way to survive. Later, it became a popular mall.
4. Abdi (2015: 147-155) documents a few pioneering women who run shops in these places, but they are rare exceptions.

3

Global and Local Identifications in Dialogue

Expressions of Somaliness in Nairobi and Johannesburg

> I am not what happened to me,
> I am what I choose to become.
>
> –Carl Gustav Jung

Haweyo is a middle-aged, well-educated woman with a PhD who left Somalia twenty years ago for Canada, where she studied, worked and lived until a few years ago, when she returned to East Africa because she didn't want her children to grow up in the West. Now she lives between Nairobi and Mogadishu. She identifies herself both as Canadian and Somali. During an interview she stated that her sense of self is based on different identifications, expressed in a performative way, and on the particular context in which she finds herself. If she is at a party with Somali women, she will behave like them, and will wear a *dirac* or other traditional costume, with henna on her hands. 'I will be completely Somali', she declared. However, at the office she will adopt certain manners and wear Western clothes. She finished the description of herself with the following statement: 'Is it healthy? They're both healthy. That's Haweyo's theory. So Haweyo is not schizophrenic.' Haweyo was describing how she consciously chooses to act depending on the context she finds herself in. As she said, this is not a schizophrenic self, but one that is able to generate different sets of identifications (Brubaker and Cooper 2000). She uses her individual agency to choose how she wants to behave to navigate different contexts. Her sense of self is not a solid, monolithic one, but fluid and dialogical (Bakhtin 1981), performed in accordance with others and with the context where interactions occur (Atkinson et al. 2008; Geertz 1973), which informs her choices of particular clothes or manners to better suit a particular situation.

However, during my research, I also talked to women like Zahara, a 28-year-old whose mother lives in Ethiopia and who has brothers living in Norway and the United Arab Emirates, and whose journey to South Africa I related in Chapter 1. At the time of her interview, she ran a small convenience shop in Mayfair, before later relocating to Limpopo with her husband. She found South Africa a hostile place, but at the time, it was the best option available for her outside of Somalia. During the interview at her shop, she explained how difficult she found South Africa and how her 'tradition' and 'culture' became the two main pillars of her identity in the new context:

> If I don't have tradition, technically I am a lost person. I need to have tradition. If not, I can follow anybody from another culture. I can follow any culture. I'm lost … It's like identity. I am called Zahara Somebody Somebody so if I come here and say, 'I will change my identity', I'll become like a Shona and all those people. It's important for me to follow my culture. As a Somalian, we don't leave our culture behind. Anywhere you go, you know this person is a Somalian. The way we dress and everything … for me it's really important. I can't leave my culture; I'm still a Somalian and I will always be Somalian.

Zahara's perception of her Somali identity seems to have some fixed and permanent characteristics inherited from her parents and passed from generation to generation. She emphasized how her culture is something that cannot be left behind and goes with her wherever she goes. Other women in Johannesburg also produced these kinds of narratives, in which certain characteristics of Somaliness seemed to be fixed identifiers; meanwhile, in Nairobi, a more fluid sense of self, like that expressed by Haweyo, was more commonly produced in women's narratives.

Having described the contexts that Somalis find in Nairobi and Johannesburg and the ways that a translocal situation generates new urban spaces, I focus in this chapter on how women renegotiate different flows of meaning in diasporic contexts, and how the different ways of being Somali are expressed through particular sets of practices and narratives in the two contexts studied. The various narratives produced by women in both cities showcased a complex scenario of identifications in which hyphenated identities, feelings of belonging and non-belonging, and reproduction of certain practices played a key role in women's expression of their Somaliness. The positioning that women adopted in relation to themselves and the world also became an expression of their agency in relation to the inhabited places and the local and translocal communities.

In line with what other multisite comparative studies on the Somali diaspora have shown (Abdi 2015; Al-Sharmani 2007), the findings of this chapter corroborate the dialogical relationship that exists between the sense of self of Somalis and the contexts in which it is performed. The chapter explores how cultural, national and ethnic identifications maintain a dialogue in the Somali collective imagination, creating a strong sense of Somaliness, like Zahara expressed, and feelings of belonging to an imagined (and real) translocal community spread around the world. A situation of transnational displacement has also generated hybrid identities that incorporate diverse sets of practices and narratives to express hyphenated senses of self that reflect different lived realities, as was the case of Haweyo. At the same time, various identifications – such as places of origin, ethnic characteristics or ways of dressing – play an important role in the sense of belonging to a collective, which these days expands across boundaries, taking place in transnational spaces around the world and in the virtual worlds of Facebook and Instagram.

Negotiating Somaliness Outside Somalia: Nairobi and Johannesburg

The sense of a strong national, ethnic and cultural identification based on a common 'tradition' expressed above by Zahara was shared by many other women I interviewed in Johannesburg, where a more static sense of self was predominant in women's narratives. Such was also the case of Lula, for example, a young respondent in a group discussion I had with several women one afternoon in Mayfair, in the room she rented in a shared flat in the neighbourhood. Although she was only 25 years old, she was already the mother of two young children and was going through a divorce with her first husband, who she hardly saw in her years of marriage as he was normally running a spaza shop in a township and only came to Mayfair once a month to buy supplies. Questioned about her Somaliness and that of her children, who were born in South Africa, she explained:

> You are born into it. Like this child, she was born here but you cannot call her South African because her mother was born there in Somalia. Our grandmothers were also born there, our origin is Somali, the culture, our culture is different. Something you cannot change. You are born within it ... Even if you have an American passport, you are still Somali.

Lula's sense of identity is quite solid, and she strongly identified as Somali; even her children, born in South Africa, are considered 'fully Somali' because of the weight of 'culture and tradition'. For Zahara and Lula, being Somali is an inherited and inflexible characteristic that entirely defines their lives.

However, in Nairobi, narratives in which 'identity isn't inscribed, forever [...] It is socially, historically, [and] culturally constructed' (Hall 2008:

347), similar to Haweyo's, were more common. Samia's perception of her identity resonates with Haweyo's initial words:

> I am a woman with two identities, actually multiple identities: I am an African. I am a Muslim. I am from East Africa, from the Horn of Africa. I am a Somali. I am a Canadian. I am a feminist. I am an environmentalist. I am a social activist.

Samia is another diaspora returnee from Canada, who went there when she was 18 years old to study. She is now in her forties, and after gaining a PhD degree, she decided to come back to East Africa, where she now lives between Nairobi and Mogadishu, running an NGO that seeks to empower Somali women. She expressed different identifications with different cultural, religious, social and geographical categories (Brubaker and Cooper 2010; Eidson et al. 2017). Both Haweyo and Samia are two educated women who have spent parts of their lives in the West, where they studied and lived for many years. Their education also makes them aware of the fluidity and performativity of their own identities.

Samia and Haweyo's senses of self are much more fluid than Zahara's and Lula's, and are based on different sets of identifications; they are aware of the multiplicities through which their identities take place and do not define themselves by strong signifiers of tradition and culture, as Zahara and Lula do. These cases showcase different expressions of Somaliness in the contemporary world. Zahara and Lula fully associate their identities with the culture, religion, ethnicity and nation that they have been born into; for them, these are static characteristics that cannot be changed, otherwise the self would get lost. Their Somali identity becomes an anchor in a world full of changes, and they stick to it in order to make some sense of it. However, Samia and Haweyo's life experiences and education lead them to recognize the multiplicity of identifications that form their selves, identifications that take place in a performative and dialogical way. To talk about Somaliness nowadays, we have to take into account these different approaches that Somali women have to expressing their identities, in which a more traditional sense of self, as part of a collective, cohabits with a more postmodern and transnational approach. In the case of Zahara's and Lula's narratives, the sense of being Somali is an immobile characteristic, 'something that you are born into' and a place in which you stay from the cradle to the grave, regardless of where you go and where you live. Their narratives showcase 'national culture' and ethnic belonging as a source of identifications, wherein 'tradition' is passed through generations. For them, the fact of being Somali encapsulates claims of origins and traditions that are continued and unchangeable across time and space, reinforcing in this way a very strong sense of collective identity. Both of them are also refugees in a hostile and xenophobic country; their lives are full of uncertainties and their Somali origin and 'way of being' is one of the few things they are fully certain about. These kinds of narratives 'construct identities which are ambiguously placed between past and future' (Hall 1992: 295). Statements like 'I was born Somali and I always will be a Somali' reinforce a sense of continuity in an always-changing and uncertain world. These narratives showcase national culture as a pillar around which identity is learned, and around which 'tradition' is passed from generation to generation.

As Cortazzi (2001: 388) points out, 'context is socially constructed and sustained interactionally', and the context that Somali migrants find themselves in in Johannesburg is extremely xenophobic and hostile. At the same time, the Somali community in Mayfair is mostly formed by refugees and asylum seekers coming from lower economic backgrounds.[1] As explored in previous chapters, feelings of insecurity, alienation and isolation were common among these Somalis. Thus, in this context, a strong collective ethnic, cultural and religious identity becomes an anchor connecting Somalis to a lost homeland, to the diasporic community living all around the world and to other Muslims in South Africa. As Abdi (2015: 27) also points out, the context that Somalis find in Johannesburg allows for 'racial, religious and gender identities [to] remain stable and secure'. This is why in this context it becomes so important to strengthen certain characteristics of Somaliness, to ensure that one has a certain place among a collective in a very hostile land. In line with Abdi's comparative study's findings, I argue that certain strengthened characteristics of Somaliness become a strategy for Somali women to navigate their identities in a very hostile place. In Nairobi, which is the meeting point of Somali refugees, diaspora returnees and Somali-Kenyans – coming from different economic backgrounds and class statuses – stronger networks of support could be found, and there was thus no need to strengthen certain characteristics of Somaliness, something that allowed for more fluid forms of identifications to emerge. This dialogic relationship between context and self becomes the basis for women's actions regarding their agency and the relationship that they adopt with the new place. Next, I focus in more detail on the cases of Haweyo and Samia in order to explore how translocal identities are negotiated across borders and cultures, generating hybrid or hyphenated identities.

The Hybrid Identity of Somaliness

Samia described herself as a woman of multiple identities; in fact, she considers herself 'hyphenated'. She declared that in all the years she spent in Canada, Somalia never left her. She returned to East Africa thinking that Somalia needed her, but realized once there that it was she who needed Somalia. When she is there, she considers herself both an outsider and an insider. As she explained:

> You become stateless. [A] Somali passport is not valid. You cannot travel with it. You don't have the state protection or access to opportunities. But then I was lucky. I worked hard, I ended up going to Canada ... and I went there to start a whole new life ... The sky is the limit ... it's up to you to build your life ... And of course, you struggle. I wasn't a white woman. I was the other ... You are always an outsider, you are always the other, you are always asked the question, 'Where are you from?'. For the way I dress and the colour of my skin, I am always seen as the other ... After twenty years of exile, I came back to Somalia and I see myself both as an outsider and as [an] insider ... Because I changed, I am wearing different glasses. Sometimes when I am in Somalia, I feel I don't belong there. And the same thing when I am in Canada, I am an insider and an outsider and I think [it] is good. It gives me advantage, room to manoeuvre.

Samia's diasporic experience has made her an outsider both in Canada and in Somalia, and although she feels that she does not belong fully to either country, this distance benefits her as she is able to successfully navigate two very different worlds. The fact that she is always 'the other', both in Canada and in Somalia, does not make her question her 'roots' or where she belongs. She admits openly that she belongs to both worlds and that this is something that works in her favour. As Stuart Hall (2008: 347) pointed out, diasporic people are:

> People from different cultural backgrounds, who have been obliged to live somewhere else but who remain in some deep ways also connected to their homes, cultures and places of origin, and consequently develop what I would call a diasporic form of consciousness and way of life [...] what DuBois called 'double consciousness'.

Hall's words resonate with other narratives of migration and belonging. Probably one of the best known is that of Gloria Anzaldúa in *Borderlands/La Frontera* (1987), in which she reflects on her multiple identities as *mestiza* and on what it means to cross borders and the multiple stratifications of cultural forms that they contain. She expresses feelings of belonging to multiple realities, something even manifested in the language she uses in the book, mixing different variants of Spanish with English and the pre-Hispanic Nahuatl language as a way to showcase the hybridity of her identity. And in the case of the Somali diaspora, as Al-Sharmani (2007:80) points out, 'different layers of identities' are claimed, especially among those who have spent time living in the West, as the cases of Haweyo and Samia illustrate: there is a hybridity of identifications with different cultures and ways of being. These women defined themselves as 'hyphenated' – a category also used in other diasporic contexts, especially among second-generation migrants, as Kebede (2017) demonstrates in relation to Ethiopian-Americans in the USA, for whom hyphenated and hybrid identities are the result of navigating two cultural environments: the ancestral place of origin and the diasporic one now inhabited. Haweyo and Samia are women who lived in the West for several years, and who use different cultural repertoires depending on the context in which they find themselves, which also has an influence on the ways they perceive themselves and are perceived by others. This hybridity, or multiple ways of being, is sometimes not well received in the homeland, which defends a 'pure' sense of identity. Some members of the Somali diaspora are sometimes accused of being too Westernized by their compatriots, who allege that they have lost their 'true Somali self'. As Haweyo explained during her interview:

> Because of the diasporic experiences, we have reinvented the country, we have reimagined women's role, and that is quite problematic, we need to define who we are and what Somaliness is. And when we define Somaliness, we have to make a space for the hybrid identity, the hybrid identity of Somaliness. The fact that we need to embrace it ... I am a Somali woman and Western at the same time. I know that invokes all kind[s] of emotions in our circles. But let's be honest and talk about that right now. I said most of my life was in Canada; if I deny that part of me, I am not being truly authentic. I like to think I am transnational.

Haweyo acknowledges the validity of both her Somali and Canadian identities, claiming a hybrid self. She is also challenging women's traditional roles, which have been reimagined in the diaspora, where many women become the breadwinners of the family (Farah 2000; Abdi 2015). She is also very aware that this is something not always welcomed in some Somali circles, where the tendency is to defend a pure sense of Somaliness, linked to its roots. However, Haweyo and Samia acknowledge their dual or multiple selves (Henriques et al. 1984), which lead them to live 'dual lives' (Anzaldúa 1987; Portes 1997); their identifications, even if sometimes contradictory, both come from their same inner selves and are a result of their transnational lives; identities here are 'negotiated within social worlds that span more than one place' (Vertovec 2001: 573). Somali women in Nairobi and Johannesburg actively navigate their identifications and act in accordance with them. These negotiations are sometimes not easy, as they confront two very different sets of values, as Haweyo went on to explain: 'I come from a culture where being old was a privilege and grew up in a culture where being old is considered senile. I negotiate between these two.' It is then up to the individual, their experiences and their lived context to negotiate between different sets of practices and values in the decisions they take throughout their life. A diasporic identity incorporates different sets of identifications to create a new 'hybrid' self that is sometimes made of contradictory practices and ways of being. This can sometimes be problematic for diasporic people looking for a fixed, united set of identifications. As

Haweyo said: 'I spent most of my adult life fighting the erroneous assumption of "you can be either or". I can be both.' But others, like Samia, actually see an advantage in this duality, as they are able to navigate different worlds and benefit from being both an 'insider and an outsider'. Therefore, the way that these Somali women negotiate their diasporic identifications is based on their transnational life experiences and how they express their relationship between local and global affinities, as 'diasporic identities are at once local and global. They are networks of transnational identification encompassing "imagined" and "encountered" communities' (Brah 1996: 196).

The 'imagined and encountered' community plays a very important part in how Somaliness is constructed and maintained across borders. Regardless of whether their senses of identity were more static or fluid, all the women interviewed in Nairobi and Johannesburg shared a strong sense of belonging to a translocal imagined community: that of 'the Somalis'. Somali collective identity flourishes all around the world in spite of the collapse of the Somalian nation state. A strong sense of Somaliness precedes the nation and still prevails after its collapse, as it is based on other collective features, such as ethnicity (Weitzberg 2017), and sustained through the implementation (or contestation) of shared cultural and religious practices and beliefs. Some of the factors that contribute to this strong sense of belonging to an 'imagined' (and real) translocal community among Somali women in Nairobi and Johannesburg are explored in the next section in relation to national, ethnic and cultural identifications.

Virtual Narratives of the Nation: 'There is No Place Like Home'

Despite all the years of conflict, in many women's narratives there was an idealized sense of home, supported by a unifying narrative of the nation that was sustained by claims of one unique language, culture and religion shared by all Somalis. These are narratives emanating from a strong national identification, in which the nation has become '*a system of cultural representation* [...] a discourse, a way of constructing meanings' (Hall 1992: 292). This narrative of the nation was especially exploited during the Siad Barre regime, which initially, following communist ideals, tried unsuccessfully to abolish the clan system and boosted the national dream of Greater Somalia (Harper 2012; Murphy 2011; Elmi 2010). Today, however, this narrative of the nation mostly takes place in the virtual world of Facebook and Instagram, and is constructed by Somalis all around the world. Images of Somalia before the war are commonly shared on social media. There is, for example, an Instagram account called 'The Best of Somalia', dedicated to posting images and comments that boost national identifications. One post shows a drawing of a camel, one of the more nationalistic symbols of Somalia that evokes the nomadic past.[2] Below the drawing, the caption reads:

> There is no place like home and especially when the world is all messed up and in wars at the moment. Somalia needs peace and stability and the only people that can do that are the Somali people. Forget *qabil* (tribalism), it is the cause of all our troubles. The only two things we as Somalis need to bring back our dignity is to love one another and our beautiful country and practice our beautiful religion of #*Islam*, the rest is nonsense. Somalia has suffered enough and we have a once-in-a-lifetime chance to bring Somalia back on the world stage. Every Somali national regardless of gender should think hard and find something they can contribute to the rebuilding of Somalia; it might be your educational background or your other life skills and experience that you think can help Somalia in any way. We live in a digital and fastly improving world where countries are competing with their economies and military improvements and we as #*Somalis* are still in the stone age and fighting these useless wars where innocent Somalis have to pay their lives with. Nations are uniting and we are busy 'invading' and 'occupying' our own cities and towns and chasing out and abusing our fellow Somalis because of *qabil*. Your tribal affiliation will not promise you heaven, we are massacring our own people for something that shouldn't be a reason to kill anyone. Let's reclaim back our country and dignity Insha'Allah. #*Somalia* #*Somali* (Best of Somalia 2015).

This caption summarizes different factors contributing to identification with a strong narrative of the nation: overcoming clan identifications, a nostalgic and idealized vision of the country from afar, Islam as a unifying factor, the wish to rebuild Somalia and a desire for national unity. It is a call for all Somalis to rebuild and unify Somalia, bringing it back to its past splendour; however, this nationalistic discourse, instead of coming from a dictatorial leader, is now mostly constructed outside the country by the Somali diaspora, and what is most interesting is that it takes place in the virtual space of Instagram, which can be accessed by all young Somalis around the world. Thus, it should also be taken into account that the 'portability of national identity' (Sassen 1998) and 'long distance nationalism' (Anderson 1992) have become even stronger as responses to a shattered country of origin. Somali collective identity is now constructed based on narratives and practices taking place all around the world and also in the virtual space of social networks. Therefore, the strong sense or feeling of Somaliness does not come from identification with the nation state, which is practically non-existent, but from the identification with certain discourses, narratives and practices based on shared structures and on the implementation of cultural and religious practices in everyday life. As Murunga (2009: 207) affirms, 'Somali identity is not imposed from above, by the state, but comes from below'. Somaliness exists independently of an original, physical place of reference – though a nostalgic mythical Somalia exists in the minds of most Somalis – and is instead based on a translocal sense of being connected. In this context, in which there is no nation state to refer to, and with the Somali diaspora spread all around the world, collective identifications are expressed and lived through different practices that, in some cases, can be exacerbated to denote the distinctiveness of Somaliness, as has been explored in relation to Somali women in Mayfair.

Purity and Belonging:
'Same Culture, Same Religion, Same Language'

As described in previous chapters, the place of origin plays an important role in the migration experience of Somali women to Nairobi and Johannesburg. As Sareedo described in Chapter 1, when newly arriving in Johannesburg, Somalis would ask for people they might know, either direct family or those connected by clan affiliations, who could help them to start their new lives in the city by showing them around, offering them accommodation and jobs or connecting them to others who might give them work. Although clan categories still plays an important role as a structure of support for new arrivals in both cities, however, clan membership did not appear to be a defining feature of women's identities during interviews and conversations with them. The above post from The Best of Somalia urges Somalis to forget about tribalism, referring to it as the source of all their troubles. This view was shared by many of the women I talked to in both cities. These words of Fadumo, one of the respondents in Mayfair, are illustrative:

> I identify more with being Somali. In Somalia there is this problem of tribalism. They politicized the tribe, they took it and made people hide behind the tribe, but that's not how Somalis are. Somalis are people who lived together for so long. We were all different tribes but we were living in harmony. There are not cultural differences between Somalis, same culture. Same religion, same language, culture is only one, we have the Islamic culture. This tribalism, you wonder where it came from and now it's a disease in Somalia.

Many Somalis considered tribalism the source of all Somalia's problems, and they frequently insisted on the importance of being Somali, and not of belonging to a clan, presenting and defending a strong unifying narrative emphasizing common factors such as language, culture and religion. 'We are all Somalis. One language, one culture, one religion' was a sentence commonly repeated during the interviews, showcasing a strong sense of collective unity.[3] Fadumo's words resonate with the distinction between the social nature of the clan as a support system, and the political tribalism, generated post-independence, that is a source of many of Somalia's maladies (Baadiyow 2001; Al-Sharmani 2007). Even if the social nature of the clan as a support system still played an important role in migration, clan affiliation per se was not used by any woman to describe her identity.[4] Thus, in line with Cawo Abdi's (2015) approach, I have consciously avoided using clan identifications as part of this work, for two main reasons: firstly, the women I talked to did not use them to define their identities when talking to me, a non-Somali. Secondly, I realized that there was a general sense of uneasiness among Somalis over always being described and defined under these terms. As the above post by The Best of Somalia states and Fadumo's words reaffirm, the politicization of clan identifications is viewed as one of the main causes of conflict in Somalia, and many women employed strong ethnic, national, cultural and religious discourses as a counter-narrative to present a unified sense of being Somali. Somalis in both cities tended to proudly explain the strong solidarity existing among them and the way that they always helped each other when in need or in adverse circumstances. I normally questioned women about the contradiction whereby Somalis demonstrated so much solidarity and were supportive of each other when living outside Somalia, but not in Somalia itself. The response was always similar: 'In Somalia everyone wants to be the president' – an affirmation that plainly explains the continuous wars that have torn down the country for years as more a problem of power and who controls the scarce resources there. Clan identification, even if useful for new arrivals and during the migration process, dissolves thereafter in some diasporic contexts (Sadouni 2009; Al-Sharmani 2010; Tiilikainen 2007), and is substituted by unifying collective narratives of national, ethnic, cultural and religious identifications.

However, in these diasporic spaces, place of origin becomes more relevant to identity in relation to those born and raised inside or outside Somalia. Somalis born outside the country receive the denominations *Dayuus baro* and *Sijuis. Dayuus baro* – the pronunciation of which resembles that of the word 'diasporas' – refers to Somalis born in the West. It is normally used as a derogatory term for Somalis who have returned to Somalia from the Western world, as the term *dayuus* in Somali refers to a person without morals and is used to denigrate Somali returnees for their supposed lax moral codes; as Haweyo noted, the possible influence of diasporic experiences on individual identities is not always welcome in certain sectors that defend a 'pure' sense of being Somali. The term *sijuis* was initially used to refer to Somali-Kenyans. Literally, the word means 'I don't know' in Kiswahili, but now it is also applied to Somalis who have lived outside Somalia for a long time, as they are also looked down on by Somalis from Somalia. As Farzana and Luul, two young respondents from Puntland residing and working in Mayfair, explained:

Farzana: *Sijuis* are those Somalians who [are] born overseas like [in] Kenya, Tanzania, Ethiopia, America, all, even South Africa ... It is someone who doesn't know the Somali language and culture properly, because they were born there and stayed there a long time and the culture changes, everything changes ...

Luul: I heard some stories about the name. Some Somali people that were staying in Kenya, long time, long time ago, *garanda, garanda*, so one Somalian guy from Mogadishu came into Garissa and he asked something, like I need that, and they said '*Sijui*'. You know? *Sijui* in Swahili means I don't know. So, this guy asked 'Do you know this family?' [and] they said '*Sijui*' [meaning I don't know]. That's why they gave that name. Those *Sijui* people cannot speak Somali properly.

F: Even we are not [the] same culture. Even here in South Africa, when they come, Somalian *Sijui*, from Tanzania or Kenya, they don't connect, they stay separate, they look after each other ... Most of them don't know Somali, they speak Swahili. We speak only one language, one culture, one religion, we are Muslims 100 per cent. Even Somali *Sijui*, even if they were born there in another county, they are Muslims, maybe their culture is a little bit different but they are Muslims.

These two respondents in Johannesburg explained that Sijuis are different because they do not know 'Somali' culture or language properly. This story emphasizes how language competence demarcates degrees of belonging and 'authenticity', something that is sometimes used to discriminate, as in the case of the few Somali Kenyans staying in Mayfair. Although they share Somali ethnicity, they are Kenyan nationals, for which they are looked down upon by other Somalis staying in the area, and they feel marginalized from the community. Here, it can be observed that place of origin is used to demarcate difference, and those born or raised outside Somalia are often looked down on by Somalis from Somalia on the basis that they 'don't know Somali culture properly', indicating different degrees of purity and belonging (Douglas 1966). As seen in previous chapters, Somali Kenyans also tend to be stigmatized or marginalized by Kenyan nationals, as the cases of Muna and Shamso showcased; thus, Somali Kenyans experience double discrimination: by Somalis, the ethnic group they identify with, and by Kenyan nationals, nationals of the country to which they belong by right of birth (Weitzberg 2017). Thus, in the two contexts studied, even if clan affiliation still played a role in the structure that supports new arrivals and the migration process, it was not expressed as a defining identity feature, and grades of belonging were established in relation to where the person was born and raised – inside or outside Somalia – and their degree of knowledge of Somali language and customs.

Ethnic Identifications:
'With the Blacks You Learn Quickly'

Perceived racial distinctions in relation to other Black Africans also came up as an identity feature among the women I talked to in both cities. One day in Amal shopping centre in Mayfair, I was chatting with some young women in a shop. At some point I made a comment to one of them about her English being very good, to which she replied that she had learned when working in town, adding that if you worked in Mayfair, you would speak Somali the whole day, but working in town made you learn faster, because 'with the Blacks you learn quickly'. This made very clear in an implicit way that she did not consider herself Black.[5] This distinction also emerged in other random conversations I had with women, and during interviews and group discussions both in Nairobi and Johannesburg. Most of the women I talked to did not identify themselves as Black, which corroborates the findings of other works that confirm that Somalis in South Africa do not identify as Black, coloured or Indian, thus not fitting into any of the categories of the highly racialized post-apartheid system (Abdi 2015; Sadouni 2019; Tewolde 2020). Tewolde (ibid.) explains that in the case of Eritrean and Somali refugees, other collective identifiers are in place. In the case of Somalis, the previously explored claims around a unifying 'national culture' were invoked. They insisted on their Arab descent and defended the unity of Somali people based on language, religion and culture. Different physical features were added to this distinction to strengthen their argument about being different to other Africans.

However, in Somalia, a Somali Bantu population is also found in the Jubba Valley in the south of the country. They are descendants of agriculturalists who lived in the Horn of Africa before pastoralist Somalis arrived, and also of slaves from the East African trade (Besteman 1993, 1996b). They are normally looked down upon by other Somalis and perceived as lower-class due to their former status as slaves and their sedentary agricultural lifestyle, and also because of their different appearance. As Besteman (1996b: 583–84) explains:

> Despite the fact that by the 1980s most descendants of slaves were fully Somali in terms of language/dialect, custom, religion, and participation in the Somali clan system (through adoption), they maintained their physical distinctiveness and are said to look more 'African' than other Somali. The physical distinctiveness is captured in the term *jareer*, which means 'hard, kinky hair'.

Although physical appearance is used by Somalis to demarcate difference and status, among themselves and also in respect to other Africans, the diasporic experience creates some interesting cases in which these dif-

Figure 3.1. The 'cultural man' of Mayfair. Photo by Salym Fayad for the project 'Metropolitan Nomads'.

ferences are either erased or even become sources of pride. For example, in Mayfair, there is a popular coffee shop run by a Somali Bantu that displays all kinds of artefacts from 'traditional Somali culture', which any Somali stopping for coffee is keen to explain very proudly to any non-Somali. This is interesting to note, as the owner is considered part of a minority, often stigmatized by their compatriots in Somalia. In a diasporic context, he has become, along with his coffee shop/museum, a kind of ambassador of Somali culture in Mayfair. Something similar could be said about a young man in the neighbourhood, popularly known as 'the cultural man', who is always present at any event taking place in Mayfair, showcasing with pride his big Afro hairstyle along with the 'traditional attire' of Somali nomads. In this context, the Afro hairstyle becomes a symbol of pride, connecting Somalis to other Africans, in place of the demeaning attitude taken in Somalia towards Somali Bantus, as exemplified by Besteman's words above.

This showcasing of Afro hairstyles can also be observed in some of the posts circulating on Instagram, which recreate a nostalgic vision of the Somali before the war, in which proud nomads stand with this hairstyle in harsh pastoralist lands, as well as depicting metropolitan men and women in Mogadishu during the 1960s. It is not the diasporic experience alone that transforms the meaning of some physical features, then, as Afro hairstyles were already present in Somali aesthetics before the breakout of the conflict. What a diasporic experience generates is a different sense of awareness that makes certain categories shift in meaning. One woman in Nairobi expressed this in a group discussion, during which seven Somali women were all declaring vehemently that they were not Black – or even African. This particular woman opposed the views of her friends, explaining that she became aware of her own Blackness when she was living in Israel and was treated as such. This made her realize, she explained, that she belonged to the African continent as much as Ethiopians or Congolese. The testimony of this woman is very different to the one expressed by the woman at the beginning of this section, who clearly defined herself as not Black; this demonstrates how racial perceptions depend enormously on the sociohistorical context of a particular place (Kusow 2006; Tewolde 2020). I was even told once in Mayfair that I was not completely white because I came from Spain, as for the men addressing me, whites were white South Africans, British, North Americans, Germans or Dutch. The fact that Spain was in the south of Europe, that the Arabs were there for several centuries, that my mother tongue was not English and that Spain had not played a major role in the colonial history of sub-Saharan Africa – with the exception of Equatorial Guinea – qualified me as 'not fully white'. Thus, the perceptions that Somalis have of themselves, of Somali Bantus, of other Black Africans or even of whites may change depending on the context. Perceived racial features are used differently as identity markers depending on the context in which Somalis find themselves. In the case of Nairobi and Johannesburg, the self-identification of Somali women as non-Black become one more argument – together with religion, culture, language and national sentiment – to present a narrative of a distinctive, united collective identity.

Dress and Identity: 'I Don't Look Somali Because I Don't Dress Like the Majority of Them Do'

The choice of how to dress was also a defining identity feature among Somali women in Nairobi and Johannesburg. Most of them chose to wear a *jilbaab* (Akou 2011). This is the outfit most people associate with a Somali refugee woman, covered from head to toe in a matching garment through which you can only see the face. The majority of women I talked to in Nairobi and Johannesburg claimed that dressing this way was a clear distinction of their Somaliness, a claim also made in other contexts, as in the case study by Hopkins (2010) among Somali women living in London and Toronto. The women I talked to in Nairobi and Johannesburg perceived this garment as 'authentic' Somali, on the grounds that other Muslim women from other places cover themselves in different ways. Many Somali women also chose to wear an *abaya*, a common garment for women across the Muslim world.

However, as Faiza, one of the women I interviewed in Nairobi, explained, the custom of wearing the *jilbaab* was not adopted until the 1990s, when the outbreak of the war took place. Faiza is in her mid-fifties and has been living in Nairobi for more than a decade, working for an NGO. She was one of the few women I talked to who was wearing 'Western clothes' when I interviewed her: jeans, a shirt and no headscarf. At some point in the interview, I asked her whether she had experienced discrimination in Nairobi after the Westgate attack. She replied that she did not because she did not look Somali: 'I don't look Somali because I don't dress like the majority of them do.' I asked her why she chose to dress like that, to which she replied: 'Because that's the way I always dressed, before the war everyone used to dress like this. I even used to wear shorts to play tennis!'

Many photos from the 1960s and 1970s, which also circulate extensively in the virtual world, portray Somali women in Mogadishu wearing high heels, big earrings, miniskirts and Afro hairstyles, with no scarfs or any other signs denoting their Muslim identity. The *jilbaab* only became 'fashionable' when the war broke out in the 1990s. As the participants in this research explained, the majority of women chose to wear it for two main reasons: it was considered 'safer and more Islamic' for them, as covering oneself became a way to be less noticeable and avoid rape in war. At the same time, as other respondents explained, wearing the *jilbaab* was a response to the popular belief that came with the re-Islamization of Somalia after the outbreak of the war, as the next chapter will explore in more detail. A form of dressing that is only twenty-five years old has now become a strong source of national and religious identification, with claims of it being 'traditional', constituting a good example of the 'invention of tradition' (Hobsbawm and Ranger 1983). Nowadays, many Somali women in the diaspora still choose to wear it daily because it has become a way of demarcating difference and easily demonstrating their Somali and Muslim identities.

Something similar happened with the *dirac*. Somali women see this outfit as more 'traditional' or 'cultural' than the *jilbaab*, and it is now mostly worn for weddings. However, as Akou (2011: 120) points out, this is also 'a new style of "traditional" dress that became popular in the 1970s'. The decision to wear the *jilbaab* and *dirac* as identity markers based on the claims that they are more 'traditional' than Western clothes demonstrates how the 'invention of tradition' in regard to collective identifications operates at the everyday level as a result of the war and the consequent mass migration of Somalis all around the world. Moreover, many Somali women in Nairobi and Johannesburg also choose to cover their faces with a niqab,[6] as a way to express their strong identification with the re-Islamization of Somalia and also to demonstrate that their Muslim identity is above their Somaliness.

However, in some cases, wearing a burka or niqab can also be a strategy to keep anonymity in daily life movements in spaces that are enormously gender segregated, as the anecdote in the preface relates. The way we dress is one of the quickest, most apparent and most direct ways to present our identity, and many women in both cities chose it as a way to denote their Somali and Muslim roots. Other women, like Farzana, even if exceptional, chose to stick to the ways they used to dress before the war and the racialization of Somalia, and others, like Haweyo, chose when to wear traditional garments depending on context. These different approaches showcase the dialogical relation with Somaliness that women maintain in Nairobi and Johannesburg, which also becomes a way to express their individual agency and how they want to present themselves to the world.

Global and Local Identifications in Dialogue

In this chapter, I have explored some of the different approaches to Somaliness expressed by women in Nairobi and Johannesburg. A more traditional sense of self – emerging from the repetition of traditions and customs and based on identifications with a common origin, a certain way of dressing and perceived physical features – cohabits with a more fluid sense of self that adopts a more cosmopolitan and performative approach. The more traditional sense of self was more widespread among women in Johannesburg, while in Nairobi women expressed a more fluid, postmodern and cosmopolitan sense of their own identities. Women in both cities positioned themselves in a certain way in relation to their local and translocal contexts. The Somali community in Mayfair is smaller and tighter, which also explains the different approach Somali women take to identity and the meaning that the identifications with which they decide to align has for them. Somali women in Johannesburg, mostly refugees with lower education levels from poorer backgrounds, tend to perceive their own identity as inflexible, based on national, cultural, religious and 'traditional' identifications with the lost homeland. They show a reinforced sense of Somaliness, based on discourses of cultural and national identifications. At the same time, the xenophobic context that they encounter in the city strengthens some identity features, as they become a unifying factor and a form of resilience in a very hostile and unwelcoming context. This is also a way to ensure their membership of the Somali community in Mayfair, to remain linked to a collective that will be the main support structure they can rely on if difficult circumstances arise. Meanwhile, among the women living in Nairobi – where a bigger population of Somalis includes Somali refugees, diaspora returnees and Somali Kenyans, belonging to different backgrounds, classes and statuses – the sense of identity that emerged during interviews and conversations was more fluid and performative. Somalis here interact with the life of the city in a very different manner than in Johannesburg, allowing more cosmopolitan narratives and ways of being to emerge. Here a dialogical and performative sense of identity becomes more noticeable, with individuals negotiating between different sets of identifications and cultural repertoires as a result of a transnational life wherein the global and the local maintain a more open and fluid dialogue than in Johannesburg, where the Somali community is more insular. This is also due to the nature of Nairobi as a 'port', more open to cosmopolitan ways of being; different expressions of being Somali cohabit in a city with which Somalis also interact more freely than they do with Johannesburg, where the isolation they find in Mayfair reinforces some of the strongest characteristics of Somaliness.

Nevertheless, although some differences were noted in how women defined themselves in the two contexts studied, in both places, a strong sense of belonging to a transnational community, with certain defining features, customs and practices, was common. Physical ethnic features, degrees of belonging and ways of implementing cultural practices, such as ways of dressing, together with a common language and a narrative of the nation constructed in the virtual world contributed to a sense of collective unity that transcended borders.

A strong sense of belonging to an 'imagined community' (Anderson 1983) is maintained through the implementation of certain cultural and social practices. This has implications for Somali women's agency, as the ways they act and behave are expected to resonate with the codes of conduct prescribed by the imagined community, which also acts as a moral one. A 'moral imagined community' (Malkki 1995: 25) regulates behaviours and practices to maintain a sense of unity among Somalis around the world, simultaneously connecting them to the ancestral home. Somali women negotiate the values prescribed by the 'moral imagined community', their Muslim identity and their individual agency in order to implement the behaviours expected from them as virtuous Somali and Muslim women, at the same time as they fulfil their individual aspirations – as the next chapter will further explore.

Notes

1. In Johannesburg, there is also a small population of upper-class Somalis who reside in the wealthy northern suburb of Sandton. Some of them regularly come to lodges and coffee shops in Mayfair to meet with other countrymen and discuss Somali politics and business. However, this group, composed entirely of men, was highly inaccessible to me, so data could not be contrasted in this regard.

2. As Mary Harper writes: 'Camels represent the very essence of Somali life [...] The Somali camel has even had its own Facebook page' (2012: 17).
3. Regarding language, although Somali has different dialects (Northern, Benadir and Maay), most Somalis see themselves as a unified language group, as most respondents in my research constantly repeated. This is also corroborated by Touval and Weltmann (1963). For more information about Somali variants and where they are spoken, see the detailed report by LandInfo (2011).
4. There is a vast literature dealing with the Somali clan system, its ever-changing subclans and all the complicated politics and conflicts associated with it. See Lewis (1965, 1994, 1998); Elmi (2010); Harper (2012); Murphy (2011); Ahmed (1995); and Gardner and El Bushra (2004), to name just a few.
5. Many Somali women have their own businesses or work for other Somalis or Ethiopians in Jeppe Street in Johannesburg's CBD, where other African immigrants and Black South Africans are also hawkers. They mostly sell fake brands of clothes, or 'Fong Kong', as it is popularly known. They buy wholesale from Chinese malls and resell in small shops or stalls in the city centre.
6. 'A very conservative and controversial head covering that diffused from the middle-east to Somalia in the 1980s; prior to that time, only the descendants of Arab and Persian settlers would have worn this kind of garment that covers the face' (Akou 2011: 75).

4
Negotiating Religious and Cultural Identifications in Diasporic Spaces

The strange phenomenon of loving culture over religion is just a reflection of the age-old struggle of loving the creation over the Creator.
—Yasmin Mogahed

A week after the Westgate attacks in Nairobi, for which the Somali terrorist group Al-Shabaab claimed responsibility, I went to Mayfair; Amal, the normally lively shopping mall, was quiet and people were worried. It had emerged on the news that one of the perpetrators of the attacks, Samantha Lewthwaite – 'the White Widow' – had lived in Mayfair before the attack, and the police and journalists had been around asking questions. People were concerned about a possible backlash; the insults they had received from Black South African citizens led them to worry about possible harassments, or that another wave of xenophobic attacks might occur. The women I talked to repeated over and over again, like a mantra, that the attack was not Islamic, that Islam was not about that, that Islam was about love and peace and not death and terror. Even if some of the perpetrators of the attack were of ethnic Somali origin, the main concern of the women in Amal was to defend and clear the name of Islam, not that of Somalis. I found this sentiment revealing as it demonstrated the deep connection between Islam and Somaliness and the way that both act as strong identifiers for Somalis.

Shortly after these events, I interviewed Fadumo, a middle-aged woman, very literate and opinionated, who had taught herself Kiswahili, English and Arabic and was an avid reader of Qur'anic texts. At the time of our interview, she was running a wholesale shop on the upper floor of Amal and waiting to be resettled in the USA by UNHRC. During the interview, she expressed her concerns about how Muslims and Islam were being portrayed in the international media after the Westgate attacks. She thought that most people believed that everyone who was a Muslim was also a terrorist. She blamed the media for hijacking the name of Islam and 'using it for their own things', meaning the discourses they built around Muslims, equating them with terrorists. I will come back to this representation of Muslims as terrorists and the implications it has for Somalis at the end of the chapter, but Fadumo's discomfort came from the meaning attached to Islam by the Western imagination, which was very different to the meaning it had for her, as for her, Islam was peace, a way of life and a sacred belief system. In her own words, it was: 'A way of ruling of the life. Our tradition, our food, our way of living, our way of doing everything. Our religion becomes our life.' She, like many other Somali women in Nairobi and Johannesburg, lives her life according to Islamic precepts, which act as a code of conduct, a set of socially constructed practices (Durkheim 1915) that regulate almost all actions in life, from how to dress to gender relations. At the same time, in the situation of displacement in which she lives, Islam connects her to the lost homeland and to other Somalis and Muslims around the world, making her feel part of a collective with shared, common practices based on a communal belief system. In diasporic contexts, Islam can also facilitate the integration of migrants into the new place, as has been explored in relation to Somalis in Mayfair, and contribute to their sense of well-being. This is corroborated in other diasporic contexts, as demonstrated by the experiences of Somalis in the UAE related by Abdi (2015), the sense of Islam as continuity and a place of comfort expressed by Somali women in Melbourne (McMichael 2002) or the role of Islam as a 'moral compass' among Somali women in Finland (Tiilikainen 2007).

As in the case of Fadumo, the identifications with Islam were so relevant for Somali women in Nairobi and Johannesburg that many of them saw no difference at all between being Somali and being Muslim, as for them one implied the other. However, other women clearly distinguished between customary and traditional cultural practices 'from the African side' (in the words of one of the women interviewed) and religious, Islamic ones. This distinction that some women made between 'culture and religion' was of interest for exploring the syncretism between Somaliness and Islam, yet what became even more relevant was how the distinction was sometimes strategically used by women as a way to exercise their own agency.

This chapter explores the interconnections between Somaliness and Islam, how the latter has become a stronger identifier among Somalis in the last few decades and how it is also regarded more highly than some cultural practices. Moreover, when a contradiction arises between the Islamic or 'Somali' way, the Islamic way is normally preferred – a belief that is also reflected in the opening epigraph of this chapter, by the Egyptian writer and public speaker Yasmin Mogahed, which was shared on the Facebook page of one of my informants in Nairobi. The original post had two thousand eight hundred likes and was shared 391 times.

The chapter also analyses how Somali women in Nairobi and Johannesburg engage with Islam in a dialogical manner and how, in some cases, the negotiations between their Somali and Muslim identifications become a strategy to exercise their agency in order to contest or discontinue certain cultural practices they disagree with (Ripero-Muñiz 2020). The differences between cultural and religious practices expressed in this chapter reflect the distinctions – or lack thereof – made by the Somali women I talked to in both cities. They used these categories to express their Somali and Muslim identifications in the diasporic places they inhabited in relation to other Somalis, other Africans and other Muslims. These categories are fluid and dialogical (Giddens 1979; Hall 1996, 1997, 2008; Bakhtin 1981), as they continually adapt to specific situations and contexts in order to express women's agency, as will be explored in relation to the ceremonies of the wedding and the *toddoba*; female circumcision; who constitutes an ideal husband; and the political implications of being perceived as a 'good' Muslim woman in a world that tends to equate Muslims with terrorists.

Somaliness and Islam

As explored in the previous chapter, Somali women's sense of their Somaliness emerged as an identification with certain discourses, narratives and practices based on shared structures, together with the implementation of cultural practices in everyday life. Nevertheless, the Muslim identification also played a very important part in how women saw themselves, with many seeing no difference at all between being Somali and being Muslim. Regarding everyday practices, the syncretism between Islam and African cultural practices makes the distinction between them not always clear (Ware 2014). As Amal – the young Somali woman who had been living in Eastleigh for a year at the time of our interview, before travelling to Ethiopia to marry her husband-to-be – declared: 'I see no difference between Somali culture and Islam; whatever we do is Islamic. Being a Somali woman means being a Muslim woman.' Something similar was expressed by Saynab, a young woman living in Johannesburg whose life story opens the next chapter, and who declared that she was born into the culture and the religion: 'I was born Muslim and I was born Somalian and from the start I was told you are Muslim and you are Somali, they go together.' In these cases, it can be observed that Islam is perceived as a pre-given structure into which you are born; 'you are told' who you are. Amal and Saynab's words resonate with what Hersi (1977) explains:

Islam as a religion and a system of values so thoroughly permeates all aspects of Somali life that it is difficult to conceive of any meaning in the term Somali itself without at the same time implying Islamic identity (Hersi 1977: 109, in Elmi 2010: 50).

Part of this is due to the strong Islamic revival that occurred in the country from the 1960s (Elmi 2010)[1]; during this decade, Somali scholars who had studied the Qur'an in the Middle East brought with them on their return to Somalia a stricter version of Islam, Wahhabism. Although Somalia was historically a Muslim country, then, Islamic interpretations and practices were formerly more relaxed than they are today. As explored in previous chapter, women would wear more casual western clothes, even shorts, and not Muslim attire like *jilbaabs*, *bui-buis* or niqabs. The stronger implementation of Islamic practices was also strengthened during the conflict in the 1990s. Deqah, a Somali woman in her late thirties who gained a scholarship to study her undergraduate degree in Italy, where she spent five years before returning to Nairobi to work as a teacher, explained the above phenomenon in the following way: 'For Somalis, [for] everything that is culture they have looked for a justification of religion. So, religion has become more important in the Somali culture. We are losing many things of our culture because of the influence of religion.' She explained that the above-mentioned scholars were very dogmatic and only taught their interpretations of Islam, which were all very radical, and that people in Somalia listened to them because they were 'the experts, the authority'. According to her, this radical interpretation of Islam was strengthened later in the 1990s, during the war, due to popular beliefs:

> The way Somalis practise Islam is very different from the people of the [Kenyan] coast or from Muslims from Western Kenya … In Somalia it is very different. People have seen the war as a punishment from Allah, because Somalis were very open before … And Siad Barre imposed a scientific socialism that did not have a religious component. Afterwards, many people said that Barre was punished because he had left religion behind … In Somalia the radicalization [of Islam] is something that suffocates you! It is not like that in other African countries, like in Senegal, there, 90 per cent of the population are Muslims but they don't dress like this, they wear their traditional African clothes, they drink alcohol ….

In this sense, Islam in the Somali context became a religion to believe in, a faith, but also a tool to create meaning. It became the foundation of a strong collective narrative with which to make sense of the war, and an ordered way of dealing with the chaos and traumas that the armed conflict and consequent forced migration brought with them (McMichael 2002). It became a way to make sense of things. As Geertz (1973: 104) notes, religion does not negate suffering, but helps with 'how to suffer, how to make of physical pain, personal loss, worldly defeat, or the helpless contemplation of others' agony something bearable, supportable – something, as we say, sufferable'.

Deqah's words also summarize in a very concise way the process of re-Islamization of Somalia and the consequences it has had for Somali society, and the way that Islamic practices are differently implemented depending on the context. Moreover, the re-Islamization of Somalia has caused Islamic practices to replace some cultural ones; a good example concerns ways of dressing, as explored in the previous chapter, as well as certain ceremonies such as weddings (as explored in the next section), in which the influence of Islam makes women and their families have to negotiate what kind of ceremony they want to host.

Thus, Islam acts as a strong identifier for Somalis both inside and outside Somalia. In diasporic spaces it provides a continuity with the place of origin, recreating even a sense of home, as McMichael (2002) has explored among Somali women in Melbourne, or Tiilikainen (2007) with Somali woman in Finland, for whom 'Islam may work as a moral and also practical compass in everyday life' (ibid.: 224). At the same time, Islam contributes to the integration of Somalis into new spaces, as in the case of Somalis in Mayfair explored in Chapter 2, or the case described by Abdi (2015) of Somalis in the United Arab Emirates, who feel a degree of integration and belonging not found in other locations, such as the USA, thanks to the Islamic connection. In this way, the relevance of the Muslim identity for Somalis made many Somali women in Nairobi and Johannesburg equate the one with the other.

However, many other women insisted on making a clear distinction between what they considered Islamic practices and 'Somali' or 'African' ones, elaborating in depth on the differences between them. Even if a distinction was acknowledged, though, Islamic identifications and practices were always given a higher status. Such was the case described by Halima, an old woman, originally from Mogadishu, who has been living in Johannesburg for more than twenty years, and who dreams of relocating to Australia sometime in the future. She owns and runs a shop in Amal, where she sells beauty products imported from the UAE and colourful *diracs* for weddings. She saw herself as a model Muslim woman, praying five times a day, fasting during Ramadan, going for prayers at the mosque every Friday and always wearing a niqab to cover her face. She was also very critical of younger Somali women who were not as rigorous in their everyday Muslim practices as she thought they should be. During the course of an interview, she declared:

> For me, religion is more important than culture. Because I'm Muslim and religion is important. I don't like culture. I like religion. We don't follow culture. The culture is from [a] long time ago, now we follow the religion. We don't

follow culture because if you follow culture you don't dress like this [she is wearing a niqab]; our culture is Muslim. We dress like Muslim[s]. So, if you dress like culture, you leave your religion. We leave the culture now and we follow the religion. Everyone in Somalia follows religion for a long time now.

She was very clear in her distinction between culture and religion and in stating that the latter was far more important. Her rejection of 'culture' in favour of religion was not unique to her; indeed, it was a common response that women gave during all the interviews, both in Nairobi and Johannesburg, regardless of their age, class or education. Their answers were simple or elaborate depending on their age and education, but their message was clear and always the same.

Samia in Nairobi gave a more detailed explanation of her relation to culture and religion. Moreover, her years living abroad in Canada and the education she received there had made her question certain aspects of her 'Somali' culture and reject those that relegate women to second place:

Culture and religion, both are important but I don't want to accept certain elements of Somali culture, I won't accept especially those that discriminate [against] women, but I fully accept Islam. Islam, unlike culture, it is divine. I cannot question. I can engage, understand and don't rely on somebody's interpretation. Culture is man-made, not divine. That's why it can be challenged. But I cannot challenge my God. But you can challenge other human beings, because they make mistakes.

Samia's words, among other things, carry with them the subtle distinction of the sacred versus the cultural (Yuval-Davis 2014) – something also observed among Bedouin women in Egypt (Abu-Lughod 1993, 2013). Samia distinguishes very clearly between what she considers culture – something 'man-made' – and religion, which is something divine. Her feminist background may make her very critical of some aspects of Somali culture, but she does not question her faith. Although Samia comes from a very different background than Halima and their life stories and experiences are very different, their words carry a similar message, which also resonates with the opening epigraph of this chapter: a distinction between culture, 'a creation' that can be changed, challenged or even rejected, and religion, which belongs to another order, that of the divine.

The ceremonies associated with the wedding and the *toddoba* are good expressions of the syncretism between cultural and religious practices and of how women navigate these practices in order to fulfil the expectations of them as Somali Muslim women. This will be explored next, together with the contestations that this distinction between culture and religion can generate as part of women's agency in relation to female circumcision and the choice of an ideal husband.

Cultural and Religious Practices in Dialogue

As was explored in Chapter 2 in relation to space, Islam regulates gender relations and roles among Somalis. Women are very much aware of this, and the way that they implement customary practices is influenced by Islamic approaches, as will be explored in relation to the wedding and the *toddoba*. Moreover, Islamic arguments are also used as a resource to challenge certain customary practices with which women disagree, such as female circumcision or not being able to choose the man they would like to marry. In this sense, Somali women make use of their religious agency as a powerful tool for the next implementation or discontinuation of certain customary practices, as next sections will explore.

The Wedding and the Toddoba

Weddings are one of the events at which cultural 'traditional' practices become more noticeable, as they are materialized in the form of music, food, costumes and dances. They are one of the few occasions on which women can leave their hair 'open' or uncovered. Women normally wear colourful *diracs* and their arms and legs are covered in beautiful henna patterns. They also display their gold earrings, necklaces and bracelets. The bride may choose between a Western white dress, a traditional Somali *gutiino* or a mix that incorporates elements of both, demonstrating the translocal syncretism among differing forms of garments.[2] For instance, Figure 4.1 shows a bride wearing a white 'Western' dress combined with henna patterns covering her body. However, some women attending weddings will still prefer to wear their scarfs and burqas for this occasion, something that happened especially in Johannesburg. The families also need to decide whether they prefer a traditional wedding ceremony, which both men and woman can attend, or a religious one, which only the bride and women attend, after the marriage has been formalized at the mosque by the father of the bride and the groom, who is also not allowed to attend the celebration and will be waiting for the bride with some members of his family and close friends at his new home. These kinds of religious weddings were becoming a trend in Nairobi at the time of this research, as Deqah explained:

> The weddings only with women, without the groom and male guests, are now a fashion among the Somali community in Nairobi. People are becoming more religious. Religion is more important now because in our original Somali culture that separation doesn't exist. We dance together, men and women.

Deqah's words describing the trend of hosting a more religious wedding exemplify the way that Islamic customs take precedence over other, more 'traditional' forms of celebration, and cultural and religious practices main-

Negotiating Religious and Cultural Identifications in Diasporic Spaces | 93

Figure 4.1. Somali bride wearing a Western-style dress combined with traditional henna patterns covering her body. Photo by Salym Fayad for the project 'Metropolitan Nomads'.

tain a dialogical relation that is materialized in events such as this. However, regardless of whether the wedding is celebrated in a more religious or traditional way, Somali music will be played and one or more women will also sing traditional *buraanburs* to the couple, on some occasions accompanied by a drum.[3] This kind of poetry is sung only by women and is repeated one week later during the *toddoba* ceremony, which is only attended by women, who bring presents to the bride and sing to her to celebrate her change of status as a married woman. In the past, if the family had some money, they would commission a woman poet who would write customized *buraanburs* for the occasion, with verses or lyrics that specifically referred to the bride and groom, her family and her clan. Today these chants are normally 'ready-made' and repeated occasion after occasion, praising the deeds and achievements of the clans involved. As one woman sings, one or two others play the drums, and the guests dance and sing in a circle until the rhythm changes, with the drums becoming stronger. Women take turns, moving into the centre of the circle, and dance covering their heads with a scarf as they turn around (as seen on the cover and in figure 4.2).

The *toddoba* is a traditional Somali ceremony that is celebrated all around the world by Somali women to praise the newly married woman and the loss of her virginity. Even if weddings can take a more Islamic or a more

Figure 4.2. Woman dancing during a *toddoba* ceremony in Mayfair. Photo by Salym Fayad for the project 'Metropolitan Nomads'.

Somali approach, the *toddoba* remains one of the traditional ceremonies that have not been replaced by an Islamic one.

Figure 4.2 shows a woman dancing during a *toddoba* ceremony in Mayfair; it can be observed that in her way of dressing, she combines Islamic elements, such as the scarf, with a Somali *bati* – a loose, long dress, normally worn by Somali women at home or below their hijab – and a more Western-style leather jacket. The way that this woman is dressed highlights how the syncretism between different traditions and backgrounds can create a unique style that transmits the different identifications that an individual engages with. Something similar can be observed in Figure 4.1, in which a bride combines a Western-style dress with traditional henna patterns on her body. The syncretism demonstrated by ways of dressing denotes the dialogical manner in which women constantly engage with religious, cultural and cosmopolitan identifications as a way to express their agency. These ceremonies were quite revealing in terms of understanding women's negotiation of cultural and religious practices. However, what is perhaps most interesting about this distinction between culture and religion is that many women used it strategically to challenge – or even discontinue – certain cultural practices they disagreed with, such as female circumcision or the inability to choose whom to marry, by using Islamic arguments to support their claims and demands, as the next sections demonstrate.

Female Circumcision

According to all the women interviewed for this book, Somali women's virginity is highly valued in Somali society and is a requisite for a woman to marry for the first time. This explains the high level of control of sociospatial behaviours and the power that gossip has in relation to the reputations of unmarried women and their families in Somali communities (Isotalo 2007), as seen in Chapter 2.[4] One of the most drastic forms of ensuring young women's virginity is the practice of infibulation or pharaonic circumcision, which has been practised for centuries in Somalia.[5] This controversial practice leaves women with physical and psychological trauma, as all respondents to this study declared. The mothers of daughters whom I interviewed in Nairobi and Johannesburg also expressed their desires to not put their offspring through this painful event and its traumatic consequences. They blamed people in Somalia for being ignorant and uneducated in this regard, and explained that migrating out of the country had opened their eyes, making them question whether it was really necessary to put their daughters through this practice. Curran and Sanguy (2001: 59) note that 'exposure to new networks with different beliefs will serve to challenge one's established world view and offer alternative value systems'. The migration experience exposes Somali women to other realities, making them realize that circumcision among women is not the norm everywhere. As Deqah, whose European experiences opened her eyes in this regard, explained:

> When you live in a place where everyone is one-armed, you believe that's the normality, but then you arrive to another place where people have two arms, then you realize that having one arm is not the norm everywhere.

Many other women declared that they became aware that circumcision was not the norm for women when they got pregnant or at the time of giving birth through contact with hospitals, medical practitioners or other women who were going through motherhood at the same time. For them, it thus became clear that circumcision belonged to the cultural realm, and therefore, as Samia put it, could be challenged. Here, the distinction between culture and religion becomes a strategy with which to discontinue a practice that women regard as cultural, and a way to exercise their own agency using Qur'anic arguments (Ripero-Muñiz 2020). As one woman stated during an interview, 'Circumcision for women is not emphasized in Islam. At least the way Somalis do it. That is Somali culture from the African side.' The fact that more women are accessing the Qur'an by themselves, or becoming familiar with Qur'anic teaching through friends or relatives, together with the years of awareness campaigns inside and outside Somalia, is changing the way that women implement or even discontinue this practice. This is a view also shared by less educated women, who do not access the Qur'an themselves but are aware of the discourses and narratives currently circulating inside and outside the Somali diaspora. Such was the case of Awa, a young refugee who left southern Somalia after a member of Al-Shabaab tried to marry her. She was sent abroad by her parents to avoid this undesired marriage and was now living in Johannesburg with some relatives. She did not know Arabic, nor had she read the Qur'an herself, but she was informed through the talks she had with other Somali women. She explained that circumcision belonged to the cultural realm and that many women wanted to stop it because of the multiple problems caused during menstruation and birth, besides the physical and psychological traumas that women go through. She said that this practice was changing now because women had become aware of the issues it created, in comparison with their mothers and grandmothers, who did not directly associate the pains they suffered with circumcision. Awa's words reflect the way that young women are gaining a new consciousness about a long-practised cultural tradition that is now being questioned. Most of these young women both in Nairobi and Johannesburg emphasized that the practice was decreasing in both places, that they were not doing it to their daughters anymore and that they blamed people in Somalia for being uneducated and backward. As Sagal and Amina, two young respondents in Nairobi who were in their early twenties but were already divorced and had a couple of young children each, explained:

> Sagal : Men actually want women who have not been touched.
> Amina: Men nowadays, the ones who are from the Somalia rural areas, they want the one who's circumcised, you know?
> S: They believe if a woman is not circumcised, she'll have very, very high hormones; she'll look for other men, because men used to travel. They were herders. So, they would go grazing [their] cattle for a long time looking for rain and greener pastures. And he comes back and doesn't know what goes on behind his back.

Sagal and Amina explained female circumcision based on Somali nomadic traditions, but others pointed to older women as being responsible for the prevalence of this practice. As Hibo , another young mother in Johannesburg, explained, it is a very old 'bad tradition' that is now changing because people are stopping it. In the past, mothers and grandmothers used to do it because they thought that young girls' virginity would be safer, but now it is those same young girls who will become grandmothers and will decide what to do. Indeed, the fact of being away from family members, especially grandmothers, helps women to question and eradicate the practice, as Fábos (2001) also explored among Sudanese immigrants in Egypt. It is true that elder women impose great pressure regarding the continuity of this practice to preserve younger women's virginity. As Luul, one respondent in Nairobi, put it:

> In Somali culture it's very complicated. It has to be a revolution from within. It is an identity that is already constructed and to deconstruct it from the outside is very difficult. Even more, there are people who keep generating that identity: the grandmothers, the mothers, the aunties ...

Luul's words demonstrate how the attempts to eradicate this practice have to come from within the community, instead of via the imposing of outside views. She emphasizes that older women ensure that this 'traditional' practice continues to be implemented. Nevertheless, even if it is mothers, aunties and grandmothers who seek the continuation of this harmful practice, they cannot be solely blamed for its perpetuation, which in fact serves the purposes of a very patriarchal society that uses certain interpretations of the Qur'an to defend the practice for its own ends. As Anzaldúa (1987:16) points out: 'Males make the rules; women transmit them.' Faiza, an activist working for a women's rights organization in Nairobi, noted that even if this practice is reproduced and implemented only by women, they do so in order to fulfil men's desires, in which women become a transaction. As she explained:

> If a man is not going to marry your daughter because she is not circumcised then you want to circumcise [her] in preparation to ensure her future place in marriage. It's like an exchange of goods. If I'm paying for this, I want to be sure that no other man has touched this, you know? How does the father ensure that his daughter is not touched? So that's the whole thing. That's the basis for it. It's also triggered [by the] egos of men and using women's bodies as goods to sell.

Faiza's words indicate the complexity of a practice that ends up commodifying women and the difficulties of deconstructing it, as it is so deeply embedded in the community. She believes that to eradicate the practice completely, despite campaigns to sensitize the population, a unified voice from the religious leaders in the country is required, condemning the practice as un-Islamic. She related how once, her organization was carrying out a campaign in a rural area of Somalia to eradicate female circumcision. They talked to the elders and then let them discuss the matter. When they met with them again to check whether they would support the campaign, the elders said no, on the basis that if they allowed this now, then women would come to demand other things, like the end of polygamy. If there was a unified response from religious leaders condemning the practice, the elders could not oppose it so easily. Moreover, as Samia stated:

> The more women have knowledge of their faith, the more chances [that] the practice of FGM will decrease. Mothers aware of the Qur'an['s] teachings won't put their daughters through that because they know [it] is un-Islamic.

In this sense, the distinction between religion and culture becomes strategic, and placing Islam above an 'African' cultural practice can be used as a strong argument to erase a harmful practice, in a more efficient way than 'Western' arguments have provided in the past. Thus, accessing Islamic texts gives Somali women power to decide certain things. This is not a phenomenon happening only in Nairobi or Johannesburg, but is in fact taking place throughout the Somali diaspora, as Hernlund and Shell-Duncan (2007) mention with regard to Somali women living in the UK, Australia, Sweden and Norway. Women accessing the Qur'an are able to interpret the verses themselves, without intermediaries, and in this way become critical of certain interpretations that have been imposed in the past. As Samia explained:

> Those who exploit, those who have more power, they want to keep people in the dark and they will decide [to translate] certain verses ... Translate the whole verse! I know because I am an educated woman but they cut, they trim it because they want people to remain where they are so they can retain their power, people don't know, so they don't question.

In this context, then, Islam can help to give women power to back up the claims they make about a practice that they want to discontinue because of its harmful effects on their physical and emotional well-being. In comparison with humanitarian efforts, which normally come from the West and tend to fail – as they try to impose a discontinuity from outside – the use of Islam to support arguments that contest this practice could become a more powerful and effective way to deconstruct it from the inside, as such arguments are harder to counter by those who insist on the practice's continuation.

The Ideal Husband: Who to Marry and Who Not to Marry

The ideal husband was described by women interviewed as someone who is respectful, responsible, educated, hard-working and able to provide a 'better life'. Many women also declared that they could marry any Muslim, not necessary a Somali man, and some of them did. However, in everyday practice, a Somali man is normally preferred and sought due to pressure from the family and community, who normally prefer such a pairing. Thus, even if the privileging of religion above culture is constant in women's narratives and discourses, when it comes to choosing a man to marry, things become slightly different. Arguments such as better understanding and 'same language and same culture' are then mobilized, as this discussion between Sagal and Amina, living in Nairobi, shows:

> Amina: For us, it is important to marry a Somali man because it makes things easier.

Sagal: We have a strong culture, and it's easier for you not to deal with all your family, cos they'll be in your business. If you married a white guy: *Oh! Is he Muslim?* Those questions will come up a lot. Also because of your culture, there are some things that are normal to you that are not normal to us.
A: My niece, she's married to an Arab from Qatar. They always have issues and problems.
S: Yes, especially with Arabs ... If you are African, they call us Black slaves.
A: We're always inferior.
S: Arabs are the worst cos they're racist.
A: They're worse than South Africans, I think, you have no rights when you live in an Arab country.

Sagal and Amina's conversation exposed the fact that despite all the constant claims made that 'religion always comes first for Somalis', it can be clearly seen in arguments defending a 'strong culture' are made to justify the preference for marrying a Somali man. They also exposed the racial stereotypes that exist about Arabs, and that being Muslim does not act as a unifying factor in this regard. On the contrary, racial, national, cultural and even linguistic differences are mobilized to defend the customary, unwritten practice of marrying a Somali man. But in fact, what really lies behind these 'racial' differences is a more complex scenario of class, economic status and cultural differences. I asked Deqah why there was this insistence that Somali women marry Somali men, and she related that her sister, who lives in the USA, was getting married, but her parents did not want even to know about it, and did not even ask about bride wealth, 'because she is crazy, mad, she always had boyfriends, a Moroccan, a Puerto Rican ... My parents had nightmares that she was never going to get a Somali husband. It is the nightmare of any Somali family.' She went on to explain why this is difficult for Somali parents to accept, as it does not affect only the family but the entire community, especially in terms of what people think about the marriage. She emphasized how difficult it is to make a decision in these cases, because it does not depend only on you, but on the entire family. She concluded by declaring: 'Those who tell you that [it] is not a problem to marry a Muslim, they are lying. Try to have one in your family; let's see what they say.'

Deqah's words make clear the implications of virginity for the asking for bride wealth; when there seems to be doubt about a woman's virginity, no bride wealth can be asked for. Moreover, her words highlight the enormous pressure from family and community to marry a Somali, and again the power that rumours and gossip play in controlling women's actions in the community. She also states that marrying a non-Somali man, even if he is Muslim, is something that families would not prefer. Apart from the cultural differences mentioned above by Sagal and Amina, which might make a marriage more complicated, the reluctance of Somali families to see their daughters marrying non-Somalis has another implicit reason: clan membership in Somali society is only inherited via the patrilineal line, and thus, a Somali with a Muslim but non-Somali father will not have a defined clan membership, and therefore no place among the Somali genealogies. This is why most families normally prefer their daughters to marry other Somalis instead of Muslims. Preferring a Somali husband is a way to ensure the continuity of Somaliness based on a common 'pure' origin. Women are generally considered the embodiment of national culture (Yuval-Davis 1993, 1997) and are expected to reproduce and even reinforce the customary structures of their community, so that continuity between past and future is maintained and a sense of 'pure' national culture is not lost generation after generation. However, young Somali women are challenging this customary practice, using again the Islamic argument that as long as they are marrying a Muslim, they are themselves behaving as virtuous Muslims; in this way, they are also exercising their individual agency. Such was the case of Hodan, a young Somali-Kenyan who was studying for her degree in international relations in Nairobi when we met. Soon after she graduated, she went to Khartoum, as she wanted to learn Arabic. After she finished the course there, her parents wanted her to come back to Nairobi and marry a Somali man. But she had other plans: she wanted to go to Qatar to live and work there for a while. Although her mother was a successful businesswoman in Nairobi who had travelled widely around the world, Hodan was aware that neither her nor her father would accept it if she ended up meeting and wanting to marry an Arab man in Qatar. But this did not worry her; she was confident that as long as he was a Muslim, she would not be behaving improperly. The knowledge Hodan had of the Qur'an, which she could access directly thanks to her knowledge of Arabic, gave her a certain degree of power to contest the politics around marriage and who makes an appropriate husband. Her knowledge of Qur'anic teachings enables her to question some customary practices with which she may not agree. This was also the case for Saynab, whose life story is presented in the next chapter, and who chose to marry a Lebanese man using the same kind of arguments.

In these cases, we can see how a deeper knowledge of Islam, as well as women's own reflexivity (Archer 2003) in discerning between a traditional customary practice and what is prescribed by Islam, becomes key to their decisions.[6] Women consider and evaluate their cultural and religious values before acting in one way or another, choosing to do what they consider to be right. Instead of passive subjects, as they tend to be perceived, Somali women strategically negotiate their religious and cultural identifications in a context of displacement. They are active agents in the reproduction, transformation or eradication of certain practices. By making use of their religious agency, they are challenging certain customary practices that they do not wish to continue. Religious agency 'is enacted in emotional, intellectual and behavioural strategies, thereby enabling individuals to negotiate overlapping and valued identities' (Leming 2007: 73). In both contexts studied, making use of their religious agency gives women a certain degree of power in the implementation or discontinuation of certain customary practices.

The 'Good Muslim' Woman

I opened this chapter with a reference to the Westgate attacks in Nairobi and the way that Somalis in Mayfair were concerned both about their possible repercussions in South Africa – in the form of xenophobic attacks – and the consequences of equating the name of Islam with terrorism, something that has been common since 9/11. Fadumo, a devoted and pious woman, pointed out that the media had 'hijacked' the name of Islam, giving it another layer of meaning very different from hers. She, and all the other women presented in the cases throughout this chapter, regardless of their positioning on culture and religion, tended to present themselves as virtuous Muslim women. Projecting the image of a virtuous Muslim woman and acting in accordance with it also has some political implications. It acts as a response to current international debates and the stereotypical portrayal of Muslims as terrorists in the global imagination (Abu-Lughod 2006, 2013; Mamdani 2004). By presenting themselves as virtuous 'good Muslims', women were also implicitly transmitting that they were not terrorists. This has special relevance for Somalis if we take into account the stereotypical narratives and discourses circulating about them, in which a prevailing representation is that of the Al-Shabaab terrorist. During my interview with Fadumo, shortly after the Westgate attacks, she claimed that the people who perpetrated the attacks were not truly Muslims, but 'abnormal people that exist in any community'. She went on to explain that the focus on Islam as terrorism after 9/11 has become an obsession in the Western world, and that every Muslim is presented as a terrorist, regardless of where they come from:

> Every Muslim is presented as a terrorist ... you're not looked at as a Somali or as an Egyptian. You're seen as a Muslim. So, when a terrorist attack happens, they blame all Muslims and Islam. But Islam doesn't teach terrorism, the meaning of Islam is peace.

She compared this with the terrorist attacks on Utøya, Norway in 2011, in which a right-wing extremist perpetrated a massive shooting; in this case, society and the media just blamed 'a crazy guy' and not an entire society or religion. She emphasized that these different discourses are created by the media and the misconceptions about Islam in the Western imaginary. Fadumo's words about terrorism and Islam reflect those of Mahmood Mamdani (2004: 15), who explains the impact of the 9/11 terrorist attack on the Islamic world:

President Bush moved to distinguish between 'good Muslims' and 'bad Muslims'. From this point of view, 'bad Muslims' were clearly responsible for terrorism. At the same time, the president seemed to assure Americans that 'good Muslims' were anxious to clear their names and consciences of this horrible crime and would undoubtedly support 'us' in the war against 'them'. But this could not hide the central message of such discourse: until proved to be 'good' every Muslim was presumed to be 'bad'. All Muslims were now under the obligation to prove their credentials by joining the war against 'bad Muslims'. Judgments of 'good' and 'bad' refer to Muslim political identities, not to cultural or religious ones.

Hence the insistence of Fadumo and many other Somali women on presenting themselves as 'good', virtuous Muslim women; for them it was important to prove to the world that they were not 'bad' Muslims, or in other words, fanatical terrorists. It also has to be taken into account that the women I talked to were addressing me, a non-Muslim, in the aftermath of the Westgate attack in Nairobi, which had strong repercussions for Somalis in Nairobi and all around the world. This attack demonstrated, in an echo of 9/11, the widespread representation of Muslims as fanatical terrorists. By presenting themselves as 'good' and virtuous Muslim women, my interlocutors were consciously positioning themselves, choosing to present themselves to the world in a certain manner, and in doing so, they were not acting as passive subjects, but engaged agents.

Negotiating Cultural and Religious Identifications

Islam is one of the pillars of Somali collective identity, and it acts as a strong identifier among Somali women in Nairobi and Johannesburg. Some of these women saw no difference at all between being Somali and being Muslim; however, many others made a clear distinction between what they considered cultural practices versus religious ones. When this was the case, the Islamic way was normally favoured and regarded as having higher status than customary practices.

The different ways in which Somali women engage with their Muslim identifications and implement religious practices in their everyday lives resonate with Talal Asad's (2009) understanding of Islam as a 'discursive tradition', according to which Islam was (and is) constructed by collective narratives spanning space and time. It is a discourse that is constantly contested and adapted to specific contexts for its implementation in the practice of everyday life. Tradition here is not to be perceived as 'static', but rather fluid and open to change, with the implementation of practices adapting to new contexts (Macintyre 1981). This could be observed during wedding celebrations and in women's choices of which men they would like to marry.

For Somalis, Islam also offers a unifying identification above the categories of clan, gender, class or even nationality, as has been explored in relation to the umma; in a context of migration, it also becomes a thread to the place of origin and helps to create a sense of home in the new destination (McMichael 2002), acting as 'a moral and practical compass' (Tiilikainen 2007: 224). Moreover, this sense of Islam as a 'moral and practical compass' empowers some Somali women, as they use arguments based on Islamic teachings to question and, in some cases, discontinue cultural practices that they no longer wish to 'perform', as in the case of the discontinuation of female circumcision or in choosing a non-Somali husband. Islam becomes a way for women to exercise their own agency, not only in relation to free will, but also to what is right, adding a moral, ethical and religious component to individual agency (Mack 2003). Moreover, it becomes a form of religious agency, whereby Islam, instead of constituting a restraining force, as it is normally perceived, is used by women to navigate their agency and express their individual will. The fact that this was the case in both contexts studied emphasizes the translocal connection between the two diasporic spaces and the unifying power of Islam across boundaries.

Finally, it was important for women to be perceived as virtuous Muslims – to present, with their actions and behaviours, a counter-discourse to Western discourses in which Muslims are normally portrayed as terrorists or threats to national security. The women's actions and the implementation of their daily practices and beliefs were also directed at proving that they were not a threat to anyone, were not terrorists and could also have a place in the 'new world order'. This desire to be part of the 'new world order', and the aspiration to improve their living conditions and those of their families, are further explored in the next chapter in relation to women's agency, the circulation of power, and transnational migration.

Notes

1. Works by Masquelier (2009) and Mahmood (2005) have also documented this process of Islamic revival taking place among Muslim women in other regions of Africa, such as Niger and Egypt respectively.
2. A *gutiino* is a traditional wrap dress (Akou 2011).
3. *Baraanbur* is a form of oral poetry composed and sung by Somali women. It is considered the most prestigious genre of the women's oral poetry tradition (Kapteijns 1999).
4. This does not apply equally to Somali men, as many have premarital sexual relations with non-Somali women. As one of the women I interviewed in Nairobi explained: 'They put us through FGM to arrive [as] virgins to marriage, but the boys want to try everything and then marry a virgin … When I was young, Somali boys used to go with other Kenyan girls, not with us.' This highlights the

double standards that normally surround this topic, in which the virginity of a woman becomes her most important value, and also where the pride and honour of her entire family resides (Yuval-Davis 1993).
5. This form of female circumcision implies the cutting of the clitoris and labia, which are sewn together afterwards, leaving a small orifice for the passing of urine and menstrual flow (Brady and Files 2007).
6. In her 2003 book *Structure, Agency and the Internal Conversation*, Margaret Archer analyses the role that reflexivity and the internal dialogue play as mediators between individual agency and social structures. The reflexivity of migrant women tends to be overlooked, but in the case studies presented here it can be observed how it can become a key component in the decisions Somali women make about their lives.

5

Somali Women of Nairobi and Johannesburg

Migration, Agency and Aspirations

> *Some women choose to follow men, and some women choose to follow their dreams. If you are wondering which way to go, remember that your career will never wake up and tell you that it doesn't love you anymore.*
>
> –Lady Gaga

I met Saynab in February 2013. She had come from Somalia to South Africa by road in 2007, crossing Ethiopia, Kenya, Tanzania and Mozambique, in a journey that took several months, as along the way she stayed for days or weeks with friends and relatives who lived in Nairobi, Dar es Salaam and Nampula. Her new husband was waiting for her in Johannesburg. They had never met before; their families had arranged and formalized their marriage when she was still in Somalia. He owned a spaza shop in one of Gauteng's townships. Saynab settled in Mayfair, 'as locations are too dangerous for women', and her husband used to come and go between the township and Johannesburg.

Saynab arrived full of dreams of a better life in the south of the continent, but they did not last long. Soon after her arrival she got pregnant and gave birth to a baby girl, but the relationship with her husband started to deteriorate quickly, as he began to chew khat on a daily basis, then stopped working, supporting neither her or their child.[1] She asked for a divorce but he did not agree to it, and even took her refugee papers away to stop her leaving. The families were not nearby to intervene in the quarrel, as is normally the custom, but after much transnational discord and talk between both families, he finally granted her the divorce. Nonetheless, he would not support her or the child. She started looking for a job and found one as a cashier in a shop in Mayfair, but she had to send her child back to her parents in Puntland as she was not able to keep looking after her on her own. After she saved some money, she invested it in 'Fong Kong' clothes that she then sold on Jeppe Street.[2] It did not work out, as the police at that time ran raids and confiscated fake branded goods. At the time I met her, she had left that business and was studying English.

After I interviewed her on a few occasions and she introduced me to other women to be interviewed, we became close and she took me around different places in Mayfair. Then one day, she disappeared. I called her and sent her messages and emails, but received no response. I could not understand her disappearance and was worried something might have gone wrong. Then, after a couple of weeks, I went to Mayfair, and the first thing women told me in Amal was: 'Have you heard? Saynab, she has married to a Lebanese! Can you believe it?' They told me that they did not understand how her family had agreed to it, that something like that was unacceptable, that maybe she had not told them or they did not talk to her any more. When I finally found her, she had moved with her new husband to a flat in Mayfair. She told me that she had met her husband in the shop that she now worked at. She showed me her wedding pictures. Her wedding dress was a white, 'Western'-style one with a Muslim touch, as the veil covering her head was arranged in the manner of a headscarf. She was aware of the gossip circulating about her in the neighbourhood, but she did not care much because she believed that she had done nothing wrong, that she had married a Muslim and her family supported her. She also told me that this husband had seemed better than the previous one. She kept working and taking care of the house, but several months after the wedding, things started going wrong, as he started mistreating her. Less than a year later, she had divorced him. She kept working as a cashier, until her parents called her back to Somalia. They told her that if she was not studying or doing something worthwhile there to improve her life, there was no point in her staying in South Africa. But she did not want to go back. She wanted to study and keep searching for a better life. Then one day, a Wednesday, I received a WhatsApp message from her, saying that she was not sure, but that she might be going to Brazil next week. This news shocked me, even though I knew that she did not want to stay in Johannesburg for ever. This was a new trend at that time among Somalis in Mayfair: a new migration route whereby many Somalis tried to reach the USA via South America. I went to see her on the Friday. She was waiting for a call from the smuggler, which could come at any time, to tell her when to go. She was nervous and scared. On Sunday she received the call, and she left, carrying her handbag with the American flag on its four sides. She made it through passport control at O.R. Tambo International Airport and through arrivals in

São Paolo. She was travelling alone, armed with just a hostel address in São Paolo. Once there she met another group of Somalis, and a few days later, they were on their way to Peru, then Ecuador. I kept track of her movements via WhatsApp. They travelled using local transport, Google Maps and the stories circulating among other Somalis. The hardest part of the journey was to be the crossing from Colombia to Panama. The Pan-American Highway stops there, due to the thick, impenetrable jungle that can only be crossed on foot with a smuggler who knows how to move around. All kinds of illegalities also cross that border. One week later she contacted me again from Panama and talked about all the hardships she went through: the smuggler abandoning them in the middle of the jungle after he asked for more money that they did not have, then the group abandoning her because she was going too slow and kept getting lost before she reached the Panama side. She even related how she had carried with her along the way, almost as a talisman, a copy of the book *A Man of Good Hope* by Jonny Steinberg, which I had given to her as a gift months ago, and how this book literally melted under the torrential rain of the tropical jungles. After recovering from this journey, she continued up to Mexico, from which she sent a farewell message stating her intention to cross into the US; she eventually made it and was put for some months in a detention centre. I heard from her again when she had left the detention centre and was living with some relatives until she could find a job. It took her a while to mentally recover from the hardships of her journey, but she finally settled, found a job in a warehouse and, a couple of years later, got married again to an American Muslim and started a new family. Thanks to the money she now earns, she has been able to help her mother and daughter to relocate to Uganda, and she sends them monthly remittances. She hopes that one day they will also be able to join her in the USA.

The challenges Saynab faced are shared by many Somali migrant women in Johannesburg, who may also experience arranged marriage, young motherhood, problems with husbands, divorce, struggles to make a living, remarriage, desires to study and, after every attempt at improvement fails, leaving South Africa in search of a 'better life' somewhere else. The desire for a 'better life' was a constant one that emerged in almost all interviews, both in Johannesburg and Nairobi. What they meant by a 'better life' was a life in which they could work or study and support their relatives back in Somalia, and in which they could freely move across borders. It also reflected their cosmopolitan aspirations. These aspirational desires are common among Somalis, and the role of the imagination is an important part in the migration process, as authors such as Cindy Horst (2016a) and Cawo Abdi (2015) have explored among Somalis in Dadaab in Kenya, and in the USA and the UAE. Horst highlights how the desire for migration and improvement is expressed through the concept of *buufis* and triggers displacement, as explored in the introduction to this book. Abdi emphasizes the important role that the imagination plays in the migration process and that 'how desired destinations are imagined is crucial on how migration is experienced' (2015: 8). The desire to belong to a world in which one can move freely, work, study and improve one's quality of material life and that of one's family becomes a very strong engine for migration, and Somali women will do everything they can to fulfil their aspirations.

Beyond her aspirations, Saynab's story also shows that Somali women's agency is informed by their personal experiences in relation to the cultural and religious beliefs and practices of their local and translocal communities. Saynab's decision to marry a Lebanese man was a personal choice, supported by the argument that she was marrying a Muslim, and thus upholding the standards of a 'good' Muslim woman.

While the previous chapter analysed the way that women used their religious agency to contest certain cultural practices, this chapter will explore how women's agency is extended to other aspects of their lives when it comes to the improvement of their circumstances, either through marriage or migration. Individual agency will be understood here as the 'the individual's ability to act according to her own best interests and to resist oppressive power relationships' (Mack 2003: 151). Individual agency is expressed as a response to social structures (Giddens 1979) and implemented through the repetition of everyday practices, or in some cases through their contestation, transformation or discontinuation (Butler 1990), as was explored in the last chapter. Here, I will focus on how the individual agency and decision-making power of Somali women have increased since the outbreak of the armed conflict and the transnational migration that followed. This is a situation that has transformed gender roles and practices both inside and outside the country (Al-Sharmani 2010; Hopkins 2010; Jinnah 2010; Langellier 2010; Farah 2000; Bryden and Steiner 1998). This, however, does not mean that expressions of women's agency did not take place in Somalia before the war or the ensuing mass migration. For example, the essays collected by Gardner and El Bushra (2004) explore the active role that Somali women played during the war, as well as the example of the legendary figure of Queen Araweelo, a female ruler who is thought to have lived in the tenth century and who became an expression of feminist contestation of patriarchy in Somali society. She imposed matriarchy during her regime, as she believed that women were more efficient leaders than men, and she became famous for the extreme measures she took to enforce it, like castrating her enemies or hanging men from their testicles to force them to get more involved in domestic chores and childbearing (see Affi 1995 and Shire 2014 for more details about this legendary queen). Still, it cannot be denied either that these expressions of agency have become stronger with the migration process and in diasporic contexts, which have made many women more independent and, in some cases, the breadwinners in their families. Cases such as that of Somalis in Italy, explored by Farah (2000), or the situation that Somalis encounter in the USA, presented by Abdi (2015), can cause some cultural and religious challenges, as they alter the traditional Islamic structures wherein men are normally the heads of the family. Despite the agency gained through the migration process, however, women are still perceived as carriers of collective culture and identity, and the politics surrounding marriage are still paramount in the lives of young Somali women, as was partly explored in the last chapter with regard to choosing the right husband. This chapter further explores how such women navigate the expectations of their families and relatives concerning what it means to be a 'good' Somali and Muslim woman, at the same time as they try to fulfil their dreams of a 'better life' in a transnational context of displacement.

The Agency of Somali Migrant Women

The previous chapter explored the ways that religious agency was navigated by women in order to challenge or discontinue certain cultural practices. In addition, expressions of agency emerged in relation to economic independence and the transformation of gender roles in the diaspora, something that also challenges the widespread representation of migrant women as victims. Non-Western women tend to be perceived as incapable of autonomy (Philips 2007) and dominated by strong patriarchal, cultural and religious power structures (Abu-Lughod 2013). And, as stated in the introduction to this book, Somali women in particular tend to be associated with the stereotype of the 'Third World Woman' as Black, Muslim, oppressed and uneducated (Mohanty 1988) – a victim without voice or choice. However, as these pages have shown, women migrate by themselves, run businesses on their own and take control of some cultural and religious practices as a way to exercise their agency. In Somalia, the role of women after the armed conflict and consequent mass migration has been directly affected, as the case of Falis demonstrates. Falis is one of many Somali women residing in Nairobi since the conflict broke out in Somalia. Divorced several times and a single mother to an extended family, she makes a living as a businesswoman and often travels to the UAE, where she buys goods such as perfumes, textiles or gold to resell later in Nairobi. As she explained, the war created a transfer of power in which women now have more access to economic freedom without depending on men:

> The Somali community survives because of the women, because women were taking care of all aspects of life as the men were busy with the war. The men in Somalia were controlling because they had money. But life is changing now. The economy is controlling, not the man. Before women didn't have anything.

> After the war the men don't work, they are confused [and] they don't know what to do, where to start ... But all the women are working, the women know how to take care of their husbands and their children, men have become a hassle. Somalis survive because of women, if not they'd have long disappeared.

Falis's case, like others presented here, illustrates that in the Somali context, the war and subsequent forced migration created a situation of transferral of power. Women became economically empowered, gaining more control over their lives and those of their families, and generating in this way new forms of social organization that benefitted the whole community (Allen 1999), even if this created some discomfort among men in certain contexts, as Abdi (2015) explores among the Somali diaspora in the USA, where gender roles are mostly altered in comparison to cultural and religious customs.

A situation of war and conflict also turned gender into a 'core organizing principle' (Boyd and Grieco 2003) in the migration process, as women are normally given preference when migrating: first, as way to avoid gender-based violence during the conflict, and second, because of the widespread belief that women tend to be more responsible and always send money back home to support other family members (Al-Sharmani 2010). As a woman, also in Nairobi, corroborated:

> Men prefer women to emigrate because they either work [and] send money home or they have children and receive benefits from the government of the countries they are staying [in]. Women have become the survival kit of the Somali society.

Most of the young, unmarried women interviewed in Johannesburg worked, either for other Somalis or Ethiopians or by running their own businesses. Back in Somalia they were dependent on their parents or relatives, but now they have had to find ways to make a living; 'here you have to learn to survive on your own', as one of the women interviewed in Mayfair put it – an assertion probably based on the women's young age and the experience of migrating away from their families, as women in Somalia also played an important role in the traditional pastoral economy (Ibrahim 2004). Married women tend to stay at home looking after their children and the house, but if their husbands' money is not enough to support the family and also send remittances back home, they try to work as well. Divorced women were the ones that seemed to struggle the most, as many did not get support from their ex-husbands, and if they worked, like Saynab, they were unable to take care of their children, with many sending them back to Somalia to be looked after by grandmothers, aunts or other close relatives. Consistent with these respondents' experiences, Abdi (2015) has emphasized the importance for Somali women of working in the South African context to maintain their independence and support their families. Farah (2000) has also illustrated this point in relation to Somalis living in Italy, where many Somali women have become the breadwinners, supporting men completely. Indeed, Somali women are a strong economic engine both inside and outside of Somalia, and in many cases, they become the main breadwinners for their families. In the context of migration, the agency of Somali women is expressed and exercised through their economic empowerment and the responsibilities associated with it, something that has repercussions for established, traditional gender roles and dynamics.

The Politics of Marriage

Despite women gaining agency and economic empowerment through the migration experience, marriage still plays an important role in the lives of young Somali women, and many expectations are built around it, as analysed briefly in the previous chapter regarding the choice of the right man to marry. Marriage can have different meanings for women, as explored subsequently, but women also attempt to achieve their aspirations to improve their lives and those of their families through marriage, which does not entirely depend on the couple that wish to marry, but involves the whole family. As Saynab explained:

> Before the marriage you are talking, you sit here and he sits there, you are not touching, if he touches your body, you cannot marry. You must be strong and say, *Ehhh, don't touch me!* You have to [pay] a lot of attention because all the men around the world are the same. They want to touch or sleep with you, but then they don't want you for the future. If Somalian men touch your body, then you cannot marry. So, you just talk, talk, talk, just talk face to face. So then when you are happy, if he is talking to you nicely, then you marry. Before, he has to talk to the family, but then you can marry. If the family doesn't like him, you cannot marry.

Saynab's words summarized, in a very honest way, the process of courtship and marriage among many Somalis and the way that it is regulated by religious and cultural precepts: prohibition of sexual relations before marriage, valuing of virginity and the involvement of the family in the whole marriage process. The families have to agree first before marriage can proceed. This process can take weeks and involves the suitor talking to various male members of the woman's family. The process can leave women with little agency if the families do not agree about the marriage, but as explored in the previous chapter, they may use their religious agency to question certain customary practices and choose a husband to their liking in order to fulfil their personal desires at the same time as creating a better life for themselves.

Even if the sense of life improving was present in the expectations that women had of marriage, it also could mean different things for them depending on their circumstances. For some it meant liberation and emancipation from their families of origin. Such was the case of Deqah, who studied for some years in Italy, and whose Italian friends used to laugh at her when she said that for her, marriage was liberating, and that she wanted to get married to emancipate herself from her parents. She was living by herself with other students because she was studying in Italy, but she would not have been allowed to do that back in Nairobi, as Somali women there are only allowed to live by themselves if 'forced by circumstances. Or you travel to another country to better your life.' These words of Deqah's highlight again the agency and freedom that the migration process can grant Somali women. After Deqah completed her studies, she returned to Nairobi to live with her parents as an unmarried Somali woman would do, even though she was 34 at that time, was economically independent and had lived by herself during her studies in Italy. Marriage also elevates the status of a Somali woman in society, as she is then seen as responsible enough to start a family and take care of it. Once a woman is married, it does not matter if her husband does not live with her. She can stay on her own, as was the case for Deqah. When she married, her husband was still working in Italy and only went to Nairobi for a couple of months a year, but she could live on her own during his absence as she was a married woman. She experienced a sense of liberation and emancipation through marriage.

However, for other women, marriage can become a kind of transaction between families in the form of arranged marriage. Arranged marriage is quite common among Somalis and many young women accept this fate, obeying the family decision and marrying a man chosen for them. Sometimes this is the only way for a young girl to survive or get out of Somalia, as was the case for Saynab, whose first marriage was arranged before she arrived in Johannesburg. There are also some situations in which young women are married against their will.[3] According to respondents, this happens especially in Somalia, where the imposition of an unwanted marriage may come not only from the girl's family but also from Al-Shabaab members, who threaten families into giving them their daughters as wives; if they refuse, the jihadists will kill the women This was the case for Awa, now living in Johannesburg, who had to leave her family overnight after a jihadist asked for her hand. However, according to respondents in both cities, more women are rebelling now against unwanted marriages. As Sagal in Nairobi explained:

> It doesn't happen in Nairobi. Most of the girls who live in Nairobi are more exposed, they see the cosmopolitan life. A friend of mine, Anisa, when she finished eighth grade, her father just told her, 'You're getting married', so the

day of the wedding, she accepted, but the night of the wedding, she ran away, she still hasn't come back, she's been away from the family till today for seven years.

Sagal's words highlight the way that the cosmopolitan experience of being exposed to other realities makes women more aware of other kinds of possibilities than a marriage that they do not want. For her, women exposed to a more 'cosmopolitan life' become more aware of the freedoms they can enjoy. Her position that migration opens a space for more cosmopolitan expression to take place echoes the views of many other Somali women interviewed for this study. These women stated that they were only exposed to certain ways of doing things in Somalia, and that the experience of living in a foreign country had opened their eyes to other realities and ways of living – as was also the case with regard to female circumcision, explored in the previous chapter.

Whether a marriage is arranged or not, the whole family tends to be involved in choosing whom the young woman will marry. In some cases, when the woman wants to marry a man other than the one chosen for her by her family, she may choose to run away with him in an arranged elopement. Deqah, whose husband was her own choice, related how difficult the agreement on her marriage was. Her father was very proud of her; he had always supported her education and even sent her to Italy to complete her studies. During her time there, she met a Somali man; they felt in love and wanted to get married, but Deqah's father opposed it on the grounds that he was a Somali that nobody in the family knew about. It took several months before he was convinced by other male members of the family and all the details of the husband-to-be's family had been checked. During this long process, Mohammed, now Deqah's husband, proposed eloping if her father did not finally agree to their marriage, but Deqah did not agree to this because she did not want to offend her father, as eloping would have meant failing him. Her father appreciated her a lot and would have taken it as a betrayal. She also explained that once a girl elopes with a man, she must stay with him; her parents will not take her back, as 'they don't know what happened between the two of them'. What Deqah means is that after an elopement, the family cannot ensure the girl's virginity any more, so they cannot try to marry her again. This has direct implications not only for the bride wealth that the parents could receive, but also for the honour of the entire family. The parents and elders of the family would be seen by the community as unable to ensure their young girl's virginity. Somali women's virginity is highly valued and ensured at all costs; this is why the extreme measure of infibulation is taken, as discussed in the previous chapter. But it is not only the family that values women's virginity; women themselves think of it as a form of self-respect, as this extract from Karen Blixen's *Out of Africa* illustrates:

> All young women had a high idea of their own value. A Mohammedan virgin cannot marry beneath her, such a thing would call down the gravest blame upon her family. A man may marry beneath him, – that is good enough for him, – and young Somalis have been known to take Masai wives. But while a Somali girl may marry into Arabia, an Arab girl cannot marry into Somaliland, for the Arabs are the superior race on account of their nearer relationship with the Prophet, and, amongst the Arabs themselves, a maiden belonging to the Prophet's family cannot marry a husband outside it […] By the time that we had become well acquainted the girls asked me if it could be true what they had heard, that some nations in Europe gave away their maidens to their husbands for nothing. They had even been told that, but they could not possibly realize the idea, that there was one tribe so depraved as to pay the bridegroom to marry the bride. Fie and shame on such parents, and on girls who gave themselves up to such treatment. Where was their self-respect, where their respect for woman, or for virginity? If they themselves had had this misfortune to be born into that tribe, the girls told me, they would have vowed to go into their grave unmarried. (Blixen 1992: 162–63)

In this passage, Blixen describes one of the observations she made among the Somali women staying at her farm – Farah's wife and relatives.[4] Here, young women expressed the fact that virginity is very much linked to the self-respect and value of a woman, who should never marry 'beneath her'; the women were horrified at the customs of some 'European tribes' that gave away their women for nothing. This also presents a counter-narrative to European lifestyles from the Somali point of view. The assertion regarding Somali men marrying beneath themselves was also confirmed by an informant during interviews, who declared that men could marry whoever they wanted, and I also heard of cases of Somali men marrying Masai women in Kenya. If a Somali man decides to marry a non-Somali woman, no one in the community sees a problem with it as long as the woman converts to Islam, in opposition to what is expected of women, who must use their religious agency if they decide to marry non-Somali men. The pressure from the family and the entire community sometimes leaves women with little room to manoeuvre, but, in some cases, they still find some agency with which to fulfil their desires, either by using Islamic arguments to defend their choices, breaking away from their families by eloping, divorcing after an unsuccessful marriage or choosing further migration, as the next sections will explore.

Divorce and Life Afterwards

Divorce is allowed in Islam. According to one respondent in Nairobi, although among Somalis divorced women are valued less – as they are not virgins any more, and the bride wealth for them will always be less or non-existent – in Islam, divorced women should be highly regarded, as the first person to convert to Islam was Khadija, a divorcee who married the Prophet Muhammad. Although a lot of expectations are placed on married life, many women start to find marriage 'stressful' soon after marrying and get divorced shortly afterwards, normally without any desire of remarrying, as Halima plainly stated in the following short exchange with me:

> Nereida: And after you divorced, didn't you marry again?
> Halima: No.
> N: Why?
> H: I don't want.
> N: Why?
> H: Because it's too much problem. I don't want a confused man again.

Halima was very clear in her short explanations that she did not want to deal with a 'confused man', a man who does not know what he wants, will not get involved and therefore causes problems; thus, she prefers to remain alone. She owns a shop in Amal, which is enough to support herself and her children, and does not need to complicate her life with a husband who will not provide for her.

The problems behind the failures of marriages among Somalis in Nairobi and Johannesburg are various, but are mainly due to men not supporting the families, the lack of respect from husbands for their wives and, in some cases, even their violent behaviour towards them. One respondent in Johannesburg explained that marriage should be based on mutual respect between husband and wife, but that many men lose that respect for their wives and transform it into power, trying to control them and treating them badly. 'That's why you see so much divorce among Somalis', she concluded.

Complaints about husbands were often heard among women, especially in Johannesburg. They lamented the extent to which Somali men changed outside Somalia, as many of them became irresponsible, chewing khat, or *miraa*, the whole day. This plant is cultivated mostly in Kenya, where the drug is legal, and is transported quickly to Somalia and all around the world, as it has to be consumed while the leaves are still fresh. This recreational, social drug has been traditionally chewed in the Horn of Africa on special occasions, or, due to its amphetaminic effects, to stay awake for long hours of work (Anderson et al. 2007). However, in recent decades it has become a drug that is consumed by many Somali men on a daily basis, inside and outside Somalia, generating an addiction that brings consequences to the family setting. Some women also chew it, but always in private spaces and in plenty of secrecy, as it is not honourable for a woman. One consequence of this addiction is that men invest all the money they earn in it and stop providing for their families, which sometimes leads to episodes of domestic violence (ibid.: 10). A respondent in Nairobi, where this conflict involving men and *miraa* frequently occurs, reported that some men spend their evenings and nights chewing with their friends, and their days at home sleeping and doing nothing. 'So, all he does is jump on you, get you pregnant, you give birth to a baby and then you have to send the child away to your parents. It's a cycle', she asserted. However, in Nairobi, the pressure of one's family nearby mitigates the conflict. In Johannesburg, most women complained that not having their families nearby to intervene and settle problems made the situation much more difficult, generating feelings of insecurity, isolation and vulnerability among women – as exemplified in Saynab's case, as her husband did not want to grant her the divorce initially, until the families intervened. Other women pointed to the early age at which they married and the ways that Somali women are changing as the main causes of divorce, as this dialogue between Sagal and Amina in Nairobi reflected:

> Amina: Somalis divorce a lot because they marry very young and then get divorced. I think when you are below 25, you have a fairy tale. You have a different perspective, but now, when you are above the age of 25, you've grown. Like me and her, we've been divorced.
> Sagal: We got married very young. I was 21 and she was 20. And it hardly works out, when you are that young.
> A: It's also about the culture, our parents got married young and they lasted more than we did. They're still married. It was the culture then; it was a mindset they had.
> S: And you know Somali women are evolving, they want careers, they want school, they want everything, they want to work. And the way the Somali man is raised is: your wife doesn't work; she doesn't do anything and you provide everything. So, there's some kind of conflict that comes from there. Because the woman wants to become independent and the man wants to provide. If you get married with that understanding, then that's okay, you two understand each other, but when you start changing how you think while you're married and you want to do other things that you didn't agree to, for example if you get married and after two years you say, *I don't want to have children*, it's going to bring problems. Or saying, *I want to start a career*, and maybe he was thinking you're going to be a stay-at-home mum. So, it brings some kind of conflict. And Somalis don't normally talk about what they want, they just get married. Not before. They normally don't. Everything is yes, yes, yes, yes, yes ... And when you marry, everything changes. It changes in the first week.

Amina and Sagal consider their young ages at the time of marriage to be one of the main reasons for the marriages' failure, as they did not know what they really wanted, and probably got married because of family and community pressure. They compare themselves with their parents' generations, which remained married for life, something that does not happen so much nowadays because Somali women are 'evolving' and want other things for their lives. However, as happens in many other societies around the world, the women are evolving faster than the patriarchal society that they belong to, and even if gender roles and relations are changing among Somalis, women still have to deal with strong patriarchal precepts that are not changing so quickly, as the transfer of power is a process that takes time to fully transform societies.

After divorce, women tend to struggle to make a living, especially in Johannesburg, where most men will not support their wives and children; the women's only chances are in remarrying or finding work to support themselves and their children. As one woman related, men would support their children after divorce if they were in Somalia because of direct pressure from their families. Here, again, the way that the lack of direct family in a diasporic context affects women can be observed, as men who divorce do not have the peer pressure to support their children, and there is nothing women can do about it but work and become independent. However, this normally implies having to send their children back to Somalia for their families to look after, as if they work, they are unable to undertake childcare as well, as was the case for Saynab. Nevertheless, and in spite of all the hardships that women face after divorce, they also gain certain freedoms: to hang around with friends after work, to study or work more, to start their own businesses. In particular, they regain the hope to improve their lives, mostly through migration to somewhere that they consider a better destination. Saynab fulfilled her aspirations for that better life, even if it meant crossing all of South America to reach the USA, showing enormous determination and willpower to get where she had always dreamed about being.

In Search of the 'Better Life'

The desire to improve their lives was a constant aspiration expressed by women both in Nairobi and Johannesburg. They believed that a better life was always possible, either through education, work, marriage or further migration. But what is that 'better life'? For Somalis, it generally implies having greater economic opportunities so that they can be independent and at the same time support their families back home through remittances; having access to education to gain new skills and higher status; and having a passport with which they can move freely around the world. Although Johannesburg is seen before arrival there as a place where they can fulfil these aspirations, when this does not happen, as is often the case, women tend to long for other destinations where they might have family or relatives. Once the feeling of *buufis* comes back again, they will do everything they can to migrate to somewhere they consider a better place to fulfil their dreams. The destinations they dreamed about were normally the USA and Canada, followed by Australia, the UK and countries in Northern Europe –

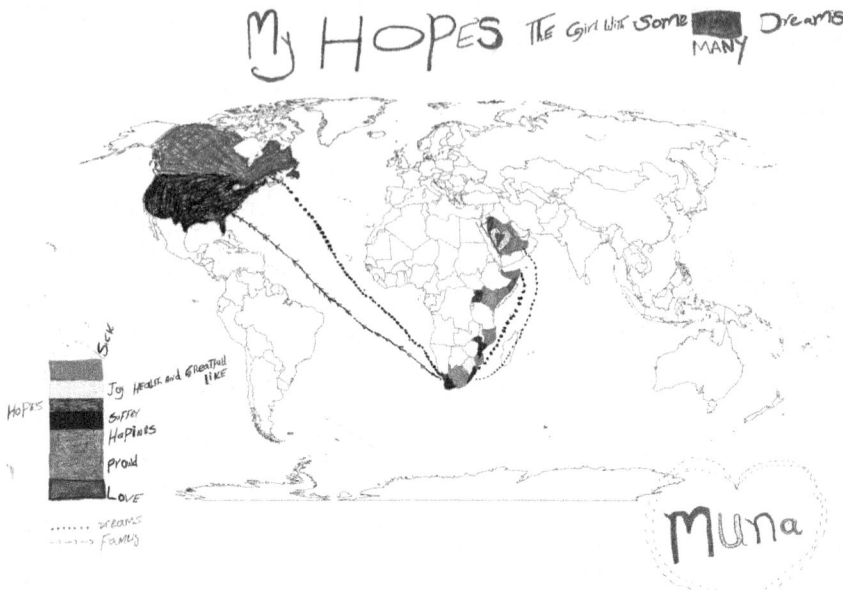

Figure 5.1. Map by participants in the workshop #EverydayMayfair. Published with permission of the participants.

although the USA stopped being so desirable during Donald Trump's presidency.

During the workshop #EverydayMayfair, one of the activities proposed to participants consisted in giving them a blank world map on which they had to indicate (1) their migration route to South Africa, (2) their desired or aspirational destinations and (3) the countries in which they already had family residing (see Figures 5.1 and 5.2). Participants firstly indicated their migration routes to South Africa by colouring the countries that they passed through to reach the south of the continent (this can be observed in the different tones of grey in Figures 5.1 and 5.2.). They gave each colour a meaning (indicated in the maps' legend) related to feelings or emotional and physical states, such as: sickness, hopes, suffering, pride, happiness and strength. Somalia normally appeared in the colour they associated with 'pride', demonstrating their patriotic feelings; Kenya was associated with 'love' or 'success', probably due to being the first country on their migration routes in search of better lives, and South Africa with 'sadness', indicating the frustration of not fulfilling their dreams in that country. Then they were asked to do the same with their desired destination countries: Canada was

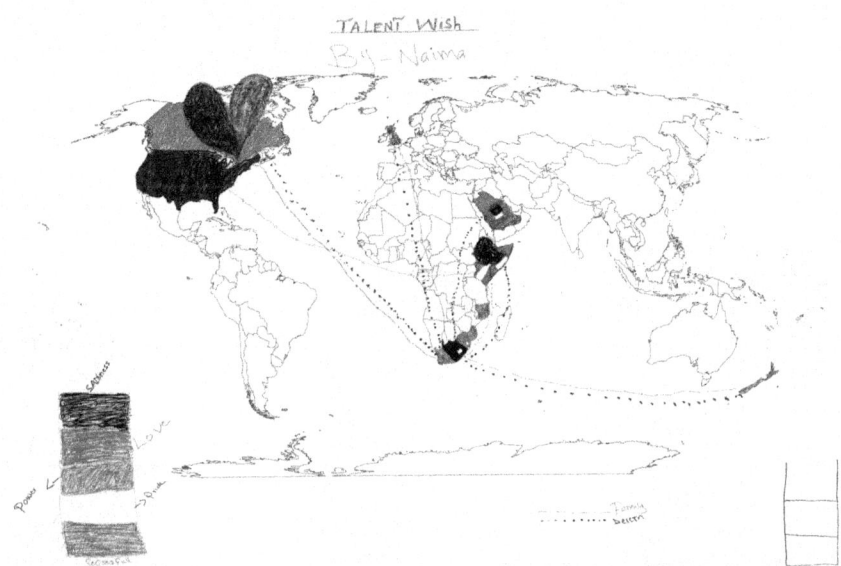

Figure 5.2. Map by participants in the workshop #EverydayMayfair. Published with permission of the participants.

equated with 'love', while the USA, even if desired, meant 'suffering' or 'sadness' due to the political situation at the time under the Trump presidency. Finally they indicated with lines where they had relatives living around the world, and with dots the countries to which they would like to migrate in the future. Family members appeared spread all around the world, showing the transnational connections among the Somali diaspora, which are also reflected in the second map at the beginning of the book. The women's desired destinations were mostly in North America, Europe, the UAE, or Australia and New Zealand. They were finally asked to give a title to their maps. All the titles reflected success, for instance 'My Hopes', 'The Girl of Many Dreams' and 'Talent Wish', reflecting again the women's hopes and desires for a better reality than that which they were experiencing in South Africa.

Some of the women who participated in the workshop actually ended up in the USA some time later, having either been relocated by UNHCR or taken the migration journey through South America, as Saynab did.

Two years after finishing the fieldwork in Nairobi and Johannesburg, I did a research trip to Minneapolis, an important enclave in the Somali diaspora in the USA, where several of the women I had met in South Africa then resided. The aim of this research trip was, among other things, to reconnect with some of these women, learn about their migration journeys and find out whether they really had found the 'better life' they had been yearning for during their time in Africa. At the time of my visit, in December 2017, most of these women were early arrivals to the USA, and they were living in shared flats with other women in the big blocks of apartments in Cedar-Riverside, a neighbourhood mostly inhabited by Somalis in Minneapolis. They had found jobs, mostly in warehouses working nightshifts for an hourly rate. They were able to support themselves and more importantly, to send remittances back home to support family members on the African continent. I met some of these women, who welcomed me into their flats in Cedar-Riverside and took me to the several Somali malls of Minneapolis and to have lunch and dinner in the Somali restaurants in the city. After all the hardship they had gone through, most of them were happy to have reached their desired destination, even if their expectations were not really fulfilled. They realized that in the USA, people just worked and worked the whole day, with no time for anything else, and that the American way of life was not like 'in the movies'. One woman who had come to the USA from Nairobi, where she used to own a small shop in Eastleigh selling textiles and perfumes, even said that she regretted the move, especially after all the difficulties she had to go through during her journey via South America. She had realized that she had no real need to leave Nairobi, as her business was doing well, and her decision to leave had mostly been to fulfil her *buufis*. After experiencing the American way of life for a couple of years, she now longed to return to Africa. Her main aim was now a short-term one, born of her legal situation: to obtain her green card so that she could regain the freedom to travel when and where she wanted. This was a desire also expressed by most of the women I talked to in Minneapolis, who longed to become transnational nomads again. This dissatisfaction with the desired life in the USA is also well documented and corroborated in Abdi (2015).

Nevertheless, these narratives of dissatisfaction in the ultimate desired destination do not normally travel back home, as the experiences narrated to family and relatives still in Africa tend to take the form of narratives of success, of having achieved one's aspirations and fulfilled one's dreams. The women longed to return home as successful diaspora returnees who had achieved their dreams and aspirations, as well as all the expectations built upon them. The sense of success reflected in their narratives was linked to individual choices and efforts to achieve desired dreams and aspirations (Konyali 2014). Relating their real experiences on the other side of the Atlantic would imply that the women failed in their pursuit of a 'better life'. Thus, the stories that do not travel back home are those of the long hours working at warehouses for minimum wage, the realization that the longed-for better life is not there and the fear of living under suspicion.

Fear and suspicion were very present feelings in the daily lives of these newly arrived Somali women in the USA, especially those still waiting to obtain their green cards. They were scared that if they made any mistakes, they would not obtain their legal status, to the point that none of them accepted to be properly interviewed and recorded, despite the mutual trust I had built with them in the past. They were happy to informally relate their experiences and hang around with me, but they felt enormous fear of being surveilled by the state; they were concerned that if they told me their stories in a recorded interview, the FBI would be able to access them in my computer. 'You cannot imagine what these people are capable of', one of them even told me. Another related that on their migration journey to the USA via South America, when they were getting closer to their destination, in countries such as Guatemala and Mexico, North Americans tried to befriend them and asked them for their names and Facebook account details. They were not travellers or backpackers; they were sure of that. Those fears were accentuated by a failed deportation of ninety-two Somalis around that time. On 7 December 2017, a plane with ninety-two Somalis on board departed from Louisiana to Somalia. Many of the people on board had been living in the USA for decades; others were not even born in Somalia, like Mohamed Hussein, a 20-year-old born in Canada who had grown up in the USA, and who described the whole situation as bizarre and extremely distressing (Ibrahim 2017). The attempt failed and once the plane landed in Senegal, the crew decided to turn back to the USA due to logistical issues. Somalis on board were mistreated during the almost forty-eight hours in which the failed deportation attempts took place (Holpuch 2017; Fortin 2017). This was the culmination of a year of controversial executive orders and travel bans on nationals from various countries, including Somalia. In January 2017 Donald Trump signed Executive Order 13769. The order, among other things, reduced the number of refugees to be admitted to the US that year, suspended the US Refugee Admissions Program and banned the entrance of nationals from several Muslim countries: Iran, Iraq, Libya, Somalia, Sudan, Syria and Yemen. Shear and Cooper (2017) note that 'During this ban more than 700 travellers were detained, and up to 60,000 visas were provisionally revoked'. The executive order was supposed to be a measure to protect American citizens against 'Islamic' terrorism, reinforcing once again the stereotypical assumption circulating since 9/11 that every Muslim is a terrorist until the opposite is proven (Mamdani 2004).

In this political climate, even if I ensured anonymity and confidentiality, the women did not accept to be interviewed. 'Who knew this crazy man was going to make [it] into power?' one of the women I had known for years in Johannesburg asked me as her reason for not being interviewed. The fear of being deported drove many of these women's lives, as it menaced not only their lives in the USA, which they had so longed for, but also the support

Figure 5.3. Mayfair. Photograph taken by a participant in the workshop #EverydayMayfair. Published with permission of the participant.

they provided to family and relatives back on the African continent through remittances. The situation that Somalis encounter in South Africa is not much better, with Home Affairs doing everything they can not to grant asylum permits and refugees status, and significant security issues arising every time a wave of xenophobic attacks takes place. However, levels of fear and suspicion were not as high there as in the US. Why? Even if conditions for Somalis are fraught in South Africa, and the complicated immigration laws and recurrent waves of xenophobia make life even harder for them, they do not feel the surveillance from the state that they feel in the USA. Moreover, Somali migrants who make it to America have invested large amounts of money from family members and undergone personal risk. It takes a lot of effort and money to get there, so they feel an enormous pressure to achieve the 'better life' that they have been dreaming of all their life, to fulfil their *buufis* and help their relatives back in Africa. The fear of failing to achieve their expectations and experience a return on their investments becomes more important than anything else. Even if what they find 'out of Africa' is not what they expected, they will never give up on their dreams and the expectations settled upon them by family and relatives. In these layered and complicated circumstances, the women's fears and insecurities were legitimate and more than understandable.

Somali Women's Agency and Aspirations

I opened this chapter with Saynab's story because it illustrates many of the situations that Somali woman face in Johannesburg and Nairobi: arranged marriage, young motherhood, failed marriage and divorce, work, study and leaving in search of a better life somewhere else. Her story resonates with those of other young women in Nairobi and Johannesburg. In the two contexts, transitional migration has increased Somali women's agency and decision-making power, as well as their economic independence; however, at the same time, they still experience a lot of hardships in fulfilling their aspirations and desires of a better life, which are normally achieved through transnational migration. Marriage, despite having different meanings for different women, is also perceived as a way to improve their life conditions. Nevertheless, many women do not find what they expect from their husbands, who often fail to provide for their basic needs, and in some cases even mistreat them. Thus, divorce rates were high among young couples in the two cities, due to women wanting different things for their lives and men not fulfilling the expectations placed upon them. This was more noticeable in Johannesburg, where women often complained about the hardships of not having their extended families nearby, both for economic support and to intervene when problems arose.

The aspirational dreams that women expressed were also realized through migration outside the African continent. I followed some of these women's lives on the other side of the Atlantic, where some had reached their desired destination. However, the culture of surveillance by the US state created a situation of fear that made these women feel extremely vulnerable, to the extent that some related a desire to go back to the African continent once their legal status had been resolved. Even if they transmitted narratives of success back home, where they were able to send some money and help their families, the realities they found in the USA were not what they expected, and their ultimate aspiration then became to go back to Africa as successful returning migrants. The widespread desire for improvement, constant in women's narratives throughout this book, was normally achieved through migration, with the Global North becoming the ultimate desired destination in which to become part of a better reality and belong to the 'new world order' (Ferguson 2006). However, once this was seemingly achieved, the aspirations of many turned to returning home with a different status, and coming full circle in their migration experience. As Abdi (2015) notes, Somali migration does not follow the binary of origin–destination, as migrants may stop and live for a while in different destinations (as this book has explored) before reaching the ultimate one, which is normally in the West. However, once this is achieved, some migrants' gazes turn back home, and they hope to return to an idealized homeland as successful diaspora returnees. It seems that feelings of *buufis* and a nomadic nature never abandon Somali refugees' cosmopolitan imagination.

Notes

1. Khat is a plant with amphetamine effects traditionally chewed in the Horn of Africa at weekends or on special occasions. Chewing khat is a social event that takes place in khat cafes or private homes. However, over the past several decades, it has become a drug consumed by many Somali men on a daily basis inside and outside Somalia, with some consequences in Somali households, as explored later in this chapter.
2. This is the name given to fake branded clothes from China that Somalis buy from Dragon City and China Mall and then resell at stalls in Jeppe Street in the Johannesburg CBD.
3. This is normally referred to as 'forced marriage', but I intentionally avoid this term due to the contestations that exist around it (Chantler et al. 2009).
4. Farah Aden is one of the main characters in Blixen's *Out of Africa*. Initially her majordomo, he became her most trusted person in Kenya. He was of Somali origin and managed the Ngong farm with her. When he got married, his wife and other female relatives lived with him on the farm.

Conclusion
Migrating in and Out of Africa

> Do not judge me until you know me, do not underestimate me until you have challenged me and do not talk about me until you have talked to me.

Days before she left South Africa for the USA to search for a 'better life', Saynab's Instagram account was flooded with motivational messages. While some of these messages were anonymous, many could be attributed to authors such as Carl Jung, James Baldwin and Martin Luther King, who shared this space with Snoopy or Lady Gaga. I transcribe some of them here:

> If you can't fly, then run. If you can't run, then walk. If you can't walk, then crawl but whatever you do, you have to keep moving forward.
> –Martin Luther King

> Making changes can feel scary but not as scary as feeling stuck in a place where you don't belong.
> –Assertiveness for Earth Angels

> You can't fall if you don't climb but there is not joy in living your whole life on the ground.

> Everything you ever wanted is on the other side of fear.

> Become friends with people who aren't your age. Hang out with people whose first language isn't the same as yours. Get to know someone who doesn't come from your social class. This is how you see the world. This is how you grow.

As mentioned in the introduction, it is common practice among young Somalis to upload these kinds of messages on a regular basis, but the frequency increases in crucial moments of their lives, such as before migration. These quotes, shared by many people from all around the world, become in this context a source of strength with which to make a life-changing decision that entails plenty of risks. They are a direct expression of the desire for improvement and to become part of the 'new world order' (Ferguson 2006). They speak directly to 'the politics of hope' (Appadurai 2013) and to young Somalis' cosmopolitan aspirations, their dreams and desires to start afresh in another place where life can be better.

Diasporic communities tend to construct narratives that look forward and backward at the same time (Braziel and Mannur 2003), and in the case studied here, the virtual space is a site where these narratives are created. These motivational quotes normally appeared accompanied by two other kinds of messages and images: on the one hand, religious messages praising Allah and being a good Muslim, and on the other hand, cultural and nostalgic images of a lost Somalia that no longer exists: women in their traditional dresses with 'open' hair, camels, traditional nomadic huts, Mogadishu in the 1960s and so on. The cultural posts, embedded with nostalgia, look back to the bright past of Somalia, before the war and conflict began, and almost seek to reconstruct a nation in the virtual space through the collective imagination. The motivational quotes look forward, building desires and aspirations for an even brighter future that reflects the dreams and desires of young Somalis. They are idealistic representations of a mythical past and a promising future respectively, products of the collective imagination of the Somali diaspora, which plays a crucial role in young Somalis' migration experience (Abdi 2015). These posts in the virtual space provided direct access to young Somali women's subjectivity, values, identifications and desires. I chose to open each chapter of the book with one of these quotes, as I believe they are a reflection in popular culture and everyday practices of some of the topics covered in these pages: strong identifications with certain cultural practices, feelings of being transnationally connected, the practice of Islam as a unifying factor and the cosmopolitan aspiration to better one's life through transnational migration.

Although forced migration is a relatively recent situation for Somalis, their traditional nomadic life generated a 'culture of migration' (Horst 2006b) that since the end of the twentieth century has taken on a larger dimension, in numbers and in scope. The fact that the Somali diaspora is nowadays spread all around the world has contributed to the creation of an 'imaginary community', with collective identities becoming deterritorialized; expressions of Somaliness recreated in in the virtual world of social media platforms, and enhanced with the implementation of cultural and religious practices in Somalis' everyday lives worldwide. At the same time, these identities become reterritorialized in the new places that Somalis inhabit, resulting in hybrid identities that allow Somalis to navigate different worlds while maintaining a distinctive 'trademark'. Cultural, religious and gendered practices are reproduced and transformed across transnational boundaries and adapted to the particular contexts that Somalis inhabit, as 'the identity of the diasporic imagined community is far from fixed or pre-given. It is constituted within the crucible of the materiality of everyday life; in the everyday stories we tell ourselves individually and collectively' (Brah 1996: 183). Thereafter, in the case of the Somali diaspora, feelings of belonging to a community are based on a strong sense of being connected through similar structures and belief systems, together with the implementation of cultural and religious practices in localized diasporic spaces around the world. At the same time, these feelings of belonging to a transnational community spread around the world generate cosmopolitan networks in which cultural and religious practices play a key role in connecting people across borders. Somalis' feelings of belonging to a collective transcend territorial boundaries, because they are the product of a collective imagination implemented through everyday practices and supported by transnational networks.

This book is a comparative study that illuminates dynamics around identity formation in diasporic spaces in the Global South. In these pages, I have analysed some of the ways Somali women navigate two diasporic urban spaces in sub-Saharan Africa: Nairobi and Johannesburg, two interconnected cities for the Somali diaspora. The hyperconnectivity between these two cities for Somalis at different levels offers a counter-narrative to hegemonic discourses that are normally constructed from a Western perspective. The fact that these two metropolises have become nodal points for the Somali diaspora in Africa and around the world also emphasizes that a translocal situation can facilitate the creation of central hubs for businesses, commerce or migration outside the homeland, as tends to be the case in diasporic communities. I have described these urban contexts using the metaphors of Nairobi as a port and Johannesburg as an island in order to understand the diasporic experience that Somalis have in them. Both cities are transitional places for Somalis on their way to somewhere else. However, they also become temporary homes: in Nairobi, due to historical and geographical links and the bigger Somali population residing in the city, Somalis develop greater feelings of belonging than in Johannesburg. In Mayfair, isolation and alienation seemed to be the most widespread collective feeling among Somalis, with the area acting more as a protective nest, especially in difficult times during xenophobic attacks. Nairobi is also experienced by Somalis as more cosmopolitan than Johannesburg, casting into question the generalizing assumption that the South African city is the epitome of modernity and cosmopolitanism on the African continent. In both places, Somaliness seems to be constructed around a sense of unity based on a common ethnicity, language, place of origin, and set of cultural and religious practices. However, the way that Somaliness is felt and performed in each place is slightly different: Somali women in Nairobi expressed more fluid senses of self and were open to different kinds of identifications, with some women even recognizing the hybridization of their identities, while in Johannesburg, a more traditional sense of self as static sets of characteristics was more commonly expressed. These findings highlight parallels with the two Hutu refugee communities studied by Malkki (1995) in Kigoma and Mishamo refugee camp: the refugees in Kigoma were creating a 'lively cosmopolitanism', in opposition to those in the refugee camp, where a heroized narrative of the nation was being constructed and became the main source of identifications. Even if Mayfair is not a refugee camp, the isolation that Somalis find there and the lack of any links to the rest of the city make it an enclosed area where cultural and religious practices are strengthened and become the main source of collective identifications. Meanwhile, the 'openness' of Nairobi, together with the cohabitation of Somalis coming from different backgrounds, allows more cosmopolitan ways of being to emerge. At the same time, in both cities, the creation of the 'little Mogadishus' of Eastleigh and Mayfair generates a particular translocal situation in which collective identity, through the repetition of cultural and religious practices, is able to transform urban spaces. The implementation of these practices in everyday life connects these places to one another, to the lost homeland in Somalia and to any other place in the world in which Somali communities have settled. Simultaneously, Islamic identification connects Somalis at two parallel levels, unifying them among themselves and connecting them to the wider Muslim community of the umma, something that dilutes local identifications in favour of a cosmopolitan way of belonging to the world. The umma can be seen here as another supra-structure of modernity and an alternative to Western cosmopolitanism, wherein particular cultural identifications are mitigated in favour of a collective Muslim identity that expands all around the world, generating a support structure on which migrants can rely for their integration and well-being – as was the case for Somalis in Mayfair. The identification with Islam also made the Somali women I met question some of their customary practices. The syncretism and negotiation of religious and cultural practices was mostly observed during traditional ceremonies such as the wedding and the *toddoba*, in which customary practices overlapped with religious ones. However, many women in both cities used the strategic distinction between cultural and religious practices to exercise their agency and challenge certain practices, for instance to choose whom to marry or resist female circumcision. The way that women renegotiate or reject these practices demonstrates how their individual agency is informed by both cultural and religious beliefs. Women's agency was also stressed in their desires and aspirations to improve their lives. The situation of forced migration faced by Somalis in recent decades has also transformed gender roles and practices, giving women more economic agency and decision-making power.

Exploring women's religious and individual agency has proved that Somali migrant women are not passive subjects, but very active agents in the decisions they make about their lives and those of their families, with the ultimate desire to fulfil their aspirations for a better life. This desire to improve their lives appeared as a constant in women's narratives. Exploring these narratives has shown the complex dynamics underlying translocal communities and the need for further attention to these dynamics to change perceptions and narratives about migrants in our interconnected world, in which the agency of migrants and refugees tends to be overlooked.

This study has also proved that migrants generate new forms of agency and mobility in interconnected diasporic spaces. Women navigate the expectations of the local and translocal communities at the same time as they try to fulfil their aspirations for a better life, demonstrating how collective and individual identities operate in contexts of displacement in the postmodern world, in which a translocal sense of being connected expands across territorial boundaries and identities are not as fixed as they used to be.

In today's neoliberal world, questions around collective identity seem a futile exercise that only takes place in the humanities departments of universities. However, a sense of collective identity and belonging to something bigger than oneself is a very powerful force and one that should be taken into account to understand the ground-level dynamics that politicians, policymakers and international agendas normally overlook. Why do collective identities still matter in the multicultural, global world in which we live today? They matter precisely because globalization and multiculturalism are not a unification of cultures, but a meeting place of different cultures and collective identities, regulated by power relations. It cannot be forgotten that identifications are always dialogical. We cannot become ourselves without 'the other', and our identities are what emerges from the dialogue we maintain with the world. What we are or are not is always established in relation to others. This is a multilayered process, which applies to the ways that both individual and collective identities interact with others in a specific place and time. In our postcolonial world, Western identities are still hegemonic, which leads other groups of people, such as Somalis, Muslims, Africans or refugees, to resist the imposition of those hegemonic identities. And although we cannot become ourselves without the other, in some cases these hegemonic identities feel threatened by others, which creates misrepresentations of non-Western identities based on stereotypes intended to keep them away from global dialogues. Even if today's world is seen as a global village, integrated with people from different backgrounds and cultural realities, it is still very much divided between those who have full membership of the new world order (Ferguson 2006) and those who are denied that inclusion because they are believed to be a threat.

I am finishing writing this book in the Canary Islands, where migrants from Africa arrive on a daily basis having endured a very perilous journey by sea that not all survive. Migrants from North and West Africa embark on this journey for the same reasons that some Somalis cross parts of sub-Saharan Africa or half of the American continent by land: they are searching for better opportunities for their lives. But they need to overcome real and imaginary borders to become part of a better reality, as ours is a world still divided into those who can move freely and those who cannot.

Collective identities are normally strengthened as a response to this situation, as a form of resistance; the more traumas or difficulties are collectively encountered, the greater a sense of collective identity will be generated. The collective identities of people not included in the new world order become a powerful tool of resilience and opposition to Western values; the desire for better opportunities and life conditions applies to entire collectives that want their voices to be heard and included in the dialogues taking place in the world today. This desire for inclusion, and these aspirations for a better life, become one of the most powerful engines of migration, which no barrier, border or policy will ever be able to stop.

References

Abdi, C. 2015. *Elusive Jannah: The Somali Diaspora and the Borderless Muslim Identity*. Minneapolis, MN: University of Minnesota Press.
Abdullahi, M. 2001. *Culture and Customs of Somalia*. Westport, CT: Greenwood.
Abu-Lughod, L. 1993. *Writing Women's Worlds: Bedouin Stories*. Berkeley, CA: University of California Press.
———. 2006. *Local Contexts of Islam in Popular Media*. Amsterdam: Amsterdam University Press.
———. 2013. *Do Muslim Women Need Saving?* Cambridge, MA: Harvard University Press.
Abusharaf, R. 2001. 'Virtuous Cuts: Female Genital Circumcision in an African Ontology', *Differences: A Journal of Feminist Cultural Studies* 12(1): 112–40.
Ahmed, A. (ed.). 1995. *The Invention of Somalia*. Trenton, NJ: Red Sea Press.
Affi, L. 2011. 'Arraweelo: Role Model for Somali Women', *Critical Mentalists*. Retrieved 10 August 2022 from https://criticalmentalists.blogspot.com/2011/09/arraweelo-role-model-for-somali-women.html.
Aidid, S. 2015a. 'Can the Somali Speak?' *Africa is a Country*. Retrieved 8 July 2022 from https://www.africasacountry.com/2015/03/can-the-somali-speak-cadaanstudies/.
———. 2015b. 'Can the Somali Speak? Open Letter to Dr. Markus Hoehne and the Somaliland Journal of African Studies', *Warscapes*, 1 April. Retrieved 8 July 2022 from http://www.warscapes.com/blog/can-somali-speak-open-letter-dr-markus-hoehne-and-somaliland-journal-african-studies.
———. 2015c. 'The New Somali Studies', *The New Inquiry*, 14 April. Retrieved 8 July 2022 from https://thenewinquiry.com/the-new-somali-studies.
Akou, H. 2011. *The Politics of Dress in Somali Culture*. Bloomington, IN: Indiana University Press.
Alexieva, B. 2002. 'A Typology of Interpreter-Mediated Events', in F. Pöchhacker and M. Shlesinger (eds), *The Interpreting Studies Reader*. London: Routledge, pp. 218–33.
Aling'o, P. 2014. 'Kenya Should Go Back to the Drawing Board to Find a Realistic Solution to the Threat of Terrorism, Radicalisation and Religious Extremism', *ISS Today*, 2 May. Retrieved 8 July 2022 from https://issafrica.org/iss-today/kenyas-current-probe-on-terror-why-operation-usulama-watch-wont-cut-it.
Al Jazeera. 2013. 'Kenyan-Somalis Speak Out', *Al Jazeera*. Retrieved 10 August 2022 from https://www.aljazeera.com/program/al-jazeera-correspondent/2013/12/15/kenyan-somalis-speak-out.

Allen, A. 1999. *The Power of Feminist Theory: Domination, Resistance, Solidarity*. Boulder, CO: Westview Press.

Al-Safi, M. 1995. 'Kenya Somalis: The Shift from "Greater Somalia" to Integration with Kenya', *Nordic Journal of African Studies* 4(2): 34–41.

Al-Sharmani, M. 2007. 'Diasporic Somalis in Cairo: The Poetics and Practices of Soomaalinimo', in A. Kusow and S. Bjork (eds), *From Mogadishu to Dixon: The Somali Diaspora in a Global Context*. Trenton, NJ: Red Sea Press, pp. 71–94.

———. 2010. 'Transnational Family Networks in the Somali Diaspora in Egypt: Women's Roles and Differentiated Experiences', *Gender, Place & Culture* 17(4): 499–518.

Amnesty International. 2014. 'Kenya: Somalis Scapegoated in Counter-Terror Crackdown'. Retrieved 8 July 2022 from https://www.amnesty.org/en/latest/news/2014/05/kenya-somalis-scapegoated-counter-terror-crackdown.

Anderson, B. 1983. *Imagined Communities: Reflections on the Origin and Spread of Nationalism*, rev. edn. London: Verso Books.

———. 1992. *Long-Distance Nationalism: World Capitalism and the Rise of Identity Politics*. Amsterdam: Centre for Asian Studies.

Anderson, D., S. Beckerleg, D. Hailu and A. Klein. 2007. *The Khat Controversy Stimulating the Debate on Drugs*. Oxford: Routledge.

Andrews, C., and M. Tamboukou. 2008. *Doing Narrative Research*. Los Angeles: Sage.

Anzaldúa, G. 1987. *Borderlands/La Frontera: The New Mestiza*. San Francisco: Aunt Lute Books.

Appadurai, A. 1995. 'The Production of Locality', in R. Fardon (ed.), *Counterworks: Managing the Diversity of Knowledge*. London: Routledge, pp. 204–55.

———. 1996. *Modernity at Large: Cultural Dimensions of Globalization*. Minneapolis, MN: University of Minnesota Press.

———. 2013. *The Future as Cultural Fact: Essays on the Global Condition*. London: Verso Books.

Appiah, K. 1997. 'Cosmopolitan Patriots', *Critical Inquiry* 23(3): 617–39.

———. 2006. *Cosmopolitanism: Ethics in a World of Strangers*. New York: W.W. Norton & Co.

Archer, M. 2003. *Structure, Agency and the Internal Conversation*. Cambridge: Cambridge University Press.

Asad, T. 2009. 'The Idea of an Anthropology of Islam', *Qui Parle* 17(2): 1–30.

Atkinson, P., S. Delamont and W. Housley. 2008. *Contours of Culture: Complex Ethnography and the Ethnography of Complexity*. Walnut Creek, CA: AltaMira Press.

Baadiyow, A.M. 2001. 'Tribalism and Islam: Variations on the Basics of Somaliness', in M.S. Lilius (ed.), *Proceedings of International Congress of Somali Studies: Variations on the Themes of Somaliness*. Turku: Centre for Continuing Education, Abo Akademi University, pp. 227–40.

Bakhtin, M. 1981. *The Dialogic Imagination: Four Essays*. Austin, TX: University of Texas Press.

———. 1984. *Problems of Dostoevsky's Poetics*. Manchester: Manchester University Press.

Barnes, V., and J. Boddy. 1994. *Aman: The Story of a Somali Girl*. London: Bloomsbury.

Beck, U. 2006. *Cosmopolitan Vision*. Cambridge: Polity Press.

Beck, U., and N. Sznaider. 2006. 'Unpacking Cosmopolitanism for the Social Sciences: A Research Agenda', *The British Journal of Sociology* 57(1): 1–23.

Behar, R. 1993. *Translated Woman: Crossing the Border with Esperanza's Story*. Boston: Beacon Press.
Best of Somalia. 2015. There is no place like home. Retrieved from www.instagram.com/p/08kYURhzRD/?taken-by=best_of_somalia.
Besteman, C. 1993. 'Public History and Private Knowledge: On Disputed History in Southern Somalia', *Ethnohistory* 40(4): 563–86.
———. 1996a. 'Representing Violence and "Othering" Somalia', *Cultural Anthropology* 11(1): 120–33.
———. 1996b. 'Violent Politics and the Politics of Violence: The Dissolution of the Somali Nation-State'. *American Ethnologist* 23(3), 579–96.
———. 1998. 'Primordialist Blinders: A Reply to I.M. Lewis', *Cultural Anthropology* 13(1): 109–20.
Blixen, K. [1937] 1992. *Out of Africa*. New York: Modern Library/Random House.
Boddy, J. 1982. 'Womb as Oasis: The Symbolic Context of Pharaonic Circumcision in Rural Northern Sudan', *American Ethnologist* 9(4): 682–98.
Botha, A. 2014. 'Political Socialization and Terrorist Radicalization among Individuals Who Joined Al-Shabaab in Kenya', *Studies in Conflict & Terrorism* 37(11): 895–919.
Bourdieu, P. 1977. *Outline of a Theory of Practice*. Cambridge: Cambridge University Press.
Boyd, M., and E. Grieco. 2003. 'Women and Migration: Incorporating Gender into International Migration Theory', *Migration Information Source*, March 1. Retrieved from https://www.migrationpolicy.org/article/women-and-migration-incorporating-gender-international-migration-theory.
Bradatan, C., A. Popanband and R. Meltonaet. 2010. 'Transnationality as a Fluid Social Identity', *Social Identities: Journal for the Study of Race, Nation and Culture* 16(2): 169–78.
Brady, C., and J. Files. 2007. 'Female Genital Mutilation: Cultural Awareness and Clinical Considerations', *Journal of Midwifery & Women's Health* 52(2): 158–63.
Brah, A. 1996. *Cartographies of Diaspora: Contesting Identities*. London: Routledge.
Braziel J., and A. Mannur (eds). 2003. *Theorizing Diaspora: A Reader*. Oxford: Blackwell.
Breckenridge, C., et al. (eds). 2002. *Cosmopolitanism*. Durham, NC: Duke University Press.
Brettell, C. 2006. 'Introduction: Global Spaces/Local Places: Transnationalism, Diaspora, and the Meaning of Home', *Identities* 13(3): 327–34.
Brickell, K., and A. Datta. 2011. *Translocal Geographies*. Farnham: Ashgate.
Brubaker, R., and F. Cooper. 2000. 'Beyond "Identity"', *Theory and Society* 29(1): 1–47.
Bruner, J. 1986. 'Life as Narrative', *Social Research: An International Quarterly* 71(3): 691–710.
Bryden, M., and M. Steiner. 1998. *Somalia between Peace and War: Somali Women on the Eve of the 21st Century*. Nairobi: UNIFEM.
Burton, R. 1856. *First Footsteps in East Africa*. London: Longman, Brown, Green and Longmans.
Butcher, M. 2009. 'Ties That Bind: The Strategic Use of Transnational Relationships in Demarcating Identity and Managing Difference', *Journal of Ethnic and Migration Studies* 35(8): 1353–71.

Butler, J. 1990. 'Performative Agency', *Journal of Cultural Economy* 3(2): 147–61.
——. 2010. *Gender Trouble*. New York: Routledge.
Campbell, E. 2006. 'Urban Refugees in Nairobi: Problems of Protection, Mechanisms of Survival, and Possibilities for Integration', *Journal of Refugee Studies* 19(3): 396–413.
Carrier, N. 2016. *Little Mogadishu: Eastleigh, Nairobi's Global Somali Hub*. Oxford: Oxford University Press.
Carrier, N., and H.H. Kochore. 2019. 'Being Oromo in Nairobi's "Little Mogadishu": Superdiversity, Moral Community and the Open Economy', in N. Carrier and T. Scharrer, *Mobile Urbanity: Somali Presence in Urban East Africa*. Oxford: Berghahn Books, pp. 76–93.
Carrier, N., and E. Lochery. 2013. 'Missing States? Somali Trade Networks and the Eastleigh Transformation', *Journal of Eastern African Studies* 7(2): 334–52.
Carrier, N., and T. Scharrer (eds). 2019. *Mobile Urbanity: Somali Presence in Urban East Africa*. Oxford: Berghahn Books.
Chant, S. 1992. *Gender and Migration in Developing Countries*. London: Belhaven Press.
Chantler, K. et al. 2009. 'Forced Marriage in the UK: Religious, Cultural, Economic or State Violence?' *Critical Social Policy* 29(4): 587–612.
Clifford, J., and G. Marcus (eds). 1986. *Writing Culture: The Poetics and Politics of Ethnography*. Berkeley, CA: University of California Press.
Cole, I., and D. Robinson. 2003. *Somali Housing Experiences in England*. Sheffield: Centre for Regional Economic and Social Research, Sheffield Hallam University.
Collins, P., and A. Gallinat. 2010. *The Ethnographic Self as Resource: Writing Memory and Experience into Ethnography*. Oxford: Berghahn Books.
Comaroff, J. 2010. 'The End of Anthropology, Again: On the Future of an In/Discipline', *American Anthropologist* 112(4): 524–38.
Cortazzi, M. 2001. 'Narrative Analysis in Ethnography', in P. Atkinson, A. Coffey, S. Delamont, J. Loflan and L. Lofland (eds), *Handbook of Ethnography*. London: Sage, pp. 384–94.
Crisp, J. 2000. 'A State of Insecurity: The Political Economy of Violence in Kenya's Refugee Camps', *African Affairs* 99(327): 601–32.
Cronin, M. 2002. 'The Empire Talks Back: Orality, Heteronomy and the Cultural Turn in Interpreting Studies', in F. Pöchhacker and M. Shlesinger (eds), *The Interpreting Studies Reader*. London: Routledge, pp. 386–97.
Crosby, D. 2008. 'Resettled Somali Women in Georgia and Changing Gender Roles', *Bildhaan: An International Journal of Somali Studies* 6(1): 68–85.
Curran, S., and A. Saguy. 2001. 'Migration and Cultural Change: A Role for Gender and Social Networks', *Journal of International Women's Studies* 2(3): 54–77.
Danow, D. 1991. *The Thought of Mikhail Bakhtin: From Word to Culture*. Basingstoke: Macmillan.
Darieva, T., N. Schiller and S. Gruner-Domic. 2012. *Cosmopolitan Sociability: Locating Transnational Religious and Diasporic Networks*. London: Routledge.
Datta, A. 2011. 'Translocal Geographies of London: Belonging and Otherness among Polish Migrants after 2004', in K. Brickell and A. Datta (eds), *Translocal Geographies: Spaces, Places, Connections*. Farnham: Ashgate, pp. 73–92.
Dreby, J. 2009. 'Gender and Transnational Gossip', *Qualitative Sociology* 32(23): 33–52.

Diouf, M., and S. Rendall. 2000. 'The Senegalese Murid Trade Diaspora and the Making of a Vernacular Cosmopolitanism', *Public Culture* 12(3): 679–702.
Douglas, M. 1966. *Purity and Danger: An Analysis of Concept of Pollution and Taboo.* London: Routledge.
Durkheim, E. 1915. *The Elementary Forms of the Religious Life.* London: Free Press.
Eidson, J., et al. 2017. 'From Identification to Framing and Alignment: A New Approach to the Comparative Analysis of Collective Identities', *Current Anthropology* 58(3): 340–59.
Elliott, B. 2005. *Using Narrative in Social Research: Qualitative and Quantitative Approaches.* Thousand Oaks, CA: Sage.
Elmi, A. 2010. *Understanding the Somalia Conflagration: Identity, Political Islam and Peacebuilding.* London: Pluto Press.
Erol, A. 2012. 'Identity, Migration and Transnationalism: Expressive Cultural Practices of the Toronto Alevi Community', *Journal of Ethnic and Migration Studies* 38(5): 833–49.
Fábos, A. 2001. 'Embodying Transition: FGC, Displacement, and Gender-Making for Sudanese in Cairo', *Feminist Review* 69: 9–110.
Farah, A. 2009. *Diaspora Involvement in the Development of Somalia.* Aalborg: DIIPER & Department of History, International and Social Studies, Aalborg University.
Farah, N. 2000. *Yesterday, Tomorrow: Voices from the Somali Diaspora.* London: Cassell.
———. 2002. 'Of Tamarind and Cosmopolitanism', in H. Engdahl (ed.), *Witness Literature: Proceedings of the Nobel Centennial Symposium.* London: World Scientific, pp. 69–76.
Fassin, D. 2014. 'True Life, Real Lives: Revisiting the Boundaries between Ethnography and Fiction', *American Ethnologist* 41(1): 40–55.
Ferguson, J. 2006. *Global Shadows: Africa in the Neoliberal World Order.* Durham, NC: Duke University Press.
Forte, M. 2014. 'Anthropology: The Empire on Which the Sun Never Sets', *Anthropological Forum: A Journal of Social Anthropology and Comparative Sociology* 24(2): 197–218.
Fortin, J. 2017. 'U.S. Put 92 Somalis on a Deportation Flight, Then Brought Them Back', *New York Times*, 9 December. Retrieved 8 July 2022 from https://www.nytimes.com/2017/12/09/us/somalia-deportation-flight.html.
Furia, P. 2005. 'Global Citizenship, Anyone? Cosmopolitanism, Privilege and Public Opinion', *Global Society* 19(4): 331–59.
Gardner, J., and J. El Bushra (eds). 2004. *Somalia – The Untold Story: The War through the Eyes of Somali Women.* London: Pluto Press.
Gastrow, V. 2018. *Problematizing the Foreign Shop: Justifications for Restricting the Migrant Spaza Sector in South Africa.* Ontario: Southern African Migration Programme.
Gastrow, V., and R. Amit. 2013. *Somalinomics: A Case Study on the Economics of Somali Informal Trade in the Western Cape.* Johannesburg: African Centre for Migration and Society.
Geertz, C. 1973. *The Interpretation of Cultures: Selected Essays.* New York: Basic Books.
———. 1988. 'Being There: Anthropology and the Science of Writing', in *Works and Lives: The Anthropologist as Author.* Stanford, CA: Stanford University Press, pp. 1–14.
Giddens, A. 1979. *Central Problems in Social Theory: Action, Structure, and Contradiction in Social Analysis.* Berkeley, CA: University of California Press.

———. 1990. *The Consequences of Modernity*. Cambridge: Polity Press.
Gilroy, P. 2005. 'A New Cosmopolitanism', *interventions* 7(3): 287–92.
Grant, R., and D. Thompson. 2015. 'City on Edge: Immigrant Business and the Right Urban Space in Inner-City Johannesburg', *Urban Geography* 36(2): 181–200.
Greiner, C., and P. Sakdapolrak. 2013. 'Translocality: Concepts, Applications and Emerging Research Perspectives', *Geography Compass* 7(5): 373–84.
Griffiths, D. 2002. 'Somali and Kurdish Refugees in London', *New Identities in the Diaspora: Refugee Survey Quarterly* 22(2/3): 478–79.
Gupta, A., and J. Ferguson (eds). 1997. *Culture, Power, Place: Explorations in Critical Anthropology*. Durham, NC: Duke University Press.
Hall, S. 1992. 'The Question of Cultural Identity', in S. Hall, D. Held and Tony McGrew (eds), *Modernity and its Futures: Understanding Modern Societies, Book IV*. Cambridge: Polity Press, pp. 273–326.
———. 1996. 'Who Needs Identity?' in S. Hall and P. du Gay (eds), *Questions of Cultural Identity*. London: Sage, pp. 1–18.
———. 1997. *Representation: Cultural Representations and Signifying Practices. Culture, Media, and Identities*. London: Sage in association with the Open University.
———. 2008. 'Cosmopolitanism, Globalization and Diaspora: S. Hall in Conversation with P. Werbner, March 2006', in P. Werbner (ed.), *Anthropology and the New Cosmopolitanism: Rooted, Feminist and Vernacular Perspectives*. Oxford: Bloomsbury, pp. 345–60.
Hannerz, U. 1996. *Transnational Connections: Culture, People, Places*. London and New York: Routledge.
Harper, M. 2012. *Getting Somalia Wrong? Faith, War and Hope in a Shattered State*. London: Zed Books.
Harris, H. 2004. *The Somali Community in the UK: What We Know and How We Know It*. London: The Information Centre about Asylum and Refugees in the UK (ICAR).
Hassan, H. 2015. 'A Somali Journal Launched without Any Somali Voices, Igniting a Debate on White Privilege', *VICE*, 2 April. Retrieved 11 July 2022 from www.vice.com/en_ca/read/somali-journal-launches-without-any-somali-voices-highlighting-another-case-of-white-privilege-in-academia.
Hassim, S., T. Kupe and E. Worby (eds). 2008. *Go Home or Die Here: Violence, Xenophobia and the Reinvention of Difference in South Africa*. Johannesburg: Wits University Press.
Hawkins, V. 2002. 'The Other Side of the CNN Factor: The Media and Conflict', *Journalism Studies* 3(2): 225–40.
Henriques, J., et al. 1984. *Changing the Subject: Psychology, Social Regulation and Subjectivity*. New York: Methuen & Co.
Hernlund, Y., and B. Shell-Duncan. 2007. *Transcultural Bodies: Female Genital Cutting in Global Context*. New Brunswick, NJ: Rutgers University Press.
Hersi, A. 1977. *The Arab Factor in Somali History: The Origins and Developments of the Arab Enterprise and Cultural Influences in the Somali Peninsula*. Los Angeles: University of California Press.
Herz, M. 2007. *Somali Refugees in Eastleigh, Nairobi*. Retrieved 10 August 2022 from http://www.manuelherz.com/somali-refugees-in-eastleigh.
Hobsbawm, E., and T. Ranger (eds). 1983. *The Invention of Tradition*. Cambridge: Cambridge University Press.

Holman, C., and N. Holman. 2003. *First Steps in a New Country: Baseline Indicators for the Somali Community in LB Hackney.* London: Sahil Housing Association.

Holpuch, A. 2017. 'Somalis Were Shackled for Nearly 48 Hours on Failed US Deportation Flight', *The Guardian*, 19 December. Retrieved 11 July 2022 from https://www.theguardian.com/us-news/2017/dec/19/somalis-shackled-48-hours-failed-us-deportation-flight.

Hondagneu-Sotelo, P. 2003. *Gender and U.S. Immigration: Contemporary Trends.* Los Angeles: University of California Press.

Hopkins, G. 2010. 'A Changing Sense of Somaliness: Somali Women in London and Toronto', *Gender, Place & Culture* 17(4): 519–38.

Horst, C. 2006a. *Transnational Nomads: How Somalis Cope with Refugee Life in the Dadaab Camps of Kenya.* New York: Berghahn Books.

———. 2006b. '*Buufis* amongst Somalis in Dadaab: The Transnational and Historical Logics behind Resettlement Dreams', *Journal of Refugee Studies* 19(2): 143–57.

Human Rights Watch. 2009a. *'Bring the Gun or You'll Die': Torture, Rape and Other Serious Human Rights Violations by Kenyan Security Forces in the Mandera Triangle.* Retrieved 11 July 2022 from https://www.hrw.org/sites/default/files/reports/kenya0609webwcover_0.pdf.

———. 2009b. *From Horror to Hopelessness: Kenya's Forgotten Somali Refugee Crisis.* Retrieved 11 July 2022 from https://www.hrw.org/sites/default/files/reports/kenya0309web_1.pdf.

———. 2010. *'Welcome to Kenya': Police Abuse of Somali Refugees.* Retrieved 11 July 2022 from https://www.hrw.org/sites/default/files/reports/kenya0610webwcover.pdf.

———. 2012. *Criminal Reprisals: Kenyan Police and Military Abuses against Ethnic Somalis.* Retrieved 11 July 2022 from https://www.hrw.org/sites/default/files/reports/kenya0512webwcover.pdf.

———. 2013. *'You Are All Terrorists': Kenyan Police Abuse of Refugees in Nairobi.* Retrieved 11 July 2022 from https://www.hrw.org/sites/default/files/reports/kenya0513_ForUpload_0_0.pdf.

———. 2014a. 'Kenya: End Abusive Round-Ups. Detainees Describe Mistreatment, Lack of Access to UN Agency', 12 May. Retrieved 11 July 2022 from https://www.hrw.org/news/2014/05/12/kenya-end-abusive-round-ups.

———. 2014b. 'Kenya: Halt Crackdown on Somalis. Thousands Arrested, Almost 100 Deported', 11 April. Retrieved 11 July 2022 from https://www.hrw.org/news/2014/04/11/kenya-halt-crackdown-somalis.

Hurst, C. 1995. *Social Inequality: Forms, Causes and Consequences.* Boston: Allyn and Bacon.

Ibrahim, M. 2017. 'For Minnesota Somalis, a Raw, Rising Fear of Deportation', *MPR News*, 17 December. Retrieved 11 July 2022 from https://www.mprnews.org/story/2017/12/13/minnesota-somali-deportation-fears-raw-rising.

Ibrahim, R. 2004. 'Women's Role in the Pastoral Economy', in J. Gardner and J. El Bushra (eds), *Somalia – the Untold Story: The War through the Eyes of Somali Women.* London: Pluto Press, pp. 24–50.

Isotalo, A. 2007. '"Did You See Her Standing in the Marketplace?" Gender, Gossip and Socio-Spatial Behaviour of Somali Girls in Turku, Finland', in A. Kusow and S. Bjork (eds), *From Mogadishu to Dixon: The Somali Diaspora in a Global Context.* Trenton, NJ: Red Sea Press, pp. 181–207.

Jakobson, R. 1960. 'Closing Statement: Linguistics and Poetics', *Style in Language* 350: 377.
Jinnah, Z. 2010. 'Making Home in a Hostile Land: Understanding Somali Identity, Integration, Livelihood and Risks in Johannesburg', *Journal of Sociology and Anthropology* 1(1): 91–99.
Jolly, S., and H. Reeves. 2005. *Gender and Migration*. Brighton: BRIDGE.
Josselson, R. 2004. 'The Hermeneutics of Faith and the Hermeneutics of Suspicion', *Narrative Inquiry* 14(1): 1–28.
Kantai, P. 2011. 'Inside Garissa Lodge, Nairobi's Somali Trading Hub', *The Africa Report Magazine*, December 2010–January 2011.
Kapteijns, L. (with M. Omar Ali). 1999. *Women's Voices in a Man's World: Women and the Pastoral Tradition in Northern Somali Orature, c. 1899–1980*. Portsmouth, NH: Heinemann.
Kebede, K. 2017. 'Twice-Hyphenated: Transnational Identity among Second-Generation Ethiopian-American Professionals in the Washington, DC, Metropolitan Area', *African and Black Diaspora: An International Journal* 10(3): 252–68, https://doi.org/10.1080/17528631.2017.1319146.
Keesing, R. 1974. 'Theories of Culture', *Annual Review of Anthropology* 3: 73–97.
———. 1990. 'Theories of Culture Revisited', in Robert Borofsky (ed.), *Assessing Cultural Anthropology*. New York: McGraw-Hill, pp. 301–10.
Kenya National Bureau of Statistics. 2019. Kenya Population and Housing Census. Volume IV. Retrieved 14 August 2022 from https://housingfinanceafrica.org/app/uploads/VOLUME-IV-KPHC-2019.pdf.
Klep, C., and D. Winslow. 1999. 'Learning Lessons the Hard Way – Somalia and Srebrenica Compared', *Small Wars & Insurgencies* 10(2): 93–137.
Kleist, N. 2004. 'Nomads, Sailors and Refugees: A Century of Somali Migration'. Sussex Migration Working Paper no. 23. Retrieved 11 July 2022 from https://www.sussex.ac.uk/webteam/gateway/file.php?name=mwp23.pdf&site=252.
Konyali, A. 2014. 'Turning Disadvantage into Advantage: Achievement Narratives of Descendants of Migrants from Turkey in the Corporate Business Sector', *New Diversities* 16(1): 107–21.
Kothari, U. 2008. 'Global Peddlers and Local Networks: Migrant Cosmopolitanisms', *Environment and Planning D: Society and Space* 26(3): 500–16.
Krause-Vilmar, J., and J. Chaffin. 2011. *No Place to Go but Up: Urban Refugees in Johannesburg, South Africa*. New York: Women's Refugee Commission.
Kushkush, I. 2014. 'Kenya's Wide Net against Terror Sweeps Up Refugees', *New York Times*, 17 April. Retrieved 11 July 2022 from http://www.nytimes.com/2014/04/18/world/africa/kenyas-answer-to-terrorism-sweeping-roundups-of-somalis.html.
Kusow, A. 2001. 'Stigma and Social Identities: The Process of Identity Work among Somali Immigrants in Canada', in M.S. Lilius (ed.), *Variations on the Theme of Somaliness*. Turku: Centre for Continuing Education, Abo Akademi University, pp. 152–82.
———. 2006. 'Migration and Racial Formations among Somali Immigrants in North America', *Journal of Ethnic and Migration Studies* 32(3): 533–51.
Kusow, A., and S. Bjork. 2007. *From Mogadishu to Dixon: The Somali Diaspora in a Global Context*. Trenton, NJ: Red Sea Press.

Lamont, M., and S. Aksartova. 2002. 'Ordinary Cosmopolitanisms: Strategies for Bridging Racial Boundaries among Working-Class Men', *Theory, Culture & Society* 19(4): 1–25.

Landau, L. (ed.). 2012. *Exorcising the Demons Within: Xenophobia, Violence and Statecraft in Contemporary South Africa*. Tokyo: United Nations University Press.

Landau, L., and I. Freemantle. 2010. 'Tactical Cosmopolitanism and Idioms of Belonging: Insertion and Self-Exclusion in Johannesburg', *Journal of Ethnic and Migration Studies* 36(3): 375–90.

LandInfo. 2011. *Somalia: Language Situation and Dialects*. Oslo: Landinfo, Country of Origin Information Centre. Retrieved 11 July 2022 from https://www.landinfo.no/asset/1800/1/1800_1.pdf.

Langellier, K. 2010. 'Performing Somali Identity in the Diaspora', *Cultural Studies* 24(1): 66–94.

LaViolette, A. 2008. 'Swahili Cosmopolitanism in Africa and the Indian Ocean World, AD 600–1500', *Archaeologies* 4(1): 24–49.

Leach, E. 1984. 'Glimpses of the Unmentionable in the History of British Social Anthropology', *Annual Review of Anthropology* 13: 1–24.

Leming, L.M. 2007. 'Sociological Explorations: What Is Religious Agency?', *The Sociological Quarterly* 48(1): 73–92.

Lewis, I. 1961. *A Pastoral Democracy: A Study of Pastoralism and Politics among the Northern Somali of the Horn of Africa*. New York: Oxford University Press for the International African Institute.

———. 1965. *A Modern History of the Somali: Nation and State in the Horn of Africa*. Oxford: James Curry/Athens, OH: Ohio University Press.

———. 1994. *Blood and Bone: The Call of Kinship in Somali Society*. Trenton, NJ: Red Sea Press.

———. 1998. *Saints and Somalis: Popular Islam in a Clan-Based Society*. Trenton, NJ: Red Sea Press.

Lewis, J. 2021. *Women of the Somali Diaspora: Refugees, Resilience and Building after Conflict*. London: Hurst.

Lindley, A. 2010. *The Early Morning Phone Call: Somali Refugees' Remittances*. Oxford: Berghahn Books.

Lochery, E. 2012. 'Rendering Difference Visible: The Kenyan State and Its Somali Citizens', *African Affairs* 111(445): 615–39.

MacIntyre, A. 1981. *After Virtue: A Study in Moral Theory*. Notre Dame, IN: University of Notre Dame Press.

Mack, P. 2003. 'Religion, Feminism, and the Problem of Agency: Reflections on Eighteenth-Century Quakerism', *Signs* 29(1): 149–77.

Mahabir, J. 2004. 'The Possibilities of Cultural Transnationalism', *Postcolonial Studies* 7(3): 359–62.

Mahmood, S. 2005. *Politics of Piety: The Islamic Revival and the Feminist Subject*. Princeton, NJ: Princeton University Press.

Malkki, L. 1992. 'National Geographic: The Rooting of Peoples and the Territorialization of National Identity among Scholars and Refugees', *Cultural Anthropology* 7(1): 24–44.

———. 1995. *Purity and Exile: Violence, Memory, and National Cosmology among Hutu Refugees in Tanzania*. Chicago: University of Chicago Press.

Mamdani, M. 2004. *Good Muslim, Bad Muslim: America, the Cold War, and the Roots of Terror.* Johannesburg: Jacana Media.

Masquelier, A. 2009. *Women and Islamic Revival in a West African Town.* Bloomington, IN: Indiana University Press.

Massey, D. 1994. *Space, Place and Gender.* Minneapolis, MN: University of Minnesota Press.

———. 2005. *For Space.* Los Angeles: Sage.

Mau, S., J. Mewes and A. Zimmermann. 2008. 'Cosmopolitan Attitudes through Transnational Social Practices?' *Global Networks* 8(1): 1–24.

Mbembe, A. 2001. *On the Postcolony.* Los Angeles: University of California Press.

———. 2007. 'Afropolitanism', in S. Njami and L. Durán (eds), *Africa Remix: Contemporary Art of a Continent.* Johannesburg: Jacana Media, pp. 26–30.

McMichael, C. 2002. '"Everywhere is Allah's Place": Islam and the Everyday Life of Somali Women in Melbourne, Australia', *Journal of Refugee Studies* 15(2): 171–88.

Mermin, J. 1997. 'Television News and American Intervention in Somalia: The Myth of a Media-Driven Foreign Policy', *Political Science Quarterly* 112: 385–403.

Migiro, K. 2014. 'More Than 1,000 Somalis Rounded up in Nairobi, Held Incommunicado', *Thomson Reuters Foundation News*, 7 April. Retrieved 11 July 2022 https://news.trust.org/item/20140407162525-4yvwx.

Miller, F. 2014. 'Kenya Deaf to Outcry over Somali Crackdown', *Mail & Guardian*, 1 May. Retrieved 11 July 2022 from http://mg.co.za/article/2014-05-01-kenya-deaf-to-outcry-over-somali-crackdown.

Mngxitama, A. 2008. 'We Are Not All Like That: Race, Class and Nation after Apartheid', in Shireen Hassim, T. Kupe and E. Worby (eds), *Go Home or Die Here: Violence, Xenophobia and the Reinvention of Difference in South Africa.* Johannesburg: Wits University Press, pp. 189–208.

Mohanty, C. 1988. 'Under Western Eyes: Feminist Scholarship and Colonial Discourses', *Feminist Review* 30: 61–88.

Morris, M., and H. Wright. 2009. 'Introduction', *Cultural Studies* 23(5/6): 689–93.

Morrison, T. 1994. *The Nobel Lecture in Literature, 1993.* New York: Knopf.

Muhumed, M. 2014. 'Cracking Down on Nairobi's Somalis', *Al Jazeera*, 22 April. Retrieved 11 July 2022 from http://www.aljazeera.com/indepth/features/2014/04/cracking-down-nairobi-somalis-201442012628685801.html.

Murphy, M. 2011. *Somalia: The New Barbary? Piracy and Islam in the Horn of Africa.* New York: Columbia University Press.

Murunga, G. 2009. 'Refugees at Home? Coping with Somalia Conflict in Nairobi, Kenya', in M. Arrous and L. Ki-Zerbo (eds), *African Studies in Geography from Below.* Dakar: CORDESIA, pp. 198–232.

Nuttall, S., and A. Mbembe. 2008. *Johannesburg: The Elusive Metropolis.* Durham, NC: Duke University Press.

Oakes, T., and P. Price (eds). 2008. *The Cultural Geography Reader.* London: Routledge.

Oakley, A. 1981. 'Interviewing Women: A Contradiction in Terms', in H. Robert (ed.), *Doing Feminist Research.* London: Routledge, pp. 30–60.

Ochs, E., and L. Capps. 1996. 'Narrating the Self', *Annual Review of Anthropology* 25(1): 19–43.

Otunnu, O. 1992. 'Factors Affecting the Treatment of Kenyan-Somalis and Somali Refugees in Kenya: A Historical Overview', *Refuge: Canada's Periodical on Refugees* 12(5): 21–26.
Palmary, I. 2011. '"In Your Experience": Research as Gendered Cultural Translation', *Gender, Place and Culture* 18(1): 99–113.
Palmary, I., et al. (eds). 2010. *Gender and Migration: Feminist Interventions*. London: Zed Books.
Pessar, P., and S.J. Mahler. 2003. 'Transnational Migration: Bringing Gender In', *International Migration Review* 37(3): 812–46.
Philips, A. 2007. *Multiculturalism without Culture*. Princeton, NJ: Princeton University Press.
Pillay, D. 2008. 'Relative Deprivation, Social Instability and Cultures of Entitlement', in S. Hassim, T. Kupe and E. Worby (eds), *Go Home or Die Here: Violence, Xenophobia and the Reinvention of Difference in South Africa*. Johannesburg: Wits University Press, pp. 93–104.
Pine, F. 2014. 'Migration as Hope: Space, Time, and Imagining the Future', *Current Anthropology* 55(9): 95–104.
Pollock, S. 2000. 'Cosmopolitan and Vernacular in History', *Public Culture* 12(3): 591–625.
Pollock, S., et al. 2000. 'Cosmopolitanisms', *Public Culture* 12(3): 577–89.
Ponzanesi, S. 2021. 'Somali Diaspora and Digital Belonging: Introduction', *Journal of Global Diaspora & Media* 2(1): 3–15.
Portes, A. 1997. *Globalization from Below: The Rise of Transnational Communities*. Oxford: University of Oxford Transnational Communities Programme.
Portes, A., L. Guaranizo and P. Landlot. 1999. 'The Study of Transnationalism: Pitfalls and Promise of an Emergent Research Field', *Ethnic and Racial Studies* 22(2): 217–37.
Ricoeur, P. 1970. *Freud and Philosophy: An Essay on Interpretation*. New Haven, CT: Yale University Press.
———. 1986. *The Rule of Metaphor: Multi-Disciplinary Studies of the Creation of Meaning in Language*. London: Routledge & Kegan Paul.
Rios, M., and J. Watkins. 2015. 'Beyond "Place": Translocal Placemaking of the Hmong Diaspora', *Journal of Planning Education and Research* 35(2): 209–19.
Ripero-Muñiz, Nereida (ed.). 2017. *Metropolitan Nomads: A Journey through Joburg's Little Mogadishu*. Johannesburg: MoVE. Retrieved 11 July 2022 from https://issuu.com/move.methods.visual.explore/docs/mn_publication_-_ebook_-_10_october.
———. 2019. 'The Port and the Island: Cosmopolitan and Vernacular Identity Constructions among Somali Women in Nairobi and Johannesburg', in Neil Carrier and Tabea Scharrer (eds), *Mobile Urbanity: Somali Presence in Urban East Africa*. New York: Berghahn Books, pp. 58–75.
———. 2020. 'Agency of Somali Migrant Women in Nairobi and Johannesburg: Negotiating Religious and Cultural Identifications in Diasporic Spaces', *African Studies Review* 63(1): 65–92.
Ruby, J. 1982. *A Crack in the Mirror: Reflexive Perspectives in Anthropology*. Philadelphia, PA: University of Pennsylvania Press.
Sadouni, S. 2009. '"God Is Not Unemployed": Journeys of Somali Refugees in Johannesburg', *African Studies* 68(2): 235–49.

———. 2019. *Muslims in Southern Africa: Johannesburg's Somali Diaspora*. London: Palgrave Macmillan.
Said, E. 1984. 'The Mind of Winter: Reflections on Life in Exile', *Harper's* 269(1612): 49–55.
Sassen, S. 1998. 'The De Facto Transnationalizing of Inmigration Policy,' in *Challenge to the Nation-State: Immigration in Western Europe and the United States*, C. Joppke (Ed.), Oxford: Oxford University Press, pp. 49-85
Shaffer, M. 2014. 'Social Control and Transnational Families: Somali Women and Dignity in Johannesburg', unpublished paper presented at *Borders, Bodies and Boundaries: Exploring Gender and Migration in Historical and Contemporary Africa*, Writers Workshop, 7 and 8 October, ACMS, Wits University.
Shear, M., and H. Cooper. 2017. 'Trump Bars Refugees and Citizens of 7 Muslim Countries', *New York Times*, 27 January. Retrieved 11 July 2022 from https://www.nytimes.com/2017/01/27/us/politics/trump-syrian-refugees.html.
Shire, M.I. 2014. 'The Legendary Queen Caraweelo: an Ethiopian Jewish Queen?', *Somali Mind*. Retrieved 10 August 2022 from http://www.somalimind.com/2014/09/legendary-somali-queen-caraweelo-ethiopian-jewish-queen.
Shweder, R. 2000. 'What about "Female Genital Mutilation?" And Why Understanding Culture Matters in the First Place', *Daedalus* 129(4): 209–32.
Sinatti, G. 2008. 'The Making of Urban Translocalities: Senegalese Migrants in Dakar and Zingonia', in Michael P. Smith and J. Eade (eds), *Transnational Ties: Cities, Migrations, and Identities*. London: Transactions, pp. 61–76.
Skrbis, Z., G. Kendall and I. Woodward. 2004. 'Locating Cosmopolitanism between Humanist Ideal and Grounded Social Category', *Theory, Culture & Society* 21(6): 115–36.
Skrbis, Z., and I. Woodward. 2007. 'The Ambivalence of Ordinary Cosmopolitanism: Investigating the Limits of Cosmopolitan Openness', *The Sociological Review* 55(4): 730–47.
Somers, M. 1994. 'The Narrative Constitution of Identity: A Relational and Network Approach', *Theory and Society* 23: 605–49.
Steinberg, J. 2014. *A Man of Good Hope*. Johannesburg: Jonathan Ball.
Tamboukou, M. 2008. 'A Foucauldian Approach to Narratives', in M. Andrews, C. Squire and M. Tamboukou (eds), *Doing Narrative Research*. London: Sage, pp. 102–20.
Tewolde, A.I. 2020. '"Racial Classification is Meaningless": Why Racial Classification in South Africa is Unintelligible for Some Eritrean Refugees', *Social Science Quarterly* 101: 514–26.
Tiilikainen, M. 2007. 'Continuity and Change: Somali Women and Everyday Islam in the Diaspora', in Abdi Kusow and S. Bjork (eds), *From Mogadishu to Dixon: The Somali Diaspora in a Global Context*. Trenton, NJ: Red Sea Press, pp. 207–33.
Thompson, D. 2016. 'Risky Business and Geographies of Refugee Capitalism in the Somali Migrant Economy of Gauteng, South Africa', *Journal of Ethnic and Migration Studies* 42(1): 120–35.
Touval, S., and S. Weltmann. 1963. *Somali Nationalism: International Politics and the Drive for Unity in the Horn of Africa*. Cambridge, MA: Harvard University Press.

UNHCR. 2014. 'Kenya: UNHCR Disturbed by Arrests and Deportations of Somali Refugees', 17 April. Retrieved 11 July 2022 from http://www.unhcr.org/534fa2c76.html.
———. 2021. Populations, Countries of origin. South Africa Multi-Country Office. Retrieved 14 August 2022 from https://reporting.unhcr.org/southafricamco?year=2021#toc-populations.
———. 2022. Kenya Operation Statistics. Kenya Infographics – 31 July 2022. Retrieved 14 August 2022 from https://www.unhcr.org/ke/857-statistics.html.
Valmary, S.. 2022. 'Somali Refugees Flock to Camps Amid Devastating Drought', *Mail & Guardian*, 26 February. Retrieved 11 July 2022 from https://mg.co.za/article/2022-02-26-somali-refugees-flock-to-camps-amid-devastating-drought/.
Venuti, L. 2000. *The Translation Studies Reader*. London: Routledge.
Vertovec, S. 2001. 'Transnationalism and Identity', *Journal of Ethnic and Migration Studies* 27(4): 573–82.
———. 2009. *Transnationalism*. London: Routledge.
Vertovec, S., and R. Cohen. 2002. *Conceiving Cosmopolitanism: Theory, Context and Practice*. Oxford: Oxford University Press.
Waldron, J. 2000. 'What Is Cosmopolitan?' *Journal of Political Philosophy* 8(2): 227–43.
Walley, C. 1997. 'Searching for "Voices": Feminism, Anthropology and the Global Debate over Female Genital Operations', *Cultural Anthropology* 12(3): 405–38.
Wandera, J., and H.A. Wario. 2019. 'Framing the Swoop: A Comparative Analysis of Operation Usalama Watch in Muslim and Secular Print Media in Kenya', in Neil Carrier and Tabea Scharrer (eds), *Mobile Urbanity: Somali Presence in Urban East Africa*. Oxford: Berghahn Books, pp. 200–18.
Ware, R. 2014. *The Walking Quran: Islamic Education, Embodied Knowledge and History in West Africa*. Chapel Hill, NC: The University of North Carolina Press.
Weitzberg, K. 2017. *We Have No Borders: Greater Somalia and the Predicament of Belonging in Kenya*. Athens, OH: Ohio University Press.
Werbner, P. 1999. 'Global Pathways: Working Class Cosmopolitans and the Creation of Transnational Ethnic Worlds', *Social Anthropology* 7(1): 17–35.
———. 2008. *Anthropology and the New Cosmopolitanism: Rooted, Feminist and Vernacular Perspectives*. Oxford: Routledge.
Willis, K., and B. Yeoh. 2000. *Gender and Migration*. Cheltenham: Edward Elgar.
Wise, A. 2011. '"You Wouldn't Know What's in There Would You?": Homeliness and "Foreign" Signs in Ashfield, Sydney', in K. Brickell and A. Datta (eds), *Translocal Geographies: Spaces, Places, Connections*. Farnham: Ashgate, pp. 93–108.
Worby, E., T. Kupe and S. Hassim. 2008. 'Introduction: Facing the Other at the Gates of Democracy', in S. Hassim., T. Kupe and E. Worby (eds), *Go Home or Die Here: Violence, Xenophobia and the Reinvention of Difference in South Africa*. Johannesburg: Wits University Press, pp. 1–27.
Wright, C. 2008. 'Gender Awareness in Migration Theory: Synthesizing Actor and Structure in Southern Africa', *Development and Change* 26(4): 771–92.
Yarwood, D. 1978. *The Encyclopaedia of World Costume*. New York: Bonanza Books.
Yeoh, B., S. Huang and K. Willis. 2000. 'Global Cities, Transnational Flows and Gender Dimensions: The View from Singapore', *Tijdschrift Voor Economische En Sociale Geografie* 91(2): 147–58.

Yuval-Davis, N. 1993. 'Gender and Nation', *Ethnic and Racial Studies* 16(4): 621–32.
——. 1997. 'Women Citizenship and Difference', *Feminist Review* 57: 4–27.
——. 2014. 'Religion and Gender in Contemporary Political Projects of Belonging', in N. Reilly and S. Scriver (eds), *Region, Gender, and the Public Sphere*. New York: Routledge, pp. 31–44.
Zack, T. 2015. '"Jeppe" – Where Low-End Globalization, Ethnic Entrepreneurialism and the Arrival City Meet', *Urban Forum* 26: 131–50, https://doi.org/10.1007/s12132-014-9245-1.
Zack, T., and Y.E. Estifanos. 2016. 'Somewhere Else: Social Connection and Dislocation of Ethiopian Migrants in Johannesburg', *African and Black Diaspora: An International Journal* 9(2): 149–65, https://doi.org/10.1080/17528631.2015.1083179.
Zack, T., and T. Govender. 2019. 'Architectures of Visibility and Invisibility: A Reflection on the Secret Affinities of Johannesburg's Cross-Border Shopping Hub', *Anthropology Southern Africa* 42(1): 29–45, https://doi.org/10.1080/23323256.2019.1575250.

Index

abaya, 66n2, 82
Abdi, Cawo, 2, 6, 16, 22n2, 43, 48, 49n5, 56, 66n4, 68, 71, 73, 77, 79, 87, 90, 107–10, 120, 124, 126
Addis Ababa, 2, 33, 36, 39, 41
Africa, xii, 2, 5–6, 9, 22, 27–28, 30–31, 38, 81, 113, 120, 122–23, 127, 129–30
   East Africa(n), 2, 20, 30, 32, 34, 38, 42, 51, 53–54, 57, 67, 70–71, 79
   Horn of Africa, 2, 26, 30, 45, 70, 79, 115
   North Africa, 130
   Southern Africa, xi, xiv, 29, 38
   West Africa, 9, 130
Afropolitanism. *See* African cosmopolitanism
agency, 6, 13, 17, 71, 87–88, 94, 109–12
   economic, 128
   individual, 67, 83–84, 100. 103, 104n6, 108, 128
   of migrants, 10, 129
   religious, 21, 92, 101, 103, 108–9, 111, 114
   of women, 6–7, 21–22, 23n7, 68, 84, 88, 91, 108, 111, 123, 128
Aidid, Safia, 16
Amal (shopping mall), 43, 46, 56–57, 59, 61, 63, 79, 86, 90, 106, 115
Anzaldúa, Gloria, 72–73, 97
apartheid, 43, 56
   post-apartheid, 46, 79
Appadurai, Arjun, 4, 8–10, 26, 126

Appiah, Anthony, 10
Asia, 9, 54
aspirations, 8–10, 17, 84, 108, 111, 117, 120, 123, 126–130
   cosmopolitan, 9, 65, 107, 126
   for a better life, 129–30
asylum seekers, 29, 42, 71
Australia, 25, 90, 98, 117, 119

Bakhtin, Mikhail, 13, 15, 18, 67, 88
belonging, 31, 36, 72, 76, 78, 83, 90
   to a collective/community, 4–6, 36, 64–65, 69, 84, 127
   ethnic, 70
   feelings of, 4, 21, 48–49, 60, 68–69, 127
   sense of, 8, 72, 74, 84
   to umma (*see* umma)
   to the world, 8, 65, 128
Besteman, Catherine, 5, 15–16, 79–80
better life (search of), 9–10, 25, 35, 42, 98, 105–11, 117, 120, 122–23, 125, 129
Blixen, Karen, 113–14
borders, 38, 52, 84, 130
   across, ix, 1, 4, 10–12, 31, 49n2, 71–72, 74, 107, 127
   colonial, 30, 34
   cultural, 9
   national, 7
Brazil, 47, 61, 106
bui-bui, 54, 89. *See also* abaya
buraanburs, 93

burka, viii, 32, 83
business, 3, 6, 25–26, 30, 42, 44–45, 59, 63, 117, 127
   people (men and women), 26, 32, 47, 51, 53–55, 63, 100, 109
   in townships, 43, 48, 59–61, 66 (*see also* spaza shops)
   in urban areas, 36, 42, 49n1, 53–54, 56, 58, 65, 85n5, 106, 110, 120
buufis, 4, 36, 46, 107, 117, 120, 122, 124

Cadaan studies, 15–16
Canada, 3, 36, 67, 70–73, 91, 117–18, 121
Cape Town, 42, 46, 61
Carrier, Neil, 2–3, 16, 27, 31, 34, 37, 53–55
Cedar-Riverside, 26, 56, 120
China, 55
   China mall, 44
civil war, 1, 29, 52, 56
clan(s), 15, 39–41, 65, 74, 75–79, 93, 99, 100, 103
Colombia, 107
community, 52, 63, 101, 110
   diasporic, 49, 71
   imagined, 65, 74, 84, 126, 127
   local, 63
   Muslim, 64, 128
   pressure from, 78, 113, 114, 116
   translocal, 6, 63–64, 69, 74
   transnational, 66, 84, 127
cosmopolitanism, 2, 4, 8, 28, 65–66, 127, 128
   African, 9, 43, 49
   from below, 9, 10
   social practice, 8
   in Somalia, 23n10
   strategic/tactical, 9
   theory, 8
culture(s), 7, 11, 14, 18, 68–79, 81, 86, 99, 109, 116, 123, 126, 129
   Islamic, 76, 94
   of migration, 4, 6, 126
   material, 65
   national culture, 70–71, 79, 100
   popular, 8, 95
   and religion, 5, 74, 76, 87, 91, 94, 98, 101

Dadaab, 20, 107
Dar es Salaam, 39, 105
dialogical, 13–16, 65, 67, 69–70, 83–84, 88, 93–94, 129
diaspora, 9, 66, 77
   Somali (*see* Somali diaspora)
dirac, 2, 22n1, 43, 67, 82, 90, 92
displacement, 2, 5–7, 12, 69, 87, 100, 107, 109, 129
divorce, 69, 96, 105–7, 109–10, 114–17, 123
dressing (way of), 34, 43–44, 55, 68, 69, 72, 81–84, 87, 89, 90–94, 106, 126
Durban, 41–42, 46

Eastleigh, xi–xii, 1–2, 6–7, 11, 16–21, 25–28, 32–38, 43, 46, 49, 51–58, 61–66, 88, 120, 128
Egypt, 26, 45, 64, 91, 96
Ethiopia, 2, 28, 38, 41, 56, 68, 78, 88, 105
Ethiopians
   in South Africa, 110, 44, 48, 58, 60–61, 63, 110
   in the United States, 5, 72
ethnography, 14–17
EverydayMayfair, 17, 39, 58, 118
Europe, 36, 81, 114, 117, 119

Facebook, 10, 14, 16, 69, 74, 87, 121
family/families, 3–4, 6–7, 9, 25–27, 33, 35–42, 44, 46, 54, 60, 63–64, 73, 76, 78, 90, 92–93, 95–96, 98–100, 103, 105–23, 129
Farah, Nuruddin, 5–6, 27, 30, 73, 108–9, 111
female circumcision, 21, 88, 91–92, 94–97, 103, 113, 128
Ferguson, James, 5, 9, 123, 126, 129
FGM, 24n16, 97, 103n4. *See also* female circumcision

Garissa, 35, 78
Garissa lodge, 55, 66n3

gender, viii, 75, 110
  identities, 71
  and place, 63
  practices (see practices)
  relations, 62, 87, 92
  roles, 16, 108–11, 117, 128
globalization, 2, 8, 65, 129
Global North, 48, 59, 123
Global South, ix, 4, 6, 9, 16, 48, 127
gold, 54–55, 63, 66n3, 92, 109
Guatemala, 121

Hall, Stuart, 69, 71–74, 88
hermeneutics (of faith and suspicion), 12
hijab, 33, 94
Hillbrow, 43, 56, 64
home, 2, 4, 72–74, 84, 92, 94, 110, 116
  away from home, 3, 48, 52
  back home, 36, 42, 63, 110, 117, 120, 123–24
  homeland, 10–11, 18, 53, 65–66, 71, 73, 83, 87, 124, 127–28
  return, 26, 55, 120
  sense of, 11, 26, 74, 90, 103
  temporary, 6, 21, 48, 65, 127
hope(s), 8, 36, 65, 117–119, 124
  politics of, 9–10, 126
Horst, Cindy, 3–4, 16, 107, 126
hostility, 28–31, 59
husband (ideal), 88, 91, 98

identity, 12–13, 18–19, 53, 65, 68, 71, 77–83, 97
  collective, 3, 21, 64–65, 70, 74–75, 81, 102, 109, 128–30
  diasporic, 73, 127
  formation, 6, 9, 11, 64
  hybrid, 71–73
  hyphenated, 68–72
  Muslim/Islamic, 66, 82, 84, 87–90, 128
  national, 75
  religious, 13–71
  sense of, 69, 73, 83–84
  translocal, 5, 49
identifications, 5, 10–13, 21, 56, 67–68, 70–75, 83–84, 94, 126–27, 129

clan, 75, 77
  collective, 4, 49, 76, 128
  cultural, 4, 21, 69, 74, 100, 128
  ethnic, 64, 69
  Muslim/Islamic, 87–88, 90, 128
  national, 64, 74–75, 83
  religious, 6–7, 21, 65, 77, 102
identifiers, 21, 68, 79, 82, 86–87, 90
Indian(s), 43, 46, 51, 53, 56, 64, 79
Indian Ocean, ix, 5, 9, 53, 55
Indonesia, 25–26, 55
immigrants, 31, 96. See also migrants
insecurity (feelings of), 46, 48, 71, 116
Instagram, 10, 14, 69, 74–75, 80, 125
Iran, 121
Iraq, 121
Isiolo, viii, 1, 35
Islam
  as a bigger structure, 64–65 (see also umma)
  as continuity for migrants, 87, 90
  as a discursive tradition, 102
  and female circumcision, 95–98
  and gender roles, 63, 92, 109
  as a moral compass, 87, 90, 103
  and Somaliness, 21, 53, 62, 86–91, 100
  and transformation of space, 61–65
  as a unifying factor among Somalis, 21, 75, 92, 103, 126, 128
  and women´s agency, 21, 88, 91, 95, 103, 114
Islamic
  arguments (to contest cultural practices), 88, 92, 94, 98, 100, 104, 114, 128
  connection, 43, 90
  interpretations, 89
  revival, 89, 103n1
  un-Islamic, 97
Islamic Courts Union, 29
imagination, 30, 107, 108
  collective, 3, 43, 69, 126–27
  cosmopolitan, 124
  global, viii, 5, 101
  Western, 87
integration, 87, 90, 128

Italy, 89, 109, 111–13

Jeppe Street, 25, 41, 44, 49n1, 58, 85n5, 106, 124n2
jilbaab, 7, 10, 23n9, 81–82, 89
Johannesburg, 2–3, 6, 9, 11, 16–21, 27–31, 38, 43–45, 48–49, 52, 58, 64, 67, 69, 95, 105, 119, 127, 128
  as an island, 21, 25, 27, 36, 42–48, 52, 61, 66, 127
journey(s), 28, 38, 42, 54, 120. *See also* migration journeys

Kapteijns, Lidwien, 16
Khartoum, 100
Kenya, 2, 19, 25, 33, 35–41, 47–48, 55, 63, 78, 89, 105, 107, 114–15, 118
  Kenyan police, 7, 20, 35–37
  Somalis in, 4, 28–31, 53, 56
khat, 44–45, 105, 115, 124n1
Kigoma, 9, 128
Kilimani, 27, 31, 34, 51
kinship, 15, 35
Kiswahili, viii, 34, 77, 86

Lewis, Ioan, 15
Lewthwaite, Samantha, 19–20, 86
life stories, 12, 14, 17, 88, 91, 100
little Mogadishu(s), xi, 6, 10, 17, 21, 49, 51–53, 56, 62, 65, 128
Libya, 36, 121
Limpopo, 40, 60, 68
London, 2, 10, 11, 19, 26, 36, 45, 81

Malawi, 38, 41
Malawians, 44, 60
Malkki, Liisa, 4–6, 8–9, 84, 128
Mandera, 35
Maputo, 38–40
marriage, 2, 63, 69, 92, 96–100, 105, 107–117, 123
  arranged, 107, 112
  politics of, 22, 111
Mayfair, 3, 6, 10–11, 16–21, 25–29, 40–71, 76–87, 90, 94, 101, 105–6, 110, 122, 127–28
McMichael, Celia, 87, 89, 90, 103

meaning(s), 27, 48, 61, 68, 74, 80–81, 83, 89, 101, 111, 118, 123
Metropolitan Nomads, 17, 23n13, 52
Mexico, 107, 121
Middle East, 54–57, 89
migrants, 8–9, 11, 27, 30–31, 38, 44, 55, 60–61, 65, 72, 87, 123–24
  African, 27, 129–30
  agency of, 10, 23n7, 129
  forced, 2, 8, 29
  Somali (*see* Somali migrants)
  undocumented, 20, 37, 70
migration, 2–13, 17, 21–22, 35, 41, 56, 65, 72, 76–77, 107–8, 113–14, 117, 123, 126–27, 130
  context of, 103, 111
  culture of, 4, 126
  desire for, 107 (*see also* buufis)
  experience, 8–9, 76, 111, 124
  forced, 27, 56, 89, 110, 126, 128
  and gender, 23n7
  journey(s), 29, 39, 42, 119–21
  mass, 82
  process, 10, 77–78, 108–112
  routes, 17, 22n3, 27, 48, 118
  transnational, 9–10, 108, 113, 126
Minneapolis, 18–19, 26, 57, 119–20
modernity, 31, 65–66, 127–28
Mogadishu, 11, 23n10, 26, 30, 35, 43, 53, 67, 70, 78, 80, 82, 90, 126. *See also* 'little Mogasdishu(s)'
Mombasa, 19, 20, 23n8, 30
mosque(s), 32, 56, 59, 61–62, 90, 92
Moyale, 35
Mozambique, 38–42, 105
Muslim(s), 8, 20–21, 43–44, 56, 63–66, 71, 78, 87–89. 100–3, 129

Nairobi, 1–3, 6–8, 16–21, 25–38, 41, 44, 46, 48–49, 53–54, 57–58, 64, 67–76, 79, 81–83, 86, 92, 95–102, 105, 107, 119–20, 123, 127–28
  as a port, 21, 25, 31–38, 48, 61, 84, 127
Nampula, 39–40, 105
Narrative(s), ix, xi, 6, 13–17, 43, 112, 70–77, 84, 88, 96, 101–2, 120, 126
  alternative, 5

autobiographical/first person, 12, 13 (*see also* life stories)
collective, 77
counternarratives, ix, 114
of migration, 72
of success, 123
nation state, 2, 4, 6, 43, 74–76
nationalism, 75
niqab, 82–83, 89–91
nomad(s), 2–3, 30, 51, 80, 120
Norway, 68, 98, 101

Operation Usalama Watch, 7, 20, 23n8, 30, 34–37
Oromo, 66n1

Panama, 107
Pangani, 32, 34
participatory research arts methods, 17, 22n3
patriarchy, 108
pastoralist, 2, 30, 79–80
pirate(s), ix, 5, 13
place, 11
  diasporic, 88 (*see also* diasporic space)
  hostile, 68, 71
  new, 53, 57, 64–65, 71, 126
  of origin, 64, 73, 76–78, 90, 127
  placemaking, 21, 49, 51, 53, 65
  transitional, 6, 21, 27, 29, 35, 48, 60, 65, 127
Postcolonial (world), 15, 129
Postmodernity, 2
postmodern, 5, 7, 9, 15, 22, 70, 83, 129
practice(s)
  cosmopolitan, 31
  cultural, 3, 6, 8, 13, 21, 34, 84, 87–88, 102–3, 108–9, 126, 128
  customary, 87, 92, 99–102, 111, 128
  gender, 6, 53, 21, 53, 108
  every day, 2, 52–53, 88, 103, 108, 126, 65, 75, 88
  Islamic, 56, 62, 64, 89–90
  and narrative(s), 13, 68–69, 75, 88
  religious, 11, 21, 49, 65, 74–75, 88, 91–92, 94, 102, 109, 126–128
  reproduction of, 6, 65, 68, 100

sets of, 68–69, 73
social, 11, 35, 84
Puntland, 25, 35–36, 77, 106

Qatar, 64, 99, 100
Queen Araweelo, 108
Qur'an, 10, 21, 44, 86, 89, 95–98, 100

refugee(s), ix, 6, 40, 121, 128–29
  camps, ix, 1, 2, 4, 35, 38
  cosmopolitan, 7–10
  status, 35
remittances, 35, 54, 107, 110, 117, 120, 122
religion, 5, 12, 64, 70, 74–79, 81, 86–101
representation
  in ethnography, 14, 15
  of migrant women, 109
  of Muslims, 87
  of Somalis, 5, 15–16, 101–2
  of Somali women, ix, 5, 17
rumours, 63, 66, 99

Saudi Arabia, 1, 2
Al-Shabaab, ix, 2, 7, 19, 26, 34–37, 86, 96, 101, 112
self, 8, 71, 73
  identification, 13, 81
  and narrative, 11–14
  narratives, 11
  respect, 113–14
  sense of, 12–13, 67–70, 83, 128
  understanding, 13
Siad Barre, 2, 74, 89
Sijui, 34, 77–78
smuggler(s), 38, 40, 106–7
Somaliland, 16, 18, 35, 114
Somalia
  Best of, 74–76
  conflict in, 2, 15, 27, 30, 35, 53, 74, 77, 81, 89, 108–9, 126
  Greater, 30, 74
  life in, 18
  nostalgic image of, 10, 75–76, 80, 126
  reconstruction of, 26, 75
  re-Islamization of, 82, 90
  return to, 37, 47, 61, 89, 124

Somaliness, 64–65, 75–76, 81, 100, 127
  across borders/ outside Somalia, 12, 69–71, 74
  characteristics, 10, 68, 71, 84
  expressions of, 21, 68, 70, 126
  and hybrid identities, 71–74
  and Islam (see Islam)
  sense of, 69, 73–74, 83, 127
Somali(s)
  American, 4, 20
  Bantus, 79–81
  born outside Somalia, 53, 69, 77–78
  Canadian, 4, 20
  culture, 4, 34, 78, 80, 88–89, 92, 97
  diaspora, 2, 11, 16, 21, 26–27, 34–38, 48–49, 53–54, 56, 63, 68, 70–76, 82–83, 96, 98, 109–10, 119–127
  ethnic, 27, 30, 51–53
  identity, 68, 70, 75
  in Johannesburg, 8–10, 12, 14, 25, 36, 41–42, 56, 68, 71, 73–84, 87–92, 96, 98, 102, 106–7, 110, 112, 115–117, 121, 123
  Kenyan, vii, 4, 27–28, 33–34, 37, 48, 51, 55, 63, 77, 100
  language, 3, 16, 78
  migrants, 29, 48, 52, 59, 60, 65, 71, 122, 124
  in Nairobi, 9–14, 34, 50, 52, 87–91, 109–117
  pastoralist way of life, 2, 30, 79
  refugees, 5, 20–21, 27–28, 34–35, 48, 53–56, 71, 79, 83, 124
  representation of (see representation)
  sense of belonging, 26–27, 41, 46, 71, 83–84, 92, 97, 99–100, 109
  from Somalia, 34, 55, 77–78
  studies, 14–16
  women (see women)
social media, 3, 11, 74, 126
South Africa, 8–9, 19, 27, 45, 78, 101, 106–7, 119, 125
  Somalis in, 17, 27–31, 43, 47–48, 56, 59–61, 64, 69, 71, 79, 105, 110, 122
  migration journeys to, 68, 38–43, 48, 68, 118

South Africans, 46–47, 52, 60–61, 81, 86, 99
South America, 106, 117, 119–121
Spain, 64, 81
space(s), viii, 3, 7, 10–12, 14, 16–17, 33, 35, 44, 47, 52–53, 57, 61–63, 65–66, 69–70, 73, 75, 77, 83, 90, 92, 102, 113, 115, 125–129
  diasporic, 22, 47, 53, 65, 77, 90, 127, 129
  gendered, viii, 61–66
  private, 62, 115
  public, viii, 63
  reproduction of, 11, 57 (see also little Mogadishus)
  urban, 10, 88, 127–28
spaza shops, 31, 49n5, 59–61, 69, 106
Steinberg, Jonny, 20, 34, 60, 107
Stereotypes/stereotypical, 5–7, 16, 23, 30, 99, 101, 121, 129
Stockholm, 1
structure(s), 35, 100
  of meaning, 15
  of power, 15, 109
  pre-given, 88, 127
  shared, 75, 88
  social, 104n6, 108
  of support, 76
supra-structure, 65, 128
Sudan, 1, 36, 96, 121
Sweden, 1, 98
syncretism, 87–88, 91, 92, 94, 128
Syria, 64, 121

Tamboukou, Maria, 11, 15
Tanzania, 2, 38, 40–41, 78, 105
terrorist(s), 5, 7, 13, 19–20, 26, 30, 36–37, 86–88, 101–3, 121
terrorism, 8, 36–37, 101–2, 121
Thika, 7
Thika Superhighway, 31–32
toddoba, 88, 91–94, 128
Toronto, 2, 26, 81
townships, 9, 31–32, 42–44, 47–48, 58–61, 66, 69, 105
tradition, 15, 68–71, 83, 87, 94
  invention of, 82

nomadic, 96, 126
traditional
  ceremonies, 92–94, 128
  costumes, 67, 80, 83, 89, 92, 126
  music, 10, 26
  practices, 87, 92, 97
  roles, 73, 111
  sense of self, 70, 83, 128
transnationalism, 2, 8, 10, 22n4
translocality, 10–11, 64
tribalism, 75–76
Tiilikainen, Marje, 77, 87, 90, 103

Uganda, 38, 39, 107
umma, 61, 64–66, 103, 128
UNHCR, 28–29, 35, 64, 119
United Arab Emirates, 55, 57, 68, 87, 90, 107, 109, 119
United Kingdom, 2, 33, 98, 117
United States of America, 18–19, 22, 26, 72, 90, 99, 106–10, 117–23, 125

Victims (victimised), ix, 5–6, 17, 23n7, 109

Wahhabism, 89
wedding(s), 1, 33–34, 82, 88, 90, 92–93, 102, 106, 113, 128
well-being, 7, 17, 87, 98, 128
Weitzberg, Keren, 2, 4, 30, 34, 37, 56, 74, 78
Westgate (attack), 19–20, 30, 37, 82, 86–87, 101–2
WhatsApp, 106–7

women (Somali)
  access to the Qur'an, 10, 21, 86, 95–100
  actions, viii, 63, 66, 71, 99, 103
  agency (*see* agency)
  contestation of cultural practices, 21, 74, 88, 91, 98, 100, 108
  decision(s), 9, 36, 73, 82, 99–100, 108, 112, 120, 126, 129
  decision-making power, 6, 17, 21, 108, 123, 128
  divorced (*see* divorce)
  empowerment, 111
  married (*see* marriage*)*
  narratives, 11–13, 68–70, 74, 98, 123, 129
  stories, 12, 14, 16–17, 19, 91, 121
  unmarried, 63, 95, 110, 112, 114
  virginity, 63, 93–99, 104n4, 111, 113–14
  voices, 16–17
  young, 8, 14, 42, 95–96, 112, 114, 123

xenophobia, 31, 49n5, 122
  attacks, 20, 27, 31, 69–71, 86, 101, 127

Yemen, 121
Yeoville, 43, 56, 64

Zambia, 38
Zimbabwe, 38
Zimbabweans, 31, 44, 60

www.ingramcontent.com/pod-product-compliance
Lightning Source LLC
Chambersburg PA
CBHW071710020426
42333CB00017B/2212